Overcoming Zionism

Overcoming Zionism

Creating a Single Democratic State
in Israel/Palestine

Joel Kovel

PLUTO PRESS
www.plutobooks.com

and

Between the Lines
TORONTO

First published 2007 by Pluto Press
345 Archway Road, London N6 5AA
and 175 Fifth Avenue, New York, NY 10010
www.plutobooks.com

and

First published in Canada in 2007 by
Between the Lines
720 Bathurst Street, Suite #404
Toronto, Ontario   M5S 2R4
1-800-718-7201
www.btlbooks.com

Distributed in the United States of America exclusively by
Palgrave Macmillan, a division of St. Martin's Press LLC,
175 Fifth Avenue, New York, NY 10010

British Library Cataloguing in Publication Data
A catalogue record for this book is available from the British Library

ISBN-13   978 0 7453 2570 5 Hardback
ISBN-13   978 0 7453 2569 9 Paperback

Library of Congress Cataloging in Publication Data applied for

Library and Archives Canada Cataloguing in Publication
Kovel, Joel, 1936–
    Overcoming Zionism : toward a single democratic state in Israel/Palestine /
Joel Kovel.

Includes bibliographical references and index.
ISBN 978–1–897071–26–7

    1. Arab–Israeli conflict—Peace. 2. Zionism—Israel.
3. Racism—Israel. I. Title.

DS128.2.K68 2007   956.9405'4   C2006–906610–8

This book is printed on paper suitable for recycling and made from fully managed
and sustained forest sources. Logging, pulping and manufacturing processes are
expected to conform to the environmental standards of the country of origin. The
paper may contain up to 70% post consumer waste.

10   9   8   7   6   5   4   3

Designed and produced for Pluto Press by
Chase Publishing Services Ltd, Sidmouth, England
Typeset from disk by Stanford DTP Services, Northampton, England
Printed and bound in the European Union by
CPI Antony Rowe, Chippenham and Eastbourne, England

If you do not expect the unexpected, you will not find it, for it is trackless and unexplored.

Heraclitus [fr 18]

Go on, builders in hope: tho Jerusalem wanders far away,
Without the gate of Los: among the dark Satanic wheels.

William Blake, *Jerusalem*, Plate 12: 42–43

Contents

PART THREE   ZIONISM OVERCOME

To my Aunt Betty, who illuminated my childhood

And to Rachel Corrie, may her name live in glory

Acknowledgements

I became inspired to begin confronting Zionism by DeeDee Halleck, whose life I have shared for the past 29 years. Soon after, I met Stanley Diamond, who became my friend and mentor for the last eleven years of his life, and provided for me the first rigorous models of extending the confrontation into the realm of scholarship. After I finally set out to do this study, the pace and scale of those who have guided, encouraged or helped me in other ways has grown exponentially, well past the point where I am able to recall all who have contributed to this effort. In some way, the greatest thanks goes to those who, over the last three and a half years, have told me on innumerable occasions how much it meant to them that somebody was finally taking on the stifling consensus about Israel. What I say in these pages, then, is said on behalf of a great number of fellow spirits, and I can only hope that the result is adequate to their trust.

Thanks to an invitation by Michael Lerner, I began this project writing articles and essays for *Tikkun* magazine. It was gracious of him to do so, inasmuch as we have disagreements, which inevitably found their way into print. The decision to go further, into the writing of this book, came out of that experience but was also sparked by Edward Said's encouragement. If this work is capable of honoring his luminous memory, it will have been worth the effort. As I went on, the pace of support accelerated. Those who have provided particular assistance have included Seth Farber, Virginia Tilley, Michael Smith, Eldad Benary, Joel Beinen, Jeff Blankfort, Elsa First, Tony Karon, Andrew Nash, David Finkel (of *Against the Current*), BH Yael, Bertell Ollman, Peter Linebaugh,

ACKNOWLEDGEMENTS

Bob Stone, Betsy Bowman, Maggie Cammer, Samir Amin, David Miller and Shannon Walsh. My trip to Israel/Palestine depended integrally on the friendship and assistance of Ingrid Gassner, Scott Leckie, Fionn Skiontis, Eitan Bronstein, Lessi and Hannah Domhe, Yehudith Harel, Ilan Pappe and Michel Warschawski. Others who have given of themselves include Brian Drolet, Kurt Berggren, Grace Paley, Bob Nichols, Steve Kowit, Gretchen Zdorkowski, Rachel Kushner, Katherine Menninger, Victor Wallis, Peter Lamborn Wilson, Mark Pavlick, Jim O'Connor, Naomi Schneider, Bruria and David Finkel, Karen Charman, Molly Kovel, Patrick Bond, Ashwin Desai, Salim Vally, Michael Smith, Kate Crockford, Gail Miller and Jenny Romaine.

I am particularly grateful to David Castle of Pluto Press for his support and editorial judgment, and to Elaine Ross and Ray Addicott for help with preparation of the manuscript.

Prologue

What do you want with this particular suffering of the Jews? The poor victims on the rubber plantations in Putumayo, the Negroes in Africa with whose bodies the Europeans play a game of catch, are just as near to me. Do you remember the words written on the work of the Great General Staff about Trotha's campaign in the Kalihari Desert? "And the death-rattles, the mad cries of those dying of thirst, faded away into the sublime silence of eternity"

Oh, this "sublime silence of eternity" in which so many screams have faded away unheard. It rings within me so strongly that I have no special corner of my heart reserved for the ghetto: I am at home wherever in the world there are clouds, birds and human tears. . . .
Rosa Luxemburg, Letter From Prison, February 16, 1917[1]

WHAT KIND OF JEW would write such a book as *Overcoming Zionism*, with its very harsh view of the State of Israel and equivalently radical recommendations for change—or what comes to the same thing, identifies with Rosa Luxemburg in her attitude about suffering and the ghetto? Not a good Jew, for sure. I ceased being that 60 years ago, with the first feeling that there was something confining about the ancestral religion. But not an uncaring one either. I wrote this book in fury about Israel and the unholy complicity of the United States and its Jewish community that grants it impunity. However, the "Jewish community" is no abstraction to me. It is the community from which I sprang, it inhabits me even if I do not inhabit it; it includes my family, and no degree of estrangement suffices to nullify the deep web of memory and conflict that links me to Jewry and shapes, however negatively, the foundations of who I am.

1

While reading Seymour Hersh's largely forgotten book about the development of Israel's nuclear bomb I was struck by an off-handed sentence that the "CIA had even been tipped off about the fact that Israel was raising large sums of money for Dimona from the American Jewish community."[2] This was by no means the most sensational of the startling revelations of Hersh's book. But not everybody who has read *The Samson Option* had a mother who bought Israel Bonds in his name and the name of his children. I had at the time winced and squirmed at receiving this "gift" (the German meaning—poison—aptly describes how I felt), and liquidated the holding as soon as I could—surreptitiously, it might be added, in order not to cause further deterioration in a relationship already strained to breaking point by conflict over Zionism. But there was little consolation in this. And learning many years later that my name could have been on funds that went into this monstrous venture only adds to the stew of emotion behind the present work.

Israel's nuclear arsenal, long helplessly accepted by the world, represents more than a strategic prize of incalculable menace. It also stands as perhaps the single greatest barrier to checking nuclear proliferation throughout the atomic era. Every American president from Eisenhower on (excluding George W. Bush, who wants Israel to have all weapons) has tried to check Israeli nuclear ambition, only to be driven back by Zionist political/financial muscle and manipulation of Holocaust guilt. Everybody in power knew this but was not to speak of it, and so the United States' effort to rein in the spread of weapons of supreme death, however compromised to begin with, became permanently crippled.

So it was not simply "making the desert bloom" with the trees my mother had planted in my name; our family could well have materially supported nuclear proliferation. I can say with reasonable confidence that mother would have thought this was right, for she had imbibed the full glass of Zionist absolutism. She would have agreed with the preponderant sentiment, that given the persecution suffered by Jews and its awful crescendo in the Holocaust, all measures, the Bomb included, had to be taken to stave off future efforts at extermination. She would likely not have gone so far as the unnamed Israeli official, enraged over President Eisenhower's squashing of the 1956 invasion of the Sinai,* whom Hersh chillingly quoted: "We got the message. We can still remember the smell of Auschwitz and Treblinka. Next time we'll take all of you with us."[3] But she would have resonated with what he meant. This was the climate in which I was raised.

Both parents had come to the United States in the early years of the last century, in the great trek from miserable, pogrom-ridden Tsarist Ukraine through the Lower East Side, Brooklyn and the Bronx, and onward to Long Island and finally the retirement communities of South Florida. Workers and small shopkeepers in the Old World, they became bourgeoisified in the New. I was the firstborn in the American Promised Land on both sides of the family, was suitably lionized as a child, and had a successful career, which led me into the medical profession, and then into psychiatry and psychoanalysis. As a youth I was never Zionist as such but felt an uneasy pride that our people had hewn a new and different kind of life out of what seemed to be an uninhabited wilderness. I celebrated with everyone else the inauguration of the State of Israel as a twelve-year-old, took my Bar Mitzvah in stride, moved in liberal Zionist circles as a rising psychiatric star, and felt panic at the threat to Israel in June 1967, then exultation at its six-day victory over what we all took to be barbaric Arab hordes.

---

* A joint venture of Israel, who wanted to strike a blow against Egyptian President Nasser; and England and France, who wanted to restore their colonial control over the Suez Canal. Eisenhower, widely taken for a golf-obsessed dolt, showed everybody just who was boss in the post-war era. But although Eisenhower must be judged as the American president least sympathetic to Israel, he had no better luck than any other in overturning security needs justified by memories of Holocaust, and so the Israeli Bomb went ahead under his watch just as it did under all the others.

How did so conventionally bred a young man reject his roots to develop ideas of the sort found in this book? My brother and eleven cousins came through similar circumstances with relatively little perturbation, more or less reproducing the values of their parents. I had had little difficulty in adapting to the ways of the world, and was well on my way toward a prominent academic career. But the pull of something within me began to supervene, "Nel mezzo del cammin di nostra vita,"[4] and continued.

Something of the process had to do with childhood relationships that formed fracture-lines in my soul. Chief among these were with my father, the saturnine Louis Kovel, and his youngest sister, my Aunt Betty. Both were contrarians, though of greatly different stripe. Lou Kovel was a good man in many ways; politically, however, he was a vile reactionary, even a kind of fascist. He seemed to disagree with everybody in our circle, which was conventionally left-of-center. Having read Oswald Spengler, father spent his days ranting about the decline of the West, the perfidy of leftists (including me as I grew into this way of thinking) and Soviet sympathizers—and the corresponding need for strong figures like Spain's General Franco, our own strongman General Douglas MacArthur, and the infamous Senator Joe McCarthy. Notably, father hated Zionism, and quarreled bitterly with my mother and everybody else in our circle about it. His reasoning on the subject was scarcely what I have come to adopt, compounded as it was from a hatred of Zionist "socialism" and a conviction, partially true but profoundly wrong-headed, that serious affection for Israel entailed disloyalty to the United States and its supreme mission of running the world for the benefit of big business. Life was trying, to say the least, with Lou Kovel, though one had to admire his fierce independence of mind and raw intellectual power. No doubt, father tutored me in the ways of dissension— both from him and through him. His disagreeability helped me to think for myself, to take nothing for granted, and to not fear going against a compact majority.

Betty was something else. She shared her big brother's independence of mind, but went in the opposite direction. Where father was a rigid patriarch, Betty was the first emancipated woman in my life, and a fount of radical verve. In the barren conformism of my family, she stood for setting forth on uncharted paths, and also for mocking authority, that is, Lou Kovel. I have no recollection what Betty's views on Zionism were, but she was notorious in the family for being a freethinking atheist. She was, in short, a Jew who did not affirm Judaism. This was to have dramatic consequences when Betty fell ill with a horrible ovarian cancer and died during my seventeenth year. Her funeral was conducted according to her wishes, in non-Jewish fashion. This seemed unexceptional to me, if tedious. But it incited a dreadful scene afterwards in which I overheard three surviving aunts denouncing Betty for her falling away from the Jewish faith, thereby depriving them of the spiritual pleasure of a proper Jewish funeral. The effect on me was apocalyptic, and sealed my heart against the ancestral religion.

The agony at Betty's funeral proved the *coup de grâce* of a long process of alienation from Judaism. As a boy I remember dissatisfaction with the rituals of the faith, boredom at synagogue, a rolling of the eyes at Seder, and a lack of interest in Judaism's theology. I considered Hebrew school to be a kind of dungeon keeping me from the streets, where true life was to be lived. I set out deliberately to not learn the language and refused to do my exercises, instead doodling football plays and fantasying about prison escapes while the instructor intoned about the Torah and the Covenant through which God had made the Jews special among the nations. In consternation, my mother sent me to a tutor, but this only worsened matters. The man was young, and his wife and children padded silently around the cramped and dim apartment as he tried to lay out for me the canons of the faith. He had a pasty look, with soft skin and hands that seemed to have never grasped more than a pencil. It seemed as though he barely ever got out of his chair, much less saw the sun. But what really impressed was the violence of his views. The words were positively spat out, bearing hatred for the *Goyim* who had persecuted our superior people, the Chosen Ones of God. And for what? "I'll tell you what," said the tutor, with blazing eyes and Old Testament wrath: "For a 'savior' who wasn't even born legitimate! That's right! His parents weren't married. The so-called god of the Christians was a bastard!" I fairly ran from the room, and from his kind. Who could have guessed that many such as him would emigrate to Israel from our neighborhood and come to play an important role in the future Jewish state?

As the years went on, my quarrel with Judaism took shape about the themes of chauvinism and entitlement, and in this way extended to the critique of Zionism.[5] The antipathy began viscerally, in the Synagogue and at my aunt's funeral, and over the years grew into a worldview. From the spiritual standpoint, I arrived at the view that to tie faith to the fortunes of a particular people is not a good idea. I have learned, slowly, fitfully, and no doubt imperfectly, that the only true foundation of faith is reaching for the infinite, not to escape the concrete here and now, but to set human existence in all its glory and shame against the immensity of the universe, the Whole of things. From this perspective, to grant a particular group Chosen status is nonsense—nonsense that may be colorful and forgiveable when the group in question is marginal, but becomes pernicious once that group links itself with the main body of power and gains control of a state. Nationalism is bad enough, but it can be sublimated through devices like the World Cup. Nationalism by divine decree—whether Judaic, Islamic, Christian or Hindu—and exercized with violent state power, is a living nightmare.

The story of Zionism is the story of that linkage and one such nightmare. The overcoming of Zionism is its dissolution. Actually, a multiple linkage and dissolution is involved: casting off the identity of the Jew as Zionist who is to redeem Israel and restore its glory, and in the process, undoing the linkage of Zion to capital and Western imperialism. Disaster without end is the result of this latter bond; and therefore also of the former. If the curse of Zionism is to be lifted, then, the identity of Jews needs to be detached from the fortunes of the State of Israel.

This differentiation gets at the core of the vexing problem of antisemitism, and its little brother, "the self-hating Jew." No doubt I will be accused of both for writing these things. So what? Those ridden by Zionist logic are bound to project the accusation of antisemitism onto whoever troubles their bad conscience. Antisemitism, a longstanding blight on humanity, occurs whenever the Jew is taken out of the nexus of historical determination, made to lose concreteness, and comes to stand for some archetype. It is a violence of abstraction, the overwriting of existence by essence. From this standpoint the Zionist who insists that the only true way of being Jewish is loyalty to the State of Israel is also a kind of antisemite, different at some levels from the the swine who scrawls a swastika on a synagogue but bound together as an exponent of violence.

We will have more to say about all this below. Concerning myself, the reader who may be worrying whether I have succumbed to the odd condition of "self-hating Jew," may rest assured that any such tendencies have been cured through the above-mentioned detachment of Jewishness from Zionism, that is, its overcoming. This does not make me a Zionist-hating Jew—though I do loathe Zionism. Rather, the lengthy process of negating the various threads of my Jewish identity has altered the very fabric of Jewishness.

The figure of who we are is formed against the ground of who we are not. Without this process of negation, nobody would exist as a distinct person, nor would any "people" have an identity. But negation that is mere repetition can eventuate in murderous cycles of revenge—as it does in the religious wars of history, each side feeding off hatred of the other. The fuller, more universal kind of being engages a negating of negation itself. This is the creative moment, the letting go and moving toward the infinite. When we let go of some possessive attachment with a good will, we are also reaching beyond. We seek in the same gesture a new object and do so non-possessively. This should extend to all aspects of our being—to property, to power, even to nature. It is what Jesus offered and why he was slain.

Tribalism is the curse of Judaism, whether as practiced by my Orthodox tutor in Brooklyn, the aunts who trampled on Betty's memory, or, in imperial form, by the State of Israel and the Zionist movement that nourishes it. It is an endless return, bound to the wheel of revenge. But there is another prospect for those who have been thrown into the world as Jews. One can negate the negation that is tribalism and accept the true glory of being Jewish, which is to live on the margin and across boundaries. Negating the negation finds a path toward the universal. The great Jewish geniuses of modernity, beginning with Spinoza, and moving through Marx, Freud, Proust, Einstein, Kafka, Wittgenstein and Rosa Luxemburg, were all of this kind. It became in each instance the mode of their achievement—observe in our epigraph to this Prologue how Rosa negated the negation that is the ghetto. Such Jews knew themselves to be Jewish, but in affirming their genius experienced the identity in varying ways as non-Jewishness. They were non-tribalized Jews, or in the phrase first defined as such by Isaac Deutscher, who was one of them, *non-Jewish Jews*.[6]

The choice emerges from the enduring dilemma of Jewishness—being alone in the wilderness, including the wilderness of human existence. It is a most interesting and wonderful way of being human, and can be so again if Zionism is let go. No ethnic homeland, no Jewish state, then, and good riddance to that, because Zionism has meant recycling the negation that is Judaism into endless destruction. Negating this negation, the wandering Jew is no longer alone. The whole earth itself and all the people and other creatures upon it come into view as our only true home.

But then there is the matter of that militarized state at the eastern end of the Mediterranean standing in the way, and the dreadful mistake that was made to get it going . . .

Part One

Coming to Zion

1
A People Apart

By the rivers of Babylon—there we sat down and there we wept when we remembered Zion.
On the willows there we hung up our harps.
For there our captors asked us for songs, and our tormentors asked for mirth, saying, "Sing us one of the songs of Zion."

How could we sing the LORD's song in a foreign land?
If I forget you, O Jerusalem, let my right hand wither!
Let my tongue cling to the roof of my mouth, if I do not remember you, if I do not set Jerusalem above my highest joy.

PSALM 137 IS ONE of the most hauntingly beautiful passages in the Bible, and a virtual anthem of the Zionist cause. Its words of longing and faith have been recited on innumerable occasions over the years, no doubt often accompanied by real weeping. But what we read above is not the whole psalm. There are three more lines, which tend to get filtered out in the consideration of this text—and, I should think, rarely get read at Seder—but must be included in its meaning. Here they are, in the New Revised Standard Version:

Remember, O LORD, against the Edomites the day of Jerusalem's fall, how they said, "Tear it down! Tear it down! Down to its foundations!"
O daughter Babylon, you devastator! Happy shall they be who pay you back what you have done to us!
Happy shall they be who take your little ones and dash them against the rock!

I have read numerous commentaries on this famous Psalm, and none of them look askance at the last two lines celebrating vengeance taken on the children of Edom. If pressed, people will most likely say, well, that was the way they talked back then, everybody accepted the necessity of revenge, the talion law of an eye for an eye. Today we live in the advanced world whose supreme moment is given by liberal democracy, where the rule of Law replaces the talion principle. What counts in the Psalm is fidelity to Zion, immortalized in the powerful State of Israel. And Israel is just such an advanced society, a bastion of the Enlightenment, the "Only Democracy in the Middle East" as one is endlessly reminded, a precious jewel of Western civilization to be protected by all right-thinking people against the forces of Oriental darkness, or as some now say, "Islamo-fascism."

As this is being written, in August 2006, Israel is bombing Lebanon, pulverising it with advanced technology provided by its mighty partner, the United States of America. The Lebanese force, Hizbullah, has retaliated with hundreds of rockets, which have caused much consternation and some loss of life, though the scale of damage, as has been the case throughout the wars between Israel and its "neighbors," is of the order of ten to one against the Arabs. This is incalculably greater when infrastructure is taken into account. The bombs have caused an oil spill that has precipitated what may turn out to be the worst ecological catastrophe in the history of the Eastern Mediterranean. Elsewhere, virtually every bridge has been destroyed in the country, which awaits the perdition of what is nicely called a "humanitarian crisis," its advent hastened by Israel's bombing of ambulances, fuel dumps, and indeed, humanitarian aid workers and UN observers. Over 1000 Lebanese had been killed by the end of the first week in August, less than 10 percent of them the combatants of Hizbullah—who are giving the Israel Defense Force (IDF) the devil of a time. Of the dead, about one-third are children. The "little ones"are sometimes dashed against the rock but more often dashed by rock-like things propelled by high explosives. So the rock comes to them, an advantage of air power, which spares the perpetrator's conscience by removing him from the scene of the crime.

This kind of distancing might be enough for the US or British Air Forces, well schooled in concepts like "surgical airstrikes" and "collateral damage." But where Israel is concerned a raw nerve intrudes that is not so easily dulled. The history epitomized by Psalm 137 bubbles to the surface and calls for more strenuous methods of moral damage control. For example, after the bombing of the Qana refugee camp in Southern Lebanon in which more than a score of children perished, a journalist published in the popular daily newspaper, *Maariv*, a sample speech of justification, which he recommended that Prime Minister Ehud Olmert deliver. A bit extreme for a PM who has to keep an international audience in mind, the speech nonetheless attracted wide attention and approval within Israel, and may be fairly brought forth as a *précis* of its basic exculpatory logic.[1] It had two main themes:

- That Israel feels really bad about bombing little children but had to do it—and will do it "today, tomorrow and the day after tomorrow. . . here, there and everywhere"— because it is facing "savages," nay, "agents of the devil [that is, Hizbullah, who have] taken over their land [that is, Lebanon] and turned the lives of our children into hell." It is Hizbullah who launched missiles from Qana, hence Israel, to protect its children, must bomb children of the Other. In other words, talion law reigns.

- But there is another, deeper narrative superimposed on this, quite specific for Israel and its Zionist ideology. This narrative overrides mere matters of fact[2] with the power of its great theme, the immemorial suffering of the Jewish people, the complicity of the rest of the world in this, the imminence and omnipresence of catastrophe, and the necessity of Israeli counterforce to prevent its recurrence. Here is some of the rhetoric:

> Ladies and gentlemen, it's time you understood: the Jewish state will no longer be trampled upon. ... Today I am serving as the voice of six million bombarded Israeli citizens who serve as the voice of six million murdered Jews who were melted down to dust and ashes by savages in Europe. In both cases, those responsible for these evil acts were, and are, barbarians devoid of all humanity, who set themselves one simple goal: to wipe the Jewish people off the face of the earth, as Adolph Hitler said, or to wipe the State of Israel off the map, as [Iranian President] Mahmoud Ahmedinijad proclaims. And you—just as you did not take those words seriously then, you are ignoring them again now. And that, ladies and gentlemen, leaders of the world, will not happen again. Never again will we wait for bombs that never came to hit the gas chambers. Never again will we wait for salvation that never arrives. Now we have our own air force. The Jewish people are now capable of standing up to those who seek their destruction ...

This narrative is foundational for Israel, and we shall take up its particulars in the pages ahead. Here we emphasize once again how far back it goes, and how steadfastly it recurs in a kind of eternal return, holding Zion within its grip. For the ancient texts are not just *about* the flow of events; they constitute events, enter their marrow, and fly out of the mouths of later generations like flocks of starlings. Ran HaCohen, an outstanding commentator within contemporary Israel, has culled some interesting specimens of recent discourse from its "liberal intellectuals" as they justify Israel's latest war. A good deal of what they say resembles the dry rationalization of apologists everywhere for crimes of state.[3] But some of the material has the sound of undigested Old Testament wrathfulness breaking through the clouds like a bloody sunset.

The editor-in-chief of Israel's largest daily newspaper demands on the front page that Israel

> wipe out villages that host Hezbollah terrorists ... [and] wash with burning fire the Hezbollah terrorists, their helpers, their collaborators, and those who look the other way, and everyone who smells like Hezbollah, and let their innocent people die instead of ours. (*Yediot Ahronot*, July 28, 2006)

Poet and self-proclaimed leftist Ilan Shenfeld writes:

> March on Lebanon and also on Gaza with ploughs and salt. Destroy them to the last inhabitant. Turn them into an arid desert, an uninhabited, turbid valley. Because we yearned for peace and wanted it, and our houses we destroyed first, But they were a wasted gift for those murderers, with beard and Jihad bands, who shout: "Massacre now!," and who have neither love nor peace, neither god nor father. [. . .] Save your people and make bombs, and rain them on villages and towns and houses till they collapse. Kill them, shed their blood, terrify their lives, lest they try again to destroy us, until we hear from tops of exploding mountains, Ridden down by your heels, sounds of supplication and lamentation. And your pits will cover them. Whoever scorns a day of bloodshed, He should be scorned. Save your people, and make war. (Ynet, July 30, 2006)[4]

And dash the little ones against the rock ... Psalm 137 is a microcosm of the Old Testament, whose beauty, grandeur and spiritual majesty coexists with a kind of hellfire celebrating every kind of violence including mass murder. It is the latter feature which thrives in modern-day Israel. Our overwrought Israeli intellectuals must have read Deuteronomy, Moses' Valedictory Address to his people and of special importance to Zionism. Here we learn that the Israelites struck down King Sihon, "along with his offspring and all his people. At that time we captured all his towns, and in each town we utterly destroyed men women and children. We left not a single survivor"—except for livestock, which were taken as spoil

[2: 33–35]. Then there was King Og of Bashan, who received the same fate, "in each city utterly destroying men, women and children," and again taking the livestock as booty [3: 6]. Later, Moses says that the enemy nations should be cleared away "little by little; you will not be able to make a quick end of them, otherwise the wild animals would become too numerous for you. But the LORD your God will give them over to you and throw them into great panic, until they are destroyed." [7: 22–23]—a passage that could well have been bandied about as plans for the ethnic cleansing of Palestinians were hatched—just as the following pertains to Israel's external wars, including, falsely, that of 2006: "Every place on which you set foot shall be yours; your territory shall extend from the wilderness to the Lebanon and from the river, the River Euphrates, to the Western Sea. No one will be able to stand against you. ..." [11: 24–25]

Among the last words of Moses to the people we find the following, which epitomize both the grandeur of the Old Testament and the deeply problematic, vengeful spirit of the Zionism that has been one of his legacies:

> I will make My shafts drunk with blood,
> and my sword will eat up flesh,
>   from the blood of the fallen and captive,
> from the flesh of the long-haired foe.
> Nations, O gladden His people,
> for His servants' blood will He avenge,
> and vengeance turn back on His foes
> and purge His soil, His people.
> [32: 42–43][5]

HOW IS ZION TO BE UNDERSTOOD?

The Judaic way of being begins with a leap of negative logic. Among the social formations of the ancient world there emerged a grouping of hill tribes whose identity was based upon refusing to be like the others. It called itself Israelite, and the notion of separateness remained, to appear throughout the Pentatuech, the five books of its chronicle, which collectively became the Torah, Judaism's precious affirmation of its history and being. In the fourth Book, *Numbers*, the seer Balaam announces the theme directly: *Behold, it is a people dwelling apart, not counting itself among the nations.*[6] The ancient Israelites were the only people who refused to grant validity to the gods of their neighbors, in contrast to what Ronald Hendel has called the "basic cultural translatability in the ancient Near East," in which peoples would freely borrow spiritual motifs from each other.[7] By affirming apartness, the tribes developed a sharply internalized identity whose spiritual reflex was to become the God, Yahweh. Thus they became the "Tribes of Yahweh," a title given to them by the Liberation theologist and historian Norman Gottwald, who saw in the Israelites' struggles with the principalities of the time a discovery of the possibility of emancipation.[8] This is plainly true.

But so is the converse: Becoming a people apart, with a godhead to match, may help account for the extraordinary durability of the Jewish identity, but it also equipped it with an enduring sense of conflict, both within itself and with other nations, and can lead to domination as well as emancipation. There is no mystery to this. Paraphrasing John Donne, we are none of us an island, thus no people can really live apart, no matter how high they build separation walls. Those who try to do so only aggravate history. They are the splinters under the skin of humanity.

Looking at the matter a bit more closely, we see the existential choice to live as a "people apart" to be a launching point for a dialectic whose further development was shaped, first, by the kinds of reactions others would have to this, and then by the counter-reactions of Israelites (later under names such as Hebrews, Jews and Israelis) in order to adapt to others. This sets into motion that process of struggle and self-definition, which makes Jewish history so interesting and varied, but also so troubled. The process could undergo lulls for considerable periods of equilibrium during which Jews were reasonably comfortable in the larger world; it could burst into spasms of terrible persecution, massacre and exile when things became destabilized; it could take forms known as "homelessness," "rootlessness," "cosmopolitanism," etc., at various points; it would allow them to play an essential role in navigating the universal alienator we call money, and so help to bring about capitalism; and it could also cause them to develop pockets of deep and dark atavisms through isolation and withdrawal from the world. We find the origins of the malaise called antisemitism in this dialectic; and we also find the reaction to antisemitism known as Zionism.

The theological reflex of being a people apart is known as the Covenant, a kind of promise bestowed by Yahweh upon his people, and first encountered in Genesis with respect to Abraham, the original Patriarch:

> Go from your country and your kindred and your father's house to the land that I will show you. I will make of you a great nation, and I will bless you, and make your name great, so that you will be a blessing. I will bless those who bless you, and the one who curses you I will curse; and in you all the families of the earth shall be blessed.[9]

The Covenant is a very conditional promise, as Abraham discovered when Yahweh asked for the sacrifice of his son Isaac as a sign of loyalty. The Old Testament is seeded with passages in which the God of the Hebrews scolds his people and threatens to bring about every kind of calamity should they disobey or forget him. We see a variation in Psalm 137's imprecation to "let my right hand wither" if the Jew forgets Jerusalem—which, turned around, means that the power to wreak vengeance, in today's world, the power of the IDF, will be restored once Jerusalem is remembered, or what comes to the same thing, if Yahweh is obeyed. Yahweh was the internal reflex of the apartness of the Israelites, and the peculiar mode of organization of their moral world made the Jewish people into the original guilt culture. Guilt is not the same, however, as recognition of wrongdoing and the taking of responsibility to bring about change. That is its overcoming. Too often, it becomes a signal calling for the replacement of responsibility with blame and accusation, and the repetition of wrongdoing, as we explore below.

The contrast between the Covenant between ancient Israel and its God, on the one hand, and animistic or Asian religions, on the other, could not be starker. In these latter, voices abound, but as a plurality that is distinct from, yet continuous with, the sensuously lived world.[10] For Judaic being there is one voice, male and dissociated from any image,[11] in other words, abstracted from the sensuous world, and experienced as a harsh command. The voice is of God, but it is also of the inner self, and of the tribe as well, whose separateness from other peoples—heathen and idolators—is ever more sharply inscribed. Obedience to a peremptory and guilt-inducing inner voice is a distinctive aspect of Judaic being, both a product of apartness and a reinforcement for apartness. It leads into a kind of moral universe where the dictates of the tribe and those of the universal deity can be conflated, especially under circumstances in which the larger society reinforces the separation of Jews from others by law or persecution. When that happens, as was the case not infrequently in the long period of wandering known as the Diaspora which followed the destruction of the Second Temple by Rome, then being apart and being chosen as exceptional became one and the same; spiritual greatness and collective narcissism flow together. Under the conditions of ghettoization that characterized the Diaspora, the ethical world can readily become organized tribally. Now the potentials for universality given by monotheism are squandered and the cycle of vengeance prevails. For if one's ethical reference point is the tribal unit, then all others are devalued, and one no longer belongs to humanity but sets oneself over humanity. The other is no longer a full person, but a thing-like repository of barbarous impulse, devoid of history and moral weight and suitable to be dashed against the rocks. This dilemma is to haunt Zionism once its state was formed and its logic of conquest put Jews in the driver's seat. But it is much older than Zionism.

To repeat, Judaic being can conduce to universality and bring forth emancipation. We should regard this as its priceless potential, if not always a legacy. However, emancipation has always, indeed necessarily, occurred in reference to a critique of, and a standing away from, the established order, including the order of Judaism itself. The Prophetic tradition within the Old Testament is certainly one of the great gems given to the world by the Jewish people, and an example of this. By definition oriented to an as-yet unfulfilled future, it is therefore grounded in critique of the given. The prophet is of the people but stands outside the city and reminds it of its falling away from the universal that is God's true being. Isaiah, the greatest, begins with a diatribe: "Israel does not know, my people do not understand . . ." Indeed, they are "utterly estranged." [1: 3, 4] He calls for a Messiah who "with righteousness ... shall judge the poor, and decide with equity for the meek of the earth." [11: 4] Equity for the meek: what can this mean but a universal vision of justice, a vision in which no one people can be "chosen" over any other, except chosen to overcome chosen-ness, to negate its negation?

The original Covenant expressed this hope, too, when Yahweh said to Abraham, "in you all the families of the earth shall be blessed." That is, there can be no people over any other in the promised, fulfilled world: all families are blessed, therefore the human family and the families of other beings come into the heaven of the universal. If it should so transpire that some people are set up over others, then it behooves us to find out why this is so, and to make a change in the circumstances of humankind so that the condition will be overcome. Abrahamic Judaism was carried out against a backdrop of tribal hill culture; but the Prophet Isaiah, and all the prophets to come, contended with a state society and its class distinctions. Hence prophetic-emancipatory Judaism is necessarily revolutionary with regard to state power.

Isaiah was the greatest Old Testament prophet; but the greatest prophet of all, and the one whose advent he prophesied, was Jesus of Nazareth. Jesus was authentically Jewish and yet a breaking point in the history of Judaism, which becomes defined thereafter by those Jews who did not follow him. Jesus was that Jew who made the Covenant universal by dissolving its tribal shell and extending it to all humanity. All spirit-forms are given shape by the concrete world in which they appear, even as they shape that world. By the time of Jesus the tribal world of Hebrew origins had become a mythic backdrop to a world of Roman imperialism, militarism, and religion served through the Second Temple. Universalism under these conditions, therefore, had to incorporate those who lived under empire and worshipped under the imperially derived authority of the Temple. These included the marginalized masses, to whose fate Jesus directed himself. He spoke to, of, and for the beggars, the whores, the rabble, the outcasts, the underlings, the nothings. His message was crafted to keep state authorities at bay by rendering unto Caesar that which was Caesar's.[12] But toward the moneyed classes, and toward the Temple hierarchy, Jesus was ruthless. He understood the exploitation of labor and of spirit, he understood how priestly authority could manipulate religious law to create mystery and alienate spirit, and how priests could be in league with money-lenders.

And so Jesus was asking for trouble, and got it. The political mapping of the time between Rome and the various factions of Jews is complex and does not concern us here. However, as a spiritual teacher, Jesus was obliged to clash with the Temple's monopoly over spirituality, as well as with Rome. The Passion of Christ is the chronicle of this world-transforming event. His constituency was the Jewish masses, very numerous at that time, and his antagonists were the rich and their Temple hierarchy. Consequently, he was done in by an alliance of wealthy, Sadducee Jews and the priests whose spiritual monopoly he threatened, while the Roman authorities looked on in continual worriment over their obstreperous Jewish subjects.

Out of the welter of factions and event, there arose that half-truth, which became the germ of the most durable of delusions, that the Jews killed Jesus. Certainly, Jews played an important role in the death of Jesus—but those who did were members of the class structure threatened by his radical message. This is the key point, perpetually buried under the blather surrounding antisemitism. The generalization of this specific moment into a blood-curse on a whole people has been one of the more pernicious turn of events to have afflicted humanity, for two reasons: the grief it gave to Jews over the centuries as accusation persisted in an undercurrent of hatred toward them within Christendom; and by the way it was exploited to occlude Jesus' radically emancipatory message—because Christ must perennially be crucified so that the world may continue on its tracks. The instrument of these baleful changes was the nucleus of what we know today as antisemitism—or what may also be called, *judaeophobia*, which is its phenomenological core, a kind of primal fear-and-loathing of the Jew *qua* Jew.[13]

A VEXING QUESTION

Nothing is more troublesome than to tease out the delusional and persecutory roots of antisemitism from the actual behavior and wrongdoing of Jews. This latter is their birthright as human beings, Jews being no more and no less capable of goodness and evil than the entire human race, though distinguished by being perpetually in the way because of their status as the people apart. Alas, many commentators, and chief among them the ideologues of Zionism, insist on keeping up the ridiculous and demeaning charade that Jews, being the most spiritually/ ethically advanced people, that is, the Chosen Ones, have been essentially innocent of all charges concocted by antisemites. Thus Howard Fast, a popular writer of strongly left-leaning convictions, wrote in his *The Jews, the Story of a People*: "Such despair and agony as the Jewish people had to endure over the past thousand years is the result, not of what they are, but of what the Christian world has inflicted upon them."[14] In other words, who the Jews are is to be simply defined by what has been done to them, as though they had no internal relationship to their persecutions, nor made any use of it for their own purposes. This is as logically defective as antisemitism itself. More recently, Marvin Perry and Frederick Schweitzer have written in their *Antisemitism: Myth and Hate from Antiquity to the Present*, that "Antisemitism has very little to do with the actual behavior of Jews or the strictures of their highly ethical religion—indeed antisemites usually are totally ignorant of the rich tradition of rabbinical writings that discuss, often wisely and insightfully, biblical themes and Jewish laws … ."[15] By proclaiming the essential innocence and moral purity of the Jew, this inversion of the antisemitic complex reinstalls the tribalist notion of "a people apart," and reinforces it with the perennial Jewish character traits of dwelling within the notion of suffering and being persecuted, and coordinated with this, having a superior ethical stature. It in fact denies the humanity of Jews by refusing to look at their reciprocal relations with others.[16]

To diagnose the malady of antisemitism, one needs to distinguish the empirical facticity of a remark about Jews from its logical content and phenomenological structure, that is, the inner state of being from which it is launched.

The logical part is fairly easy to do, though all too rarely undertaken. One need only ask the question: is this statement about Jews a *concrete* one, or is it made as a proposition about an underlying general *essence* of Jewishness? The method here is strictly historical; that is, is one looking at concretely situated people subject to the whole range of historical determinations and recognizable therefore as living individuals? Or do we encounter them as pasteboard figures carrying about some sign of Jewishness—avariciousness, cunning, etc.—and *essentially* standing in for that?

The phenomenological inquiry is more difficult, but only because it requires some knowledge of the state of mind from which the judgment of Jews proceeds. Chiefly, this consists of being able to determine the affect with which the judgment is made, and whether it is deeply felt and enduring as well as hateful. If the answer to these questions is affirmative this tells us that antisemitism is going on and that it is an effort to deal with a lesion in the being of he who launches the charge against the Jew; the accusation against Jews itself is no more then than a cloak to cover up this relationship, though needless to add, often enough highly destructive. In this respect, Jewishness is a statement about something unresolved in the self of the antisemite. In its broadest aspect, we would say, then, that the miserable antisemitism that has perfused Christendom is a manifestation of its unlived life, and its failure to realize Jesus. (We set aside here the pressing question of judaeophobia within Islam, except to say that it is a definite issue, though less deeply corrosive than what has taken place within Christendom.) Finally, it should be recognized that in the real world judaeophobic statements are complex and often refer to subtle layerings of truth and falsehood stuck together with every which kind of human foible.

One would be hard put to say which of the three Abrahamic religions has most betrayed its prophets. All have a lot to answer for, nor can any degree of explanation as to why this was done take away the stain of the doing. In the case of interest here, that of the People Apart, Perry and Schweitzer's propagandistic evocation of the "rich tradition of rabbinical writings that discuss, often wisely and insightfully, biblical themes and Jewish laws," deserves some scrutiny. This is quite a tall tale in view of the very checkered record of classical Judaism under the influence of the Rabbinate who replaced the priestly class of antiquity during the long Diaspora—and whose important relationship to modern Israel we take up in some detail below. There is needless to say, much spiritual and aesthetic wealth in the rabbinical tradition. But there is also a lot of dross, and beyond that, things weird and frankly destructive. What else can be expected in so great a range of enclosed and weak societies surrounded by a hostile world and presided over by a male authority system?

The great Israel Shahak, fearless critic of Zionism, made a study of the odd results of this system as it took hold in Europe from the medieval to the early modern period. Here is something of what he learned:[17]

- that according to the Talmud (that is, the teachings of the rabbis), "Jesus was executed by a proper rabbinical court for idolatry, inciting other Jews to idolatry, and contempt of rabbinical authority. All classical Jewish sources that mention his execution are quite happy to take responsibility for it; in the Talmudic account the Romans are not even mentioned." Other, more popular accounts accuse Jesus of witchcraft; the very name is "a symbol for all that is abominable, ..." [97–98]

- Jews are forbidden to praise gentiles; rather are they asked to utter curses when passing by gentile cemeteries, or large gatherings of gentiles. [93] Similarly, they are not to give gentiles gifts, while being directed to charge gentiles maximum interest in their money-lending activities.

- Sexual intercourse between Jewish men and gentile women is not considered adultery but bestiality, since gentile women are not considered human and are therefore incapable of matrimony. This does not let the gentile woman off the hook. She must be executed even if raped: "If a Jew has coitus with a gentile woman [writes one authority who shall be discussed below], whether she be a child of three or an adult, whether married or unmarried, and even if he is a minor only nine years and one day—because he had wilful coitus with her, she must be killed, as is the case with a beast, because through her a Jew got into trouble." The Jew himself must be flogged, as befits one who has had sex with a beast. [87]

In sum, the dark record of antisemitism includes not just the racist-imposed sufferings of Jews but the imprint of certain counter-racisms. The presence of these and similar statements should not be used to label Judaism as such, or even its Orthodox proponents. They are only parts of a much more complex whole. But they are also parts that can be seized under particular circumstances, including those pertaining to the history of Zionism, which has incorporated them in ways we discuss below in order to advance the notion of Jewish exceptionalism in a malignant form.

A great deal of attention is given within classical Judaism to the supreme importance of saving human life. This has become regarded as a centerpiece of the ethical superiority of the Jewish people. There is a qualification, however, inasmuch as only Jews are considered human. The Kabbala, that profound tradition of Jewish mysticism much beloved by New Age savants and stars like Madonna, and highly influential among Hassidim and ultra-right wing Israeli groups like Gush Emunim, states that "Souls of non-Jews come entirely from the female part of the satanic sphere. For this reason souls of non-Jews are called evil, not good, and are created without [divine] knowledge." From which it follows that "it is plain that those prospects and the scheme [of salvation] are intended only for Jews."[18] Rabbi

Abraham Kook the Elder (1865–1935), an important figure in the Zionist tradition and "revered father of the messianic tendency of Jewish fundamentalism ... said 'The difference between a Jewish soul and the souls of non-Jews ... is greater and deeper than the difference between a human soul and the souls of cattle.'"[19] Similarly, Rabbi Menachem Mendel Schneerson, the adored leader of the Lubovitcher Hassidim, writes that

> The difference between a Jewish and a non-Jewish person comes from the common expression: "Let us differentiate." Thus we do not have a case of profound change in which a person is merely on a superior level. Rather we have a case of "let us differentiate" between totally different species. This is what needs to be said about the body: the body of a Jewish person is of a totally different quality from the body of [members] of all nations of the world ... .[20]

From which it follows logically, in the words of Rabbi Yitzhak Ginsburgh in the *Jewish Week* of April 26, 1996, that "If every single cell in a Jewish body entails divinity, and is thus part of God, then every strand of DNA is a part of God. Therefore, there is something special about Jewish DNA."[21]

This kind of thinking is laced through the Talmud and other documents of the Halakhah, the foundation of Jewish Law and the cement of traditional Jewish identity and society. The contradictions become particularly severe around the question of the saving of gentile lives by Jewish physicians. It is inscribed, for example, in the Talmudic maxim that "Gentiles are neither to be lifted [out of a well into which they may have fallen] nor hauled down into it." [80] The Hippocratic Oath—product of the Hellenism that discomfited Jews in the three centuries directly before the Common Era—prescribes that the doctor try to save all human life irrespective of the identity of the person who happens to be alive. This however runs afoul of the classical Jewish precept that the difference between Jews and non-Jews is greater than that between humans and cattle, and that therefore non-Jews are not human. Given the primacy of rabbinical authority in traditional Jewish society, then, it should come as no surprise to read the following:

> As for Gentiles with whom we are not at war ..., their death must not be caused, but it is forbidden to save them if they are at the point of death; if, for example, one of them is seen falling into the sea, he should not be rescued, for it is written [Lev: 19–16]: "neither shalt thou stand against the blood of thy fellow"—but [a Gentile] is not thy fellow ... [80]

It does however come as a surprise to learn that the author of these jarring words is none other than Moses Maimonides—who also wrote the passage above about putting to death gentile women with whom Jewish men have had sexual relations, along with others in this vein. Maimonides!? The most revered and prodigiously learned of Jews, physician to the court of the great Saladin (who is exempt from the prohibition of treatment, as the kind of authority a prudent Jew would not want to cross), the contemporary of St Francis and his moral equivalent for the Jewish people, and one of the greatest of those medieval Aristotelians whose intellectual synthesis points the way for the Age of Science and Reason.

The contribution of Maimonides to the practice of withholding medical treament to gentiles resurfaced in the infamous case of Baruch Goldstein, an immigrant physician from Brooklyn who massacred 29 Muslims (wounding 100 others) at prayer in the Patriarch's Cave in Hebron on February 25, 1994. Submerged in the history of this sensational event is the prior story of Goldstein as a doctor in the Israeli army, where he repeatedly breached military regulations by refusing to treat Arab soldiers and was more than once reassigned on this basis. Two things stand out in this episode: first, that though Goldstein repeatedly violated direct military orders, he was never court-martialled, evidently because of protection by higher-ups fearing adverse publicity by Israel's ultra-right religious parties. And second, when confronted with refusal to treat a wounded Arab, Goldstein declared: "I am not willing to treat any non-Jew. I recognize as legitimate only two [religious] authorities: Maimonides and [Meir] Kahane."

It is therefore not possible to dismiss the moral oddities of the Halakhah as a mere peccadillo. As extreme as he may have been, Baruch Goldstein certainly mattered within Israel, as shown by his elevation to the status of a heroic martyr after his death, and more generally, by the remarkable rise in the status and influence of the ultra-Orthodox in Israel.[22] It follows that the two names, Moses Maimonides and Meir Kahane, the former a veritable saint and the latter as violent a figure as has ever appeared in Jewish history, are drawn together by the logic of Zionism, which has rooted itself, for reasons we now explore, in the most archaic and vengeance-ridden strata of Judaic being in order to advance a thoroughly modern agenda.

2

The Unnatural History of a Bad Idea

"It's no bad thing," said M. de Charlus when he had finished questioning me about Bloch, "to have a few foreigners among your friends." I told him that Bloch was French. "Is that so?" said M. de Charlus, "I took him to be Jewish."
Marcel Proust, *The Guermantes Way*.[1]

A TRAGIC DILEMMA LEADS TO A BAD DECISION

BY THE END OF the nineteenth century, Europe's Jews were in an increasingly difficult situation. Their population had increased from 2.75 million in 1825 to over 8.5 million in 1900, far faster than the rate for Europe as a whole.[2] A small fraction had done exceptionally well, while most by far were desperately poor and jammed into cities under distinctly unwholesome conditions. This was markedly accentuated in Eastern Europe, where the vast majority of Jews lived, and where the impending crack up of Czarist absolutism had led to a sharp increase in violent antisemitism, frequently state-sponsored. Everywhere, great social forces were grinding like tectonic plates presaging an earthquake to come. Jews sensed that they lived along the fault lines and could be consumed in the catastrophe. The awareness stimulated a heightening radicalism and a marked increase in emigration, mainly Westward.

32

The emancipatory side of Judaism was greatly stimulated by this conjuncture of forces. Revolutionary socialism, especially that of Karl Marx, that unreconstructed "non-Jewish Jew" who drew deeply from the prophetic and messianic tradition, seized the imagination, whether as the Bolshevism that would emerge victorious in the great Russian Revolution to come, or the Bundist movements of Eastern Europe, which were dedicated to a kind of radical and autonomous syndicalism. The possibility of liberal reforms within the bourgeois state remained as well, although these were open to an ever declining fraction of the Jewish people of Western Europe.

And then there was national renewal, which could readily be seen in an emancipatory light. Great numbers of Jews were on the move within the terms of the Diaspora. Why not, then, reasoned some, move outside these terms, and reclaim Jewish nationhood? Throughout the centuries of Diaspora, Jews had regarded themselves as a kind of nation; that is how, after all, they survived in the pores of other societies. The gathering *fin de siècle* crisis had greatly energized Jewish culture, especially in its Yiddish form, and further stimulated this line of reasoning. Thus a Zionist urge, which had for centuries marginally occupied the Jewish mind, began to gestate as a real possibility.

At first glance the Zionist movement seems the very antithesis of the dark tribalisms that haunt Jewish history. Zionists were, manifestly, thoroughly modern "New Jews." Indeed, no antisemite could surpass the loathing of some of them for the backwardness and superstition of the Jewish masses. Yet Zionism's dynamic was drawn from the most tribal and particularistic stratum of Judaism, and its destiny became the restoration of tribalism in the guise of a modern, highly militarized and aggressive state. In other words, both of the Covenant-al paths open to Jewry, universalism and chauvinistic tribalism, were used by Zionism, but toward markedly different ends: the former as a fig leaf for the latter, which became the real driving force of the movement.

The reason for this is perfectly obvious. Jews may have *thought* of themselves as a nation, but thought and reality are not the same. To be a nation, a people has to have an organic relation to a territory, and this the Jews lacked. They had instead a *fantasied* relation to a *mythic* territory, the Biblical Israel, which had to stand in for the real, habitable territory until this was gained. And that has been the fatal flaw in Zionism, both before and after the conquest, and why we call it, ungenerously but truthfully, a bad idea.

The choice of Palestine as national home enabled the quest to proceed along mythically defined lines, at the cost of situating the dream of Jewish renewal in the very center of Islam. This was very foolish, and will one day bring Israel down. But wherever the Zionists would have gone, they would have encountered severe resistance. Habitable land has a way of being already inhabited, and inhabitants have a way of being attached to place. It is just one of those nagging features of human nature. A tremendous struggle would be necessary, therefore, if the Zionists were to dislodge these inhabitants, and only a tremendously concentrated desire could suffice to energize that struggle. This concentration of desire would have to contend with three great difficulties: the resistance of those who stood in the way and would have to be displaced; the exigencies of geopolitics; and one's own inner being, which would have to be retooled from the self-image of an ethical victim to that of a ruthless conquerer.

All of these obstacles could be dealt with by signing onto Western imperialism and capitalism. A great deal came the Zionist's way as a result: money, the imprimatur of Great Powers, and a full deck of moral excuses reaching back to the Crusades, the *mission civilisatrice*, and the White Man's Burden—all these fell into the Zionist lap, with long-term consequences we trace below. But what remained unique to

Zionism was the way the imperial mantle fit over the archaic tribalism.

Only an immensity of Jewish suffering could compensate for the moral contradictions inherent to the drive for land. As a result, a subtle but profound shift took place with respect to the persecutions that the Jews had suffered. The burden of antisemitism, which was the perceived stimulus to Zionism, became integrated into Zionism as an essential condition for it. Judaeophobia acquired an ominous kind of necessity: rather than stimulating the drive to transform the social conditions from which judaeophobia arose, antisemitic persecution was drawn into service; it became a useful, and even necessary, wheel in the machinery of Zionism.

Zionism might be called an artificial nationalism. The passions that drove it were all too real, but the reality was that of a collective fantasy animating a people who, as Jean-Christophe Attias has put it, "never defined themselves simply as Jews: they were Jews from the country where they lived; Jews of the particular language they spoke." Even Moses Maimonides, for example, who left Spain for Egypt as a young man because of persecution and spent the rest of his life in what is now Cairo, never ceased "characterizing himself as a Sephardi, a Spaniard, or even an Andalusian!"[3] For Jewish nationalism to become "really real," these particular concrete histories had to be annihilated, then an alternative homeland would have to be hewn out of an obdurate world through a process that would utterly transform the character of Judaism, bringing ancient tribalism and modern statehood together in strange juxtaposition.

This set into motion a vicious cycle. Those who were aroused to become Zionists had to invent themselves for the task. Jewishness had to be placed front and center, and the path of self-invention gravitated to that moment when the Jew arose, as this was expressed in the ancient texts of the Covenant processed by centuries of Halakhah. And here lies the foundation of the bad idea: collective narrative is essential to nationalism, but the narrative employed by Zionist nationalism did not ground itself on the actual, collectively lived life of the Jewish people. It stemmed rather from the mythos according to which Yahweh granted the Israelites exceptional status among the nations. A redemptive, messianic desire arose, enormously powerful but also blind and delusive, in which weakness as a nation was nullified by greatness conferred by God, and moral claims were accentuated even as an amoral path was entered. The mythic power "established" in the Zionist mind a regime of desire, which overrode mere details such as the lack of a legitimate claim. All the historiographical exertions by generations of Zionist apologists cannot confer legitimacy on a project in which a variegated people held together by texts and a common faith, and whose actual ethno-national genealogies had been formed all over the map, suddenly decide after two thousand years that they have a real claim on a part of the earth just because it is the center of their Biblical identity. A two thousand-year-old claim would be laughed out of any secular court—all the more so for the Ashkenazi Jews who comprise the main body of Zionists and have little discernable link to the ancient inhabitants of Palestine.[4]

Other nationalisms—let us set aside for now the particular reasons that drove them—had far less difficulty in defining the territory that was to be the object of their desire. It was, simply enough, the land they had been inhabiting as a people, which habitation made it possible for the people to become a nation. Moreover, their goal was coherently defined as just by the fact that the reclamation of their land required the expropriation of an imperialist usurper. No one could deny that the English had seized Ireland and India, and that therefore there was something righteous in the struggle by the Irish and Indians to throw them out, however complicated and imperfect these campaigns may have been in practice. So, too, did the great power maneuvers that placed Britain in charge of Palestine give the Zionists some moral purchase in their struggles, even when these took luridly terroristic shape, as in the bombing of the King David Hotel by the Stern Gang in 1946, which wiped out a good deal of the British High Command. But one can only take this so far before running into the brutal facts; first, that the objects of Zionist expropriation were Islamic people, themselves victims of empire, who could by no stretch of the imagination be held responsible for the trail of Jewish suffering that eventuated in the struggle for Palestine; and second, that however its origins may have been ascribed to the ancient expulsion from Palestine, in real life, the trail of suffering had been inscribed not in Palestine but in the West, in Europe and among the Christians. And it was the same West and Christendom to whose empire-building the Zionists signed on to fulfill their dream. Accordingly, the manifold sufferings and persecutions inflicted on the Jews became inexorably used as justifications for the aggression inherent to the Zionist project. In the process, their moral value was corrupted and replaced with instrumentalisms that fool no one but the suitably deluded.

The very weakness of the real claim caused a totalization of the desire, with the result that Zionist nationalism became not the restoration of a land but the establishment of Jewish control over that land, and, coordinatively, the elimination of its indigenous inhabitants. This was unlike normal nationalisms. As Ze'ev Sternhell describes in his essential work, *The Founding Myths of Israel*, a twofold "methodological necessity" for Zionist nation-building was rooted in the fact that Jews in the nineteenth century were not actually a nation with a common relation to territory, but a collection of peoples united by a set of writings as interpreted by a Rabbinate. First, "hatred of the diaspora and a rejection of Jewish life there"; and second, that everything, all hope, all truth, all effort, had to be vested in Palestine.[5] The former gesture included a contempt for "assimilation" as well as the old ways. In the service of creating a national Judaism, Zionism therefore cut Jews off from what history they did possess and led to a fateful identity of interest with antisemitism, which became, with deadly irony, the only thing that united them. In this way the identity of Palestine was sealed as not simply an actual refuge and homeland, but as a magical place that had to be fully, absolutely possessed by Jews and no one else if it was to be possessed at all. It is essential to grasp this point, which stands in stark contrast to the public face that the Zionist settlers just wanted to live in peace side by side with their Arab hosts.[6] The whole history of the movement gives the lie to this benign interpretation, and is still evidenced by the uncompromising, desperate tendency embedded in the conduct of Israel, including the notorious disregard for the rules of international conduct, which abundantly persists to the present day in "special claims," such as never disclosing the existence of its nuclear arsenal, refusing to take down the "apartheid wall" despite the verdict of the International Court of Justice, and innumerable other slaps in the face of world opinion.

As a magical realm, Palestine must have no other real people than Jews, else the Jewish people themselves would lack reality. Hence the collective delusion of "a land without people for a people without land," which aggravated the normal ethnocentrism of European colonialism, with severe implications for indigenous Palestinians. The Zionist intrusion into Palestine was therefore a very different matter from the ordinary expansion of empire and required a much greater degree of denial and mystification, which lent its ruthlessness an almost surreal character. Although everyone who was directly engaged in being a Zionist settler knew perfectly well the necessary contours of what lay before them if they were to achieve their goal, the official founding documents of the Zionist movement are virtually silent about the difficult fact that others lived in and had developed the land it coveted. This befits a project whose subject itself, the Jewish nation, had to be created by the invasion of another's land, and where recognition of the presence of real people in Palestine would detract from the construction of the new national identity—not least because it would shatter the high ethical self-regard of the Jewish people. The quintessential statement of this came from the legendary Golda Meir, shortly before she became prime minister in 1969: "It was not as though there was a Palestinian people in Palestine considering itself as a Palestinian people and we came and threw them out and took their country away from them. They did not exist."[7] A slip of the tongue this may be, but any acquaintance with Zionism will confirm the authenticity of its basic sentiment.

In the plans for the new nation, its territory is specified as "Eretz Israel," the magical kingdom that occupies the Zionist imaginary. Eretz Israel is not, however, the actual kingdom of ancient Israel, founded in the the tenth century BCE, but the Promised Land offered in Covenant with Yahweh. Thus the State of Israel is to reign over mythic, unbounded territory. Theodor Herzl writes in his diary (Vol II: 711) that the land he had in mind extended from "the Brook of Egypt to the Euphrates"—essentially the notion of Moses as recounted in Deuteronomy 11: 24–25. Such was the germ of "Greater Israel," a dreamland whose western border includes Egypt east of the Nile, whose eastern perimeter cuts halfway through Iraq, that extends southward into the Arabian desert and northward to the edge of Turkey. This is far greater than the Biblical Kingdom. But in for a penny, in for a pound, as the saying goes: if one is to make the outlandish claim of a territory controlled 2500 years ago by one's putative ancestors, one might as well go for broke and claim the whole region, thereby folding into the substance of the Zionist project what the ignorant goyim call Syria, Jordan and Lebanon along with chunks of Egypt and Iraq. Ariel Sharon is said to have uttered in a fit of youthful enthusiasm the dream of Zionist suzerainty all the way to Algeria.

As the Zionist dream drives the Zionist reality, so does Greater Israel animate Israeli foreign policy—and something of United States policy as well (see Chapter 6). Beneath the claim that all that matters is security from Arab hordes who refuse to tolerate the democratic haven for the Jewish people, lies the primordial Covenant in its tribal interpretation. This, holds Zionism, is what Yahweh promised; and the obligation is on the Jewish nation to become so great and redemptive as to rescue the land from the dull and backward people who know nothing of the messianic promise. As Sternhell has pointed out, the liberal and utilitarian view that sought a kind of practical refuge against Jewish insecurities became swept away by the tribally driven notion that Eretz Israel was the "culmination of Jewish history" and the "rescue of the [Jewish] nation" rather than that of any particular individual or set of individuals.[8] This latter conception prevailed as the central dynamic of Zionism, not because it was ethically better, or even more popular, than the liberal/utilitarian conception, but because it was necessary, because the nation had to be created for the huge task of settling another's land. This interpretation of Zionism, called "political," was to sweep all others before it.

THE HERDING OF JEWISHNESS

There is no one way of being Jewish—either racially,[9] culturally, or religiously. That is the glory of the faith, imposing as it does a permanent condition of marginality and radical opportunity. The same dialectic would end up in the hands of antisemites as the label of "rootless cosmopolitanism," used to task Jews with the burdens of modernity. As a street person in pre-war Vienna, the young Adolf Hitler saw what he took to be "rootless Jews," read into them the projection of his own disintegrating psyche, and learned to hate them as a way of holding himself together. This synthetic drive within judaeophobia finds further expression in the immemorial ascription of conspiracy to the

Jews; that is, the Jews are accused of putting together what the antisemite cannot. For Hitler, his self-creation at the expense of Jews incorporated the socialist threat; Hitler began thinking in terms of "Judaeo-Bolshevism," and the ideological linchpin of Nazism had been forged.[10]

A germ of misplaced truth lies within many delusions, for Jews have indeed been primed to see things differently, and hence to be troublemakers. Centuries of being forced to rely on texts instead of land as the source of authority opens onto the endlessness of possible interpretation, and hence the possibility of radical practice. There had long been a Jewish "underground," for the simple reason that to be Jewish was to be already underground. The radical potential had been confined during the epoch of classical Judaism under the Diaspora, finding its channels in various hermeneutic and ecstatic spiritual movements. Some of these persist within the life-worlds of the ultra-orthodox, while others have been given shape by thinkers such as Gershon Scholem and Martin Buber in ways that link Jewish mysticism and Kabbalism to the spiritual movement of modernity.

By far the largest body of radical practice by Jews, however, took place outside the purview of religion, once the varied Jewish communities had been released from feudal restriction through the acquisition of civil rights that fitfully took place in post-Napoleonic Europe—their so-called "emancipation." Once embedded in the soil of civil society, the multivalence of Judaic being gave rise to remarkable achievement. This was prefigured in the seventeenth century by Baruch Spinoza, who made the first and perhaps the most radical break with Covenant Judaism, negating it so severely as to demolish the notion of a personalistic God *tout court*. Spinoza's extreme, monistic universalism caused him to be excommunicated by the Rabbinate of Amsterdam (to which city his Converso family had fled from Portugal in order to reconnect with Judaism), and hence to pass out of the Jewish tradition altogether; but he prepared the ground for the more mediated universalisms of modernity.

These may be said to have begun in 1743, with the entrance into Berlin of the boy Moses Mendelssohn through the only gate of the city open to Jews—and, significantly, cattle. Mendelssohn began Talmudic study, then broke with it by teaching himself the languages of Europe. He became the "German Socrates," the first Jew to achieve European prominence and a progenitor of the Enlightenment itself.[11] His example was later epitomized by figures as brilliant and diverse as Heine, Marx, Freud, Luxemburg, Einstein, Proust, Kafka, Schoenberg and Wittgenstein, along with thousands and thousands of others, who variously contributed to civilization by accepting Jewish marginality as a creative challenge rather than trying to abolish it through nation-building.[12]

The Zionist way was fundamentally different. It sought to channel, or as we will say, *herd* the many creative potentials inherent to Jewish being into the search for a state, as though these potentialities were the equivalents of the cattle with whom Mendelssohn was forced to enter Berlin. Somehow, they reasoned, the homeland of Israel would enhance the potentials revealed under emancipation even further once the wandering Jews had settled down to redeem the land. They found it hard to conceive that having one's very own state could impose another regime of repression, especially if the land it controlled had to be usurped from others.[13] Meanwhile, this paramount, overriding consideration led them to instrumentally make use of every fragment of Jewishness for the purpose at hand.

Given the certainty that state-building in Palestine would lead to trouble of all sorts, and that this was going to be carried forth within the vast upheavals of the twentieth century, it is scarcely surprising that a continual though fitful drift would take place in Zionist institutions, one in which their messianic, idealistic and utopian character would tend to get replaced with ever coarser and more brutal aspects. In the process, no element of Jewish culture or identity could escape unscathed or uncorrupted; all were herded into the pen of nation state building.

The *Zeitgeist* at the close of the nineteenth century was principally defined by protracted economic crisis and the resulting imperialist frenzy that was to lead to global war and revolution. The rise in antisemitism that entered into the particular crisis of the Jews belongs to this larger crisis, which in its deepest reaches was a civilizational reaction to the spiritual poverty and dislocation of capitalism. The nationalisms of the time were efforts to relocate a communal self in a world redefined, as Marx and Engels had written as far back as 1848, by the fact that, under the impact of capitalist production, all "fixed, fast-frozen relations, with their train of ancient and venerable opinions, are swept away ...." The resulting transvaluation of all values produced at its outer edges the delusional recuperation signified by Jew-hating and, in the early-twentieth century, its extensions into fascist malignancy. Accompanied by imperialist expansion and militarism, this set the stage for the twentieth century to become by far the most brutal and murderous in history.

Zionism, nationalism with a Jewish face, was both a reaction to these morbid developments and an instance of them. All forms of aggressive nationalism are dependent on a hated Other; they thrive in the dark and collapse as soon as human beings are seen in a universal light. So it has been for the antisemites, and so it has been for the Zionist reaction to antisemitism, which, like its demonizing and demonic Other, itself fell into the ways of imperialist expansion and militarism, and showed signs of the fascist malignancy.

None of this happened symmetrically, or smoothly, or uncontestedly. Zionism was not the exact antipode of antisemitism, just as Israel is not the mirror image of Nazi Germany. Antisemitism and the Zionist reaction to it were

bound together in fear and hate, and, in the instance of
Zionism, carried out in the shadow of the immense horrors
visited upon Europe's Jews in the first half of the twentieth
century.

This collective nightmare blurred the imperial character of
Zionism, which, in the final and agonal stage of the founding
of Israel, became fully eclipsed by the overriding moral effect of
the Holocaust. Moreover, in its early days, the movement was
little more than a curio on the world stage and could scarcely
have aroused much consternation. Herzl moved among genteel
circles, was careful to couch his plan in deliberately harmless
terms, and while showing a very different awareness in his
diaries, remained purposefully vague on the fate of the actual
inhabitants, and even on whether the new state would be
exclusively Jewish or not.[14]

Such settlements as occurred under the aegis of the
Zionist organizations would have for some time appeared
to the inhabitants of Palestine as not very different from the
innumerable ethno-religious collectives that had immemorially
gathered in this ancient crossroads of world religion.
Communities of Jews had lived continuously in Palestine since
Biblical days. They were chiefly pious and considered harmless,
because in fact, they were. Jewishness was not the issue posed
by Zionism, but only its emblem. The indigenous population
had little problem with Jews as such. But they refused to
tolerate the presence of a people who came onto Palestinian
land in order to take it for their own national purposes.

There is substantial evidence that at least a significant
fraction of the actual people who made Zionism happen
knew quite well that they were engaged in a fight, the goal
of which was the annihilation of the indigenous people as a
national entity. These settlers entered Palestine with a clear-
headed appreciation of what had to be done and a remorseless
will to carry this out. As Benny Morris, a leading member
of the revisionist school of Israeli history (and who will be

considered below in a different context) has put it, from well before the founding of the official Zionist movement in 1897, the earliest settlers in Palestine "tried to camouflage their real aspirations, for fear of angering the authorities and the Arabs. They were, however, certain of their aims and of the means needed to achieve them." Thus Vladimir Dubnow, in 1882: "The ultimate goal is, in time, to take over the Land of Israel and to restore to the Jews the political independence they have been deprived of for these two thousand years ... The Jews will yet arise and, arms in hand (if need be), declare that they are the masters of their ancient homeland." Or as Ben-Yehuda, who settled in Jerusalem in 1881, put it in a letter written the next year: "The thing we must do now is to become as strong as we can, to conquer the country, covertly, bit by bit ... We can only do this covertly, quietly. ... We will not set up committees so that the Arabs will know what we are after, we shall act like silent spies, we shall buy, buy, buy." This was bound to greatly reinforce the exclusionary impulses within Judaism. As Ahad Ha'Am, who became one of the first critics who feared that in winning their Homeland Jews might lose their soul, wrote in 1891, the settlers had begun "a tendency to despotism as happens always when a slave turns into a master," adding two years later that "The attitudes of the colonists to their tenants and their families is exactly the same as towards their animals," indeed that they referred to the local Arabs as mules. He might have added that they were only following the Talmudic comparison between asses and Canaanite slaves.[15]

All this took place before Herzl created official, or "political Zionism," by promoting the colonization of Palestine through acquiring internationally recognized legal rights and building a permanent international organization for the purpose. Herzl's fame is deserved, for he took the necessary steps, beyond the speculations and dreams of the nineteenth century, for the ultimate goal of building the Jewish state. He also forged the fateful link between Zionism and Great Power imperialism.

In contrast to the Zionist emphasis on a monolithic judaeophobia facing all Jews in the Western world, many among the more advanced thinkers of the later nineteenth century saw in the Jews not only an oppressed people but one capable of exerting a redemptive function. Charles Dickens changed his depiction of the Jew from the evil Fagin of *Oliver Twist* to the gentle and virtuous Riah of *Our Mutual Friend* (a pasteboard figure and artistic failure) under pressure from such liberal opinion. And ten years later, in 1876, that magnanimous spirit, George Eliot, published her last novel, *Daniel Deronda*, whose protagonist was not only lofty and idealist, but an ardent Zionist. Joseph Salvador, a half Sephardic-Jewish philosopher, had set forth such a benignly messianic rendering of Zionism as far back as 1860. As Walter Lacqueur has written, Salvador held "that the basic ideas of Judaism were, on the one hand, the unity of the human race, its equality and fraternity, and on the other, a new and higher messianism, called upon to establish a new order replacing Caesars and Popes. To that end he advocated the establishment of a new state between Orient and Occident, on the coast of Galilee and Canaan."[16] Thirty-six years later Herzl was saying essentially the same thing, while linking Zionism to the inexorable march of progress in his *The Jewish State*: "We shall not revert to a lower stage but rise to a higher one. We shall not dwell in mud huts; we shall build new, more beautiful, and more modern houses, and possess them in safety."[17]

And then there was the matter of money to fund all this, to "buy, buy, buy" the land, as Herzl put it, and do all the myriad things necessary to get a modern society going. Jewish pioneering labor was going to do a lot of the job, but Jewish capital was necessary as well. Zionism could never have got off the ground had not a substantial Jewish bourgeoisie arisen to finance it. Herzl saw himself as the catalyst of this process. Through a frenzied campaign that would exhaust him and cost him his life after eight years, Herzl gained the ear of the Jewish "rich, who enjoy a comprehensive acquaintance with all technical advances [and] know full well how much can be done for money."[18] He doggedly pursued them in the years remaining to him, and an expanding network of Zionist organizations continued the work from then on.[19] It was this money that bought up parcels of absentee-owned land in Ottoman Palestine for the Zionist settlers to legally use; and it was to the system of generating wealth without end that Herzl and the Zionist movement appealed.

Apologists for Israel like Alan Dershowitz in his *The Case for Israel* make much of how innocent, indeed beneficial, this was. He attempts to refute the accusation that Jews expropriated Palestinian lands with the finding that before 1948 much of the land was legally purchased from landlords, and that the Jews, being European, brought a higher standard of living, raised the economic level, provided superior health services and sanitation, and generally were a boon to the miserable ingrates they found.[20]

There is a twofold problem with such reasoning. Firstly, the fact is that Zionists dealt with absentee landlords, not the direct inhabitants of the land, who were essentially tenant farmers. Caught in a vice between a feudal and capitalist system, the fellaheen tended to lose all rights once the land changed hands, suffering the landless fate of billions of peasants since the modern world began.[21] Secondly, the larger implications of the money raised by Herzl and subsequent generations of Zionists need to be clarified.

It is well known that money does not grow on trees. It is the abstracted value of past human labor, capable of being stored and transferred from place to place. He who accumulates a significant stock of funds, therefore, has at his disposal the collective power of past labor and the power to control future labor. The more money, the more does the self become aggrandized, and the 'others' whose labor has been exploited become reduced, their humanity dissolving into a thing-like

Otherness. And the more that money is used for the particular
gain of one faction while others are seen as being merely in
the way, the more malevolent becomes the will whose power
money expands. In any case, there can scarcely be a worse
error than to assume that money is neutral and bears no charge
of history.

Herzl certainly realized that the money he was raising was
far from neutral, though he prudently saved such reflections for
the privacy of his diary while reserving his public statements
for lofty rhetoric. Here is an entry from 1895:

> We must expropriate gently the private property on the state
> assigned to us. We shall try to spirit the penniless population across
> the border by procuring employment for it in the transit countries,
> while denying it employment in our country. The property owners
> will come over to our side. Both the process of expropriation
> and the removal of the poor must be carried out discretely and
> circumspectly. Let the owners of the immoveable property believe
> that they are cheating us, selling us things for more than they are
> worth. But we are not going to sell them anything back.[22]

These musings were to become the nucleus of the system
by which the Palestinian economy was destroyed while all
desirable land was to be placed in perpetuity into Jewish hands,
even as the Palestinians were "spirited across the border," that
is, ethnically cleansed. As for the "progress" brought to all
Palestine by this, one needs only to take a look at its Occupied
Territories.

Zionism also identified itself as socialist to the core, this not
unrelated to the fact that socialism was Jewish to the core.
Indeed, every Jew in those years had to take socialism seriously.
Practically speaking, this meant the conscious building of
radical movements of, by, and for, working people, which is
to say, those who produce under conditions of exploitation.
Through advance and retreat, triumph, betrayal and eventual
collapse, the socialist challenge to capitalist domination was

a main dynamic of world history until the break-up of the Soviet empire in 1989.

It was also essential to Zionist history. The actual builders of the *Yishuv*, or Zionist community in Palestine, espoused a kind of socialism and, forming the nucleus of the Labor Party, gave political Zionism its predominant meaning of "Labor Zionism" until the mid 1970s. Labor Zionism envisioned Israel as a Jewish state of the most advanced human relationships whose society was to be constructed along collective lines. This had great ideological value. Nothing could be better devised than socialism to persuade that in the Zionist project, Jews had broken with their narrow tribal past and moved into the bright sunlight of universalism, thereby redeeming the expanded meaning of Covenant. Diasporic Jews, urbanized, bookish, and suffocating in their ghetto existence, could look with pride and envy on institutions like the kibbutzim agricultural collectives, with their suntanned, muscular, gender-equalized cadre of *Sabra* "making the desert bloom," and believe that in Labor Zionism their people were truly making a Brave New World.

There was one problem, however: Marx had proclaimed *class* struggle, and not *national* liberation, as the defining feature of and pathway towards the universal, socialist realization of humanity. The reason for this was that only the proletariat, created yet oppressed by capitalism, contained within itself the germ of a universal realization of human powers. There were ample numbers of Marxian socialists to remind the Zionists of this, chiefly in Russia, where the majority of the world's Jews lived during this time, and where the disintegration of the Czarist regime had produced both appalling antisemitic violence and powerful socialist movements. Here Marxist Jewish workers had formed the Bund, a consciously anti-Zionist organization that challenged the socialist bona fides of Zionism, insisting instead that the obligation of Jews was to overturn the class relations of their given societies and to universalize from that point. The basic threat of Bundism to

Zionism was to affirm that authentic Jewish identities could be built on grounds other than creating a nation state.[23] In response, Labor Zionism took comfort in the doctrine of Ber Borochev, who argued that the Jewish settlement of Palestine would create the "primitive accumulation" for capitalism in Eretz Israel, after which the terms of struggle would shift away from nation-building to class conflict. The Jewish and Palestinian working masses would then come together, struggle for their common emancipation, and thereby move toward the universal betterment of humanity.[24]

Berochev was a brilliant man. But ideas have to be tested in the furnaces of the real world, and in this real world, none of his ideas were to be realized. The reason, again, is transparent to those who would look at the main project of Zionism, the building of an organic nationalism for Jews, and Jews alone. This could never open onto a larger vision of humanity. There was to be no sharing of a common fate and struggle between peoples in the building of Israel. It was to be Us versus Them in spades: the buying of the land, for sure, and its reservation for Jews alone; but also—and this would be crucial to the corruption of the socialist content of Labor Zionism—the reservation of the upper registers of labor for Jews, and therefore the construction of a class system that was to block any emergence of a universalizing force from below.

The socialist pioneers who went off to build Eretz Israel (and especially those of the so-called "Second Aliyah," or migration, which began in the early 1900s) were bent on redeeming the inalienable land through the "Conquest of Labor."[25] This entailed negating centuries of Jewish labor centering on the ways of the book and epitomized by the calculatedness of the userer. These unhealthy practices were, the Zionists postulated, predicated on separation from the soil; curing them, therefore, required the reclamation of productive connection with the earth. The spiritual leader of this tendency was Aaron David Gordon, himself anti-socialist but very influential in shifting Zionist socialism away from class struggle and toward an organic and mystical unity with Eretz Israel through collective labor. But once again redemption of the Jews meant expropriation of the Arab, in this case from labor as well as land, all of which was formally put into the constitution of the Jewish Agency, the official body set up by Britain to administer the Yishuv.[26] The kibbutz, that shining star in the ideological firmament of Zionism which proclaimed to the world the collective and cooperative character of social relations in Israel, figuratively had inscribed over its gates the words, "Arabs Stay Out!"

And so two separate worlds took shape in Palestine, with very different visions for labor, and where one was destined to conquer the other. The depth of the difference was already revealed in the nineteenth century when the first settlers "forcibly denied local shepherds the use of traditionally common pasturelands."[27] In other words, people from a different culture entered Palestine, often as self-proclaimed socialists, to destroy the foundations of the "commons" upon which the indigenous folk had built the ground of collective social existence. We need not moralize here. Destruction of the commons is a simple necessity if land is to be commodified; and Eretz Israel had to be commodified in a double gesture within the overall subsumption of Zionism into capitalism: to sell (or lease) it to Jews, and also to prevent Jews from selling it to anybody else.

Meanwhile other Zionist immigrants continued the practice of usury, lending money at as much as 40 percent interest to the peasants. Overall, then, the settlers were demolishing the preconditions of socialism in the name of Labor Zionism. Such socialism as would remain would be for one segment of the population alone. However, as Sternhell has forcefully argued, without universalism "socialism" cannot be a socialism; just as a democracy for some fraction of the population cannot be a democracy. He calls this by its true name: Labor Zionism was

no socialism built around the emancipation of labor, with its
universal implication; it was, rather, a *nationalist socialism*—
socialism that had, as Sternhell puts it:

> lost its universal significance and became an essential tool in the
> process of building the nation-state. Thus, the universal values
> of socialism were subordinated to the particularistic values of
> nationalism. In practice this was expressed by a total rejection of
> the concept of class warfare and by the claim of transcending social
> contradictions for the benefit of the collectivity as a whole.

The Labor Zionist leadership saw no contradiction between
nationalism and socialism. As Berl Katznelson, chief ideologue
of the movement, put it at a party convention in March,
1919:

> It is as if, in the reality of the worker in Eretz Israel—and not in
> the deceptiveness of words—there could be a nationalism without
> socialism, or a socialism without nationalism! As if there were
> workers among us whose Zionism condoned the oppression and
> exploitation of workers, or there were workers in this country
> whose socialism looked toward alien horizens and was indifferent
> to the revival of the people or the building of the land![28]

Well, it could—if the majority of the population where one
lived were not regarded as beings with a common human nature.
Another implication of the identity between nationalism and
socialism would be that the customary aim of socialist transformation, namely, that it would entail a radical alteration of
the capitalist system, was to become shelved. What was the
point of worrying about such a goal when the paramount task
was to "revive" the people—that is, bring in as many Jewish
immigrants as possible, and set them to work—collectively, to
be sure—to build the land? Class warfare—without which the
capitalists could never be displaced—would get in the way of
this, and so would any attitude that might alienate the powerful
capitalists upon whose good will the Zionists depended.

Nationalist socialism, as Sternhell points out, was not unique
to the Zionist campaign in Palestine, indeed, its roots extended

back to the the mid-nineteenth century doctrine of Pierre Proudhon. What was unique was the quality of the nation being built and the settler-colonial conditions under which its building took place. The former imposed for-Jews-only tribalism as the condition for national identity; while the logic of settler-colonialism would see to it that the indigenous people who had to be displaced would gather around and between the settlements, increasingly sullen, hateful, their humanity erased by the "socialist" polity developing within.

THE ARLOSOROFF CASE

Fitfully but inexorably, the balance in Palestine shifted toward the settlers. The Great War was a war of realignment, and amongst its most important legacies was the collapse of the Ottoman Empire and its replacement in the Middle East by the European powers, chiefly Britain and France. Western hegemony placed Zionism in a new light, as an instrument of imperial expansion. It also tended to formalize the contradictory relations between the West and the Zionists, who were eager to break loose from Europe while being utterly dependent on it. The Balfour Declaration of November 2, 1917, recognizing the Jewish right to a "national home" in Palestine, put the imprimatur of Western empire on the Zionist project. And through the fog of its diplomatic obfuscation one can also foresee the downfall of Arab/Muslim Palestine.[29]

But many pitfalls and crises were to lie ahead. In August 1929, terrible riots erupted in Hebron and elsewhere, with substantial loss of both Jewish and Arab life.[30] This was also the year that a global economic crisis such as had never before been seen first began to gather. The combined effects would weigh heavily on Zionism and the future State of Israel.

Chaim Arlosoroff was an outstanding young leader of the Zionist movement in Israel. As head of the political office of the Jewish Agency, he was a kind of Secretary of State for the government-in-waiting. Arlosoroff was anti-Soviet, anti-American, anti-materialist in general, and on the whole, spiritual in his approach to politics, yet with a capacity to take a hard look at difficult realities. He was appointed to his high position because of his conciliatory character and acceptability to the Arabs, whose fears he was able to allay. But in mid 1932 he was coming to a troubling conclusion, which he haltingly transmitted in a lengthy letter to Chaim Weizmann, head of the World Zionist movement.[31]

Arlosoroff couched his letter—"a somewhat strange literary creation"—as "an abstract essay on Zionist policy," but it was stimulated by growing unease. He found the present policy of the Labor Zionists to be "palliative and that it would be difficult, perhaps even impossible, to attain the political ends of Zionism in this manner." It is, he went on, a view shared by all Zionists that "if we do not wish to reestablish Diaspora conditions in Palestine we must strive toward the quickest possible settlement of hundreds of thousands of Jews in order to assure at least a rare equilibrium between the two peoples in the country." But this will not happen under present policy, which assumes the method of attaining "our aims gradually, step by step." This may have made sense in the past, and built the Jews up to the point of being able "to preserve their present positions [although] without possessing sufficient strength to assure the constant growth of the Jewish community ..." But since the Zionist dream is wedded to the idea of constant growth, something will have to be done about this, else the entire project was going to founder. This will require such a relationship between the two communities "as to preclude any possibility of the establishment of an Arab state in Palestine."

How to attain this next "stage" was the question. Arlosoroff reconsidered the essentially gradualist, evolutionary method used to this point by Zionism, and found it wanting. For this requires ignoring "all the hardships and interference, to overlook bitterness and disappointments, and to continue diligently to add one asset to another" until the next 'stage' is attained. Under present circumstances, however, "I am inclined to think that [this] is not possible." The financial means are not there, and the British authorities are not going to put themselves out "for the sake of settlers of a 'foreign' people." The Balfour Declaration notwithstanding, "it is in the nature of things that the [British] administration should be considerate of the sensibilities of the Arabs and Moslems to such an extent as to prevent an active policy in our favor." Furthermore, there are no more "government lands available for Jewish colonization," and simply too many regulations and restraints on support for developing existing Jewish settlements.

Even so, continues Arlosoroff, one might recommend continuing the present cautiously incremental policy

> if I forsaw the likelihood of some decades of peace and more or less stable conditions in Palestine, during which we would have the opportunity to grow slowly. But unfortunately the world political situation is so upset and the tensions in the Middle East are growing at such a rate, that there exists but a tenuous basis for such an optimistic assumption.

Indeed, the Arab movement is growing, and "has meanwhile learned all the political practices of Zionism." It can no longer be effectively marginalized and ignored. Moreover "the non-Jewish population of Palestine is increasing at a rapid rate." In 1922, 500,000 Jews would have constituted a majority; in 1932, it would take 800,000; looking ahead to 1947, 1,500,000 will be required. All of this is going to be greatly exacerbated by the imminence of another world war, which, it so happens, is "as certain as that winter follows autumn." Under wartime conditions, all mandates will collapse, and Britain will likely move toward full imperial incorporation of Palestine, and make an alliance with the Arab states, sacrificing Israel in the process.

And so, what is to be done? Arlosoroff sees four possible paths, of which only the last has any merit:

- "… hold tight and do nothing, in the hope that something good may turn up. This is a characteristically Jewish attitude … but it is definitely not a Zionist attitude … which I have always looked upon as a rebellion against Jewish tradition" and its fatalism.

- Give up on Zionism, and recognize it to be objectively impossible as a political goal.

- "cling to fundamental Zionist principles but … contract the geographic limits of their realization"; that is, settle for a smaller Eretz Israel. This, too, is to be considered impossible, given geostrategic and demographic factors (and the magical appeal of Eretz Israel, observed above).

- finally, strike off on a new path, through "a transition period during which the Jewish minority would exercize organized revolutionary rule." This requires that such a minority would control "the state apparatus, the administration, and the military … in order to eliminate the danger of domination by the non-Jewish majority and suppress rebellion against us …" This radical, and even desperate path raises questions which Arlosoroff does not intend to consider in the letter. But he needs to say that "I will never become reconciled to the failure of Zionism before an attempt is made whose seriousness corresponds to the seriousness of the struggle for the revival of our national life and the sanctity of the mission entrusted to us by the Jewish people."

Arlosoroff finishes by emphasizing that this new venture does not constitute a coming around to the position of the revisionist faction—headed by Vladimir Jabotinsky—which had been pressing the Zionist movement to take more extreme measures for a decade. "Now, too, I consider that the tactics, the policies, and the educational principles of Revisionism are madness" and guaranteed to wreck the Zionist cause. We labor Zionists, by contrast, "have the real strength of the *Yishuv*," namely, the "organized labor movement, which is destined to be the 'iron legion' of Zionism irrespective of the policies followed." And with that, Arlosoroff signs off.

The letter calls three things to our attention—that political Zionism was in grave crisis by the early 1930s; that the movement had become deeply factionalized between two groups: the labor Zionists who were in control of its existing institutions, and Jabotinsky's revisionist camp, so named because of impatience with the respectable, temporizing tactics of official Zionism; and that Arlosoroff, one of the top leaders of Labor Zionism, was reluctantly reaching the same conclusions as his bitter enemies even as he continued to denounce them.

I do not know what became of this remarkable document, but what became of Arlosoroff is worth pondering. On June 14, 1933, less than a year after posting his letter to Weizmann, Arlosoroff returned to Palestine from Germany where he had been negotiating with the Hitler regime over transferring German–Jewish assets to Palestine. The next day an enraged polemic appeared in a revisionist journal attacking Arlosoroff and the Labor Zionists for

> The cowardice to which the Palestine Labor Party has stooped in selling itself for money to the biggest Jew-hater, [and which] has . . . no parallel in all Jewish history ... The Jewish people has always known how to deal with those who have sold the honor of their nation and their Torah, and it will know today also how to react to this shameful deed. ...[32]

The evening following, June 16, 1933, Arlosoroff was assassinated by two gunmen as he and his wife strolled near the beach in Tel Aviv. Although no one was ever convicted of the crime, presumptive evidence pointed to figures in Jabotinsky's faction. This conclusion was in any case roundly believed by the labor Zionist majority, thus further deepening the schism between the groups. And yet, by the end of the decade, Labor and the revisionists, while still externally antagonistic, had converged into a common "forward" strategy. How are we to account for this?

Comprehensive study of the Byzantine interrelations between the various Zionist factions, as well as their external relations to the Arabs, the British, the United States, the fascist powers, etc., is well beyond the scope of this work, and would only obscure the main issue, which is the internal logic of Zionism and its "herding" effect on various manifestations of Jewishness under the pressure of events, including those it felt obliged to set into motion. From our standpoint, the differences between factions, however necessary for the fine-grained understanding of the history of Israel, is less significant than what brought them together in the ever more aggressive pursuit of Zionism as Jewish tribalism. Caught in a maelstrom of their own making, where from one side they are sucked down by the practical exigencies of building an ethnically pure Jewish nation in the midst of Arab territory, and from the other, psychological side, buffeted by the internally contradictory identities resulting from this, Zionists became trapped in a spiralling state of emergency in which "extremist elements" were—and continue to be—constantly enhanced.

This is no metaphor: the State of Israel has had to declare a "state of emergency" for every one of its years, with no relief in sight. What we mean by "extremist elements" is to be understood at multiple levels—within individuals, between individuals, in the composition of groups and institutions, in the ideologies by means of which all these become conscious of themselves and represent themselves to the world, and in the nation and nation state itself. Vladimir Jabotinsky was, as a whole person, such an extremist element, brought forth by the logic of Zionist struggle and articulating its maximalist position at a time when to do so estranged him from the mainstream of the movement. Chaim Arlosoroff was not an extremist person, quite the opposite; he might be said to epitomize and represent the mainstream, as a "moderate," the liberal and talented Jew who was the salt of the Zionist earth. But as a realist embroiled in the actual statecraft of the Zionist project, he had to encounter the awful facts bearing down on it: the never-ending demographic worry about Arabic population increase; the maddening reliance on cynical and opportunistic Great Power imperialism; and the newly looming cloud on his horizen, of fascism and the Great War he accurately foresaw. All these, recall, are consequences of the fatal decision to pitch the Zionist tent in Palestine, a decision made imperative by the logic of nation-building on the basis of fantasy.

At some point, equilibium breaks down, something snaps, and a new idea emerges. Not a drastically new idea, but a critically different rearrangement of elements that had held together the Zionist project in Arlosoroff's mind. Because Zionism has become inscribed in his identity, he cannot give up the "sanctity of the mission entrusted to us by the Jewish people." And because he senses the stagnation of the previous path, and because stagnation is forbidden to the Zionist, Arlosoroff begins to see things in a different light. A new, *forward* strategy suggests itself:

> a transition period during which the Jewish minority would exercize organized revolutionary rule. [This requires that such a minority would control] the state apparatus, the administration, and the military ... in order to eliminate the danger of domination by the non-Jewish majority and suppress rebellion against us ...

Let us ponder this: "a transition period . . ." Transition to what? Surely not a new equilibirum; there is no light at the end of this tunnel. What is offered—"organized revolutionary rule"—may foster Zionist power, but at the cost of destabiliza-tion for an indefinite period. Who is to do the organizing? The

Jewish minority, yes, but also a minority of the Jews: a group cut off from other Jews and more radically than ever, from the larger world, a group controlling "the state apparatus, the administration, and the military," in other words, a kind of secret society dedicated to force, indeed, violence. Though secret in its operations, this aggressive body would remain bonded to Judaism by the enduring power of Covenant tribalism, the Promise of Yahweh to the Jews and to the Jews alone. Or rather, the rest of Judaism would become bonded with it to the degree that absolute tribalism was bonded into their own identity. Thus the original land-possessing logic of Zionism, that all of Palestine must be had, or none at all, now decisively expands: all of the Jews, everywhere, must join in the aggressive possession of all of Palestine, and anyone who opts out of this is not a real Jew. It is at this point that the identity of Zionism with Judaism as such acquires real force. Forged in the compact with aggression, "defense" of Israel becomes defense of aggression, and part of the definition of what it is to be Jewish.

This body proposed by Arlosoroff would comprise a clandestine state in advance of the legally recognized state; and it would impart its character to the legal, above-ground state precisely because it would remain shielded off from humanizing and universalizing influences by what Jabotinsky was to presciently call the "Iron Wall," which is really only another name for the radicalization of the notion of a "people apart." But how else is one to "eliminate the danger of domination by the non-Jewish majority and suppress rebellion against us." Here is where the forward strategy comes in: the group must be pre-emptive, proactive, risking all and stopping at nothing. In plain words, the political director of the Jewish Agency recommends that Zionism, beginning as an idealistic and humanistic dream, turns itself into organized terrorism. And this came to pass.

There had been preparations. From the early 1900s the settlers had to think in terms of armed defense. At first sporadic and reactive, the forces gradually took shape, coalesced and formed themselves into militias, and then into the Haganah ("defense" in Hebrew) under the control of Histadrut, the umbrella labor organization. Jabotinsky had tried in the 1920s to introduce an enhanced capability, but the effort, along with all attempts to develop the Zionist military beyond the informal level, were squashed by the British authorities. Nonetheless the process went on clandestinely, even including secret armories for producing light weapons. After the riots of 1929, matters now appeared in a radically different light, and preparations for enhancing the military to include the entire Yishuv went forward. Arlosoroff, along with David Ben-Gurion, played a leading role in this.[33] Meanwhile, the military itself was not sitting back. By 1930 a clique within Haganah calling itself "Irgun Bet" that is, the "B" squadron began developing plans for an aggressive, retaliatory line to replace the original emphasis on defense. As Benny Morris puts it, "Within months the group veered rightward and in April 1937 renamed itself the Irgun Z'Vai Leumi (national military organization; IZL or Irgun), effectively affiliating itself with the Revisionist movement and becoming its military wing."[34]

In this manner Arlosoroff's vaguely articulated and secretive notion of moving from a defensive to a forward, aggressive phase had acquired its material embodiment from his arch-adversaries and presumed murderers. Add another contradiction to the overstocked bin of Zionism, one, however, that also completes the fundamental structure according to which the conquest of Palestine is to move forward and the State of Israel is to be organized. Although most of the visible and dramatic history of Israel is to lie ahead—the great Arab uprising of the late 1930s, the ever-more entangled relations with Britain, and later the United Nations, the extraordinary year of 1948, which signalled Zionism's victory and acquisition of state power and the coordinated *Nakhba* of the Arabs, and all that has followed until the present day—it may be said that the essentials had been put into place by the mid 1930s. There will be, from that time on, two apparently disarticulated entities connected by the profound dualism of Covenant Zionism, whose various features they manifest. On the surface and to the world, the humanistic, universalizing *faux* socialism, later to turn into "the only democratic state in the Mid-East"; and on the inside, the stop-at-nothing, lawless terror apparatus strictly responsive to the needs of the only real human beings on the planet, God's Chosen People.

Some of these matters will be approached below. Here we need only point out the following: that the constant state of emergency and extremism sets up the dynamic wherein ever more violent and reactionary elements come to the fore. Even as tough-as-nails Ben-Gurion was denouncing Jabotinsky as "Vladimir Hitler," elements of his own coalition were dismissing Jabotinsky as passé and adopting the more forward terrorist strategy. People such as Avraham Stern saw Jabotinsky as soft on the question of violence. Stern had the unusual distinction, at least in the history of Judaism, of having a "Gang" named after him. Under ordinary conditions this would signify Stern and his followers as "gangsters." But under the logic of Zionism, with its pact between "sacred terrorism"[35] and democratic statecraft, a number of these individuals became prime ministers and other high officials of the new Jewish state, and it was their extreme tribalist position that would come to direct its affairs. We return to the theme in Chapter 7.

One should not think simplistically about the development of these "elements" of violence and terror, as though they would grow linearly in size, like a tree. Each such element exists in a manifold of conflict, and according to the flux of events will wax and wane, combining and interacting with others. The Stern Gang, for example, was an extremist splinter of the Irgun, which was an extremist branch of the Haganah. At no point did the Stern Gang enjoy the approval of all elements of the Zionist movement, even the radical right wing. And, as so often happens, it was itself composed of bizarre and contradictory individuals, who could be self-destructive as well as destructive to others. After Stern was killed by British police in a shoot-out, the Gang collapsed, only to transmogrify and reconstitute itself. And once the State of Israel had been formed the contours of violence changed as it entered the zone of officialdom. The point to grasp is how, beneath the ever-changing vagaries of its historical development, the Zionist project became subjected to a *structural* tendency, a kind of induction according to which the tribal end of the Covenant selects and pulls various elements of individuals, movements and institutions into its orbit, where they become reassembled into new formations. These are constantly reconfigured about that great, unsurpassable contradiction, that in order to survive, the Zionist project has had to violate its universal aspiration through the expropriation of another people. And so we descend from the noble aspirations of Joseph Salvador, Ahad Ha'Am, and the Prophets to the ethical level of Ariel Sharon and the ultra-right settlers.

Today, a traveler in Tel Aviv's fashionable North side may traverse in quick succession three parallel East-West avenues, named successively for David Ben-Gurion, Vladimir Jabotinsky and Chaim Arlosoroff, and commemorating the profound unity of the Zionist plan.

3
The Spectre of Shoah

Z IONISM HAS NEVER LACKED detractors, among whose ranks we can find some of the great moral leaders of the age. Tolstoy, although an inspiration to the back-to-the-land pioneers, was harshly dismissive of their project, telling them, as Lacqueur puts it, "that Zionism was not a progressive but basically a militarist movement; the Jewish idea would not find its fulfillment in a territorially limited fatherland. Did the Jews really want a state on the pattern of Serbia, Rumania, or Montenegro?"[1] In 1938, Gandhi was even harsher in his assessment.[2] Fully aware of the "inhuman treatment meted out" to these "untouchables of Christianity," and despite his "lifelong" friendships with Jewish comrades from the days of struggle in South Africa, Gandhi nevertheless wrote that such "sympathy does not blind me to the requirements of justice. The cry for a national home for the Jews does not make much appeal to me." For it is "wrong and inhuman to impose the Jews on the Arabs. What is going on in Palestine cannot be justified by any moral code of conduct ... The nobler course would be to insist on a just treatment of the Jews wherever they are born and bred." As for the Jews in Palestine (at the time the Arabs were waging a fierce but losing battle against what seemed to be an entente between the British forces and the Jewish settlers),

I have no doubt that they are going about it in the wrong way. I am not defending the Arab excesses. I wish they had chosen the way of non-violence in resisting what they rightly regarded as an unwarrantable encroachment upon their country. But according to the accepted canons of right and wrong, nothing can be said against the Arab resistance in the face of overwhelming odds.

These words are eerily continuous with the predicament of the Second Intifada and the latest wars in the region. But Gandhi was also writing just after Kristallnacht, the most violent episode of a Nazi pogrom until the Holocaust, proper, and he was obliged to call attention to the looming shadow of "the German persecution of the Jews [which] seems to have no parallel in history. The tyrants of old never went so mad as Hitler seems to have gone." How, then, are the Jews to resist this "organized and shameless persecution"? Gandhi, true to himself, sees the clear path as one of spiritual affirmation and resistance.

> No person who has faith in a living God need feel helpless and forlorn ... [such a God] is common to one and all ... as the Jews attribute personality to God and believe that He rules every action of theirs, they ought not to feel helpless. If I were a Jew and were born in Germany ... I would claim Germany as my home even as the tallest gentile German might, and challenge him to shoot me or cast me in the dungeon ... [with] confidence that in the end the rest were bound to follow my example. ...

Similar advice is given to the Jews in Palestine, once it is realized that the

> same God rules the Arab heart who rules the Jewish heart. They can offer Satyagraha* in front of the Arabs and offer themselves to be shot or thrown into the Dead Sea without raising a little finger against them.

Gandhi also wrote a letter to Hitler around this time, a forlorn copy of which can be seen in the museum that was his home in Mumbai, India, asking the Nazi dictator to desist

---

* The Gandhian practice of "insistence on truth"—showing tolerance and goodwill coupled with firmness in one's cause through non-violent passive resistance and non-cooperation.

from the warlike path. No response is known, and the horror
unfolded: a worst-case scenario that puts to the test all powers
of human comprehension, and still reverberates.

One certainty about the Holocaust ("burnt offering"), or
Shoah ("desolation"), is that it put the matter of Zionism
on a radically different footing. What had been a turbulent
side-event in the welter of international politics up until 1938
suddenly found itself in the center of the world stage as the
scale of Nazi persecution became known. The Zionist question
was turned into a supreme test of the human conscience itself,
and all matters pertaining to coming to grips with the Nazi era
were transferred into its terms. From the labyrinth of moral,
philosophical and legal considerations, one dominating theme
emerged: an overriding value given to the Zionist resolution
of the "Jewish Question." How could anybody question, after
what had transpired during the twelve years of the Third
Reich, that the Jews had to have their national home? And very
few people did question this. Today, more than a half-century
on, to look at the images of concentration camp suffering and
follow this by images of seeing refugees disembarking at Haifa
in 1946, a great tide of relief surges. Tears of joy are catching,
and such tears—along with those of remorse, grief and bitter
accusation—watered Israel aplenty in the years following
the Second World War. By 1948, roughly half the Jewish
population of Palestine were Holocaust refugees, and the
Jewish state had acquired the reputation and role of a savior.
From a purely instrumental standpoint, the Shoah proved
the greatest asset ever acquired by Zionism, one sedulously
cultivated over the years.

It may be impossible to overestimate the emotional charge
set loose by the Shoah. The Jewish tradition was from its
beginnings not conducive to a sense of security. Its origins were
inscribed in a wilderness, which underscored the aloneness and
contingency within human existence. The Israelite's Yahweh
was a fearsome deity, and in the demand made upon Abraham

to sacrifice his son disclosed an order of sheer terror: "fear and trembling," Kierkegaard called it. Under conditions of Diaspora, this became routinized; the landlessness that eventuated in the peculiar difficulties of Zionist nation-building also contributed to the chronic state of insecurity that came from being dependent, both for sustenance and protection from danger, upon an authority alien to oneself. When judaeophobia surged toward the close of the nineteenth century, Jewish fearfulness surged with it. However we may criticize the choice of Zionism as a path of resolution, there can be no argument with the existential ground of the anxiety that stirred Zionism into life ... nor with the mounting dread as the situation in Germany turned into the unfathomable malignancy of a willful extermination.

Each genocide is unique in its own way, whether that of the indigenous in the New World, the Africans in the Congo under Leopold of Belgium, the Armenians under Turkish rule, and so on to genocide in Cambodia and Rwanda. It is grotesque to compare genocides, saying, in effect, the mass slaughter of my people is worse than yours. However, they all have their signatures, which in the case of Shoah drew itself into a long-wrought narrative and concentrated the affect of unfathomability, thus rousing all the monsters set down over three thousand years. This complex of feeling still persists, and, turned into guilt, shadows the debate on Israel, making even committed anti-imperialists and champions of justice into crypto-Zionists, who despite themselves, end up following the Israeli line. The complex has crippled a good deal of politics in Europe and the United States.[3]

Those to whom befell the task of sorting through the wreckage after the Second World War had to contend with the agitated state of mind and the shock waves it represented. This became elaborated in rousing fictional form—for example, Schwarz-Bart's *The Last of the Just*, Kosinski's *The Painted Bird*, and later, D. M. Thomas' *The White Hotel*—

and more recently, in films without end, endless memorials, conferences, academic programs, endowed chairs, and official commissions, the enshrinement of certain figures like Elie Wiesel as professional arbiters, and, inevitably, to the growth of what Norman Finkelstein has grimly called the "Holocaust Industry," set up to sort through the grim and unending question of reparations.[4] In view of the magnitude of the events and their elaborations in our culture, it is hopeless to expect the Shoah not to have become politicized. It is all the more necessary, then, to understand the particular politics that have emerged to structure the collective mind with respect to the Holocaust—politics, which, in sum, have operated across the spectrum to generate support for Zionism.

The chief themes set forth by the discourse surrounding the Holocaust were first, the essential victimhood of the Jews and their essential innocence;[5] second, and contradicting this in part, an endlessly accusatory debate over collusion and resistance that fractured Israeli politics for many years; third, the essential guilt of the Christian West for not helping Jews in their hour of need and more deeply, for spawning such a monster within its borders as Nazism—for the conclusion could not be avoided that this was no fluke, nor a peculiarly German mutation, but rather expressed something systemic that the Nazis exploited to the hilt. And finally, that the trail ends in the ancient land of Palestine, from which the Jewish people had been expelled and through the return to which they would be saved, at last protected, by their state, from the beast that had hunted them down through centuries of exile. The supreme corollary was that the magnitude of the Holocaust trumped all competing moral claims, including certainly those of the displaced Palestinians whose actual suffering could readily be seen as peripheral to the great drama over the appropriation of the memory of Jewish suffering.[6]

The Shoah did not determine the inner drive and logic of Zionism, but it had the highly important result of allowing this to be shown outwardly in a benign light that drew in vast degrees of support for what had hitherto been considered a marginal and dubious idea. Both the Jewish community and world opinion were greatly affected. In the outpouring and the rescue, the considerations developed in the previous chapter, that Zionism had developed a forward, terroristic strategy to achieve its goals, which in both means and ends was inherently violative of the ethical integrity of Judaism, became blurred and largely lost from view. The Shoah, in other words, allowed the perception of a highly evolved Zionist aggression, which dated from before the war, to become eclipsed, turned around, and seen as defensive and therefore necessary. Once Israel had been established as the sole guarantor of the survival of the Jewish people, it was granted a blank check: anything it was to do could be automatically justified by the immensity of what it stood against. In the same gesture, what had been inflicted by the Nazis became seamlessly transferred to the threat posed by the bloodthirsty Arab hordes surrounding little Israel and ever threatening to drive its Jews into the Mediterranean Sea. All this was achieved despite warnings not to politicize the catastrophe, even though this had already happened because the extremity of events had worked to suppress critical thought.[7]

Mindful of the tremendous moral weight this notion still enjoys, we are yet obliged to question its foundations. For it must be asserted as a moral axiom that the unfathomability of a collective trauma by no means translates into a blank check to do whatever one presumes necessary to prevent its recurrence. Because one is deeply injured does not, in effect, make it all right to injure someone else in return—especially when that someone had committed no injury beyond trying to shake off the invasion of his land. Yes, Israel had provided a tremendous forum for those who had suffered Nazi brutality, a place where the Holocaust could be brought into active awareness. But this boon cannot provide more than the beginning of an assessment. We need to go further and ask: what does the concurrence of the formation of the State of Israel with its role in providing a haven for victims of the Holocaust tell us about its fundamental legitimacy, popularly expressed as its "right to exist"? If in fact the claim of Israel as the savior of Holocaust victims and the defender against Holocaust recurrence is warranted, this would tend to force the legitimacy of the Jewish state no matter what else has transpired. For such to be the case, however, all of the following claims often made on behalf of Zionism need to be substantiated:

- That the Holocaust sprang from an immemorial and essential judaeophobia, that it could only be accounted for in this way, and that its recurrrence is a never-ending potentiality. If this was the case, then inasmuch as the key determining factor is Jewishness as such, only a Jewish state, with its mobilization of Jewish force and perpetually on guard against antisemitism, can suffice to guard against a recurrence;

- That Israel, and before its founding, the Zionist movement, has proven its bona fides as the provider of a haven, in other words, that protectiveness toward Jews facing oppression was based on more than momentary or instrumental factors but was inherent to Zionism itself; and that

- Israel has made good on its promise to safeguard and liberate the Jewish people.

The first point, that the sufficient cause of the Shoah is Jewishness as such, is related to the previously mentioned unfathomability. For if there is no understanding of the Holocaust as the product of specific historical conditions, then it is only possible to explain it by generalizing its manifest content, the genocidal hatred of Jews. Without a context, this is necessarily seen as arising from the abyssal depths of the Christian—and now Arab—soul, and to require a counter-affirmation of Jewish strength to be put down.

It is important to be clear about the distinction between the subjective sense of unfathomability concerning the Shoah, which is a state of mind, and the actual, objective case, for the understanding of which subjective dispositions are important factors, but no more than that. There are other phenomena, nuclear war for example, which surpass our limited human powers of comprehension, and where we take account of this fact but do not rest with it. If we all sat back and threw up our hands at trying to understand the political dynamics of the nuclear arms race because of the unique and unfathomable nature of what happpened at Hiroshima, the world would be at even more risk for nuclear annihilation than it is already. Alternatively, we would cede control of the situation to those who elaborate apocalyptic religious explanations for nuclear war instead of trying to deal rationally with the problems it raises—which, when one thinks about it, is not that dissimilar to what has happened in the case of Israel viewed as the bulwark and haven against a recurrence of the Holocaust.

One of the first problems with the idea that the Holocaust was essentially an orgy of judaeophobia resides in the fact that Jews shared victimhood with others such as homosexuals, leftists and "mental defectives." Nor were Jews the only ethnic group singled out for genocidal extermination, given the inclusion of Romani in that category. According to propagandists for Israel like Elie Wiesel,[8] Jews still are special, for even if not all the Holocaust's victims were Jews, all Jews were the victims of the Holocaust, from which the conclusion must be drawn that Jews should use the experience for the purposes of drawing together as a nation, under, it goes without saying, the aegis of a Jewish state.

But if I stand in horror at what the Nazis did to Jews, why should this diminish the horror of what they did to Romani and the rest? And should I not grant an equal measure of

horror to the other cases, especially if by doing so I will break
with the tribalist tendencies that, corrupting the German mind,
spurred the Holocaust itself? Does not the extension of an
equivalent collective worth to all the victims break with the
cycle of vengeance, and beyond that, enhance the worth of
the real individuals sacrificed to this beast, Jews and non-Jews
alike? Why should I not want each of these classes of victims
to experience the same fellow-feeling toward the Jews who
perished? But if I do so then I must ask the Jews to reciprocate,
and not remain locked into a nationalism that, like all elements
of the Zionist complex, has been generated for the occasion
rather than from the complex of lived history.

There is a kind of penumbra, a gradient of compassion
according to the actual ties one has had with those who have
suffered violence. If someone near and dear to me dies at the
hands of a brutal aggressor, I am bound to *feel* more for that
person than for the other human being next to her who has
suffered the same fate but whom I do not know, simply because
a flood of memories are released in the one instance and not in
the other. One can take this a step further: there were members
of my family who perished under the Nazi regime, some of
whom I never knew, and others I never even knew existed. I
can still have a degree of "special" feeling for them because
it cements a community I know close at hand and whose
value I affirm. But the affectual side of this is already much
weaker than in the first instance and becomes increasingly
abstract or imaginary, and so no longer possesses the same
degree of *immediate* value: thus a gradient of compassion
necessarily exists according to history, which as we know, is
also necessarily subject to degrees of interpretation. At some
point in this gradient the concern begins now to belong to
a more general feeling, about people bound together, and
to oneself by membership, say, in a tribe, or ethnicity, or, as
Zionism would have it, a nation, that is, by some *intermediate*
value; and beyond that, according to the immortal principle

Menachem Begin may well have been an important example, as we discuss in Chapter 7. We are not talking about full-blown Nazism. But given the circumstances, some impulsion in this direction would be highly likely. Inundated by a flood of unassimilated feelings of fright, grief, rage and mortification that swirled through Jewry as a result of Nazi crimes, it would have taken a miracle to block a degree of "identification with the aggressor," the mental construction of which could be applied to the Palestinians, already humanly devalued as they were, who stood in Zionism's path of redemption. Such a miracle did not occur.

That the Holocaust could not have been the simple unfolding of judaeophobia was demonstrated in its actual development, the lessons of which have scarcely been appreciated despite the superb historical treatment by Arno Mayer, himself one of its victims.[12] There can be no doubt that Jews were extremely important victims of the unfolding Nazi aggression. However, they did not become so *qua* Jew according to the traditional self-understanding of Judaism, or even in the understanding of Zionism. From the beginning of Hitler's delusional career of Jew-hating, the future victims were typically hyphenated into "Judaeo-Bolsheviks." By linking a prime enemy with the archaism of Jew-hating, the Nazis were embarking on a consciously chosen political strategy with incalculable destructive potential. In any case, the fury Hitler evoked by stoking the fires of judaeophobia was meant to be directed against the radical left and, ultimately for geostrategic reasons, the Soviets, against whom he launched the most horrific war in history. Before that, in the process of consolidating Nazi power the Nazis filled the first concentration camps with leftists, the crushing of whom was the first order of business for the Third Reich. At this time, Jews, though experiencing revilement of all sorts, were not singled out as particular victims. If a Jew landed in a concentration camp from 1934 to 1938 it was because he or she was a labor official, or a Communist, or a socialist or an anarchist—categories into which, it must be added as a matter of fact (and for me, also as a matter of pride), many did fit.

As Mayer develops the theme, the mass murder of Jews evolved from two additional factors, both consequences of the violent expansion of Nazi Germany. First, came the lurch Eastward and the relatively sudden acquisition of territory, chiefly Poland, in which the majority of the world's Jews happened to live. Needless to say, the sudden acquisition of three million delusionally hated people posed a serious dilemma for the Nazi overlords. But even then the "Final Solution" did not take shape until the invasion of Russia, or to be more exact, until that invasion began to run into trouble on the road to Moscow thanks to the unanticipated resistance put forth by the Soviets. It was then, with yet more millions of Jews in the newly invaded lands (chiefly Ukraine), and with the first presentiment that the mad scheme of world conquest was not going to happen as planned, that the pressure-cooker of Nazism began to germinate the scheme of mass extermination, and followed it through with all the nihilism, race-hatred, industrialization, sadism and cold malevolence that was the Nazi trademark.

It may be said, therefore, that limiting oneself to "bearing witness" to the unfathomable Shoah is not the best way of building a world where Holocaust-like events will not happen again. There is no question that directing energy to eliminating the roots of antisemitism is essential, but no question either that an equivalent degree of energy should be given to overcoming anti-communism, imperialism, militarism, and authoritarian male-dominated capitalist states under conditions of extreme crisis. These are not either/or propositions, since judaeophobia, whatever else it may be, is also a toxic product of male-dominated social relations. In this regard, Nazism can be seen as a terroristic degeneration of Prussian Junkerism, driven by extreme fear and loathing of the flowing liquid female principle. It is not a trivial afterthought to point out that the Jew had been forced into assuming this feminized role within Europe, in respect of which Zionism may be interpreted as a drastic negation of the castrated/feminine position assumed by Jewry, turning Hebrews from "girlie-men" (to use a phrase of a contemporary politician with Nazi roots) to "Tough Jews" never to be pushed about again.[13]

This brings us to the second proposition: How did Zionists actually behave with respect to the Shoah? Did their behavior merit the trust and confidence the world placed in the State of Israel as guardian against supreme evil? There are two questions to be differentiated here: How many Jews were saved from the Holocaust itself? And how many survivors of the Holocaust were able to end up in Israel? The second enterprise was more successful than the first. Tom Segev has written:

> There had been about nine million Jews in Europe on the eve of the war; about six million were killed, leaving three million alive. Most of these were saved by Germany's defeat in the war. Some were spared thanks to help they received from various governments and organizations such as the Joint Distribution Committee and from thousands of good-hearted people in almost every country—the "righteous gentiles." There were dramatic rescue operations such as the flight across the Pyrenees from France to Spain and the convoys of Jews that sailed from Denmark to Sweden. Only a few survivors owed their lives to the efforts of the Zionist movement.[14]

In good measure this was due to the weak position of Zionism during this period, beset as it was with problems concerning Great Britain and the Arabs. But it would be foolish to ignore the following remark made in 1938 by the ever-outspoken David Ben-Gurion:

> If I knew that it was possible to save all the children in Germany by transporting them to England, but only half by transporting them to Palestine, I would choose the second—because we face not only the reckoning of those children, but the historical reckoning of the Jewish people.[15]

Zionist apologists have tripped all over themselves trying to avoid the implications of these words, claiming that the leader of the Yishuv didn't really mean it, that he was prone to exaggeration, that he said different things at different times and that, of course, he only spoke this way because he knew there was no real option of the sort. But that is to entirely miss the point. No one would expect Ben-Gurion to actually do such a thing, or to have such an option. But the very preposterousness of the choice allowed him to express what he *really felt*, free from the inhibiting effect of actual consequences. And what he felt was Zionism's defining feature, that the "historical reckoning of the Jewish people" was at stake and that this was paramount in their hearts; in a word, that the living Jewish people were less important than the forming of the Jewish nation—and later a Jewish state. There have been two aspects to the problems faced by Zionism: the question of acquiring the land for nation state building; and that of acquiring sufficient people of the right sort—"good human material" was the preferred Zionist construction, with ominous overtones[16]—to build that nation state upon the land, and keep it Jewish. Chaim Arlosoroff, in his letter to Weizmann, is explicitly aware of the dual nature of the problem. And in the ruin disclosed by the downfall of Nazism Zionists found an unprecedented opportunity for capitalizing upon Jewish grief.

But there is something else. For the fact that no one would *expect* Ben-Gurion to actually sacrifice Jewish children on the altar of Zionist nation-building does not mean that he didn't in fact set out to *do* just that on a smaller scale. Indeed, the Zionist apparatus did exercise just such an option when the opportunity arose to bring "good human material" to Eretz Israel in the wake of Nazi collapse.

An overture appeared toward the close of the war when FDR, mindful of the difficulties in opening the doors of the United States to refugees from Nazi persecution,[17] estimated that there were some 500,000 Jewish survivors of the Holocaust and conceived a bold scheme to bring them to new homes around the world after the surrender of the Third Reich. The plan had two components: to win commitments from a number of nations to accept Jewish refugees; and to administer the program so that every refugee had a free choice within the framework of quotas. These included a total of 200,000 from an assortment of nations, and 150,000 each from the bellwethers of the Allies, England and the United States. The British agreed readily; but the United States was another story. Knowing he would have his work cut out to persuade his chronically isolationist and nativist Congress to ratify his humanitarian idea, Roosevelt delegated the prominent Jewish (though non-Zionist) lawyer, Morris Ernst, to travel about the country to help build support for the plan among Jewish leaders. This Ernst set out to do, full of enthusiasm because he knew that his cause was just and that the most popular and charismatic president in modern American history was behind him. We may follow the story in his own words.

"It did not work out," Ernst writes in his memoirs.[18] The sticking point was not, as anticipated, the gentile nativists and their antisemitism, however, but the Jewish leadership. "I do not intend to quote F.D.R. ... But to me it seemed that the failure of the leading Jewish groups to support with zeal this immigration program may have caused the President not to push forward with it at that time." For despite the fact that "no Jews . . . would be compelled to go anywhere and certainly not to any assigned nation" according to the plan, it received a cold shoulder. Worse, "I was amazed and even felt insulted when active Jewish leaders decried, sneered and then attacked me as if I were a traitor. At one dinner party I was openly accused of furthering the plan for freer immigration in order to undermine political Zionism. Those Jewish groups which favored opening our doors gave little more than lip service to the Roosevelt program. Zionist friends of mine opposed it."

This odd reaction makes perfect sense according to the logic of Zionism. The mass of Jewish refugees at the end of the war constituted more than half the population of the Yishuv in Palestine. Getting all, or the great majority, of these to emigrate to Israel would be an incalculable boon for the cause; contrariwise, to see the refugees slip out of Zionist hands, especially if they were to find their way to hated England, would have been a serious blow to both ideology and demographics.[19] And so a no-holds-barred campaign under Ben-Gurion's leadership was launched in the refugee camps to persuade, insist upon, organize and even force refugees in the direction of Palestine. This encountered, yet also overrode, two serious problems: first, conditions in the camps were by and large dreadful, especially for a people who had gone through such an ordeal as had the Jews; and second, that many of the survivors didn't want to go to Palestine. Some were not interested in Zionism, or even hostile; some gave token support for the purposes of helping Israel, but had other plans in mind; still others were too broken to choose. As individuals, they would have been better served by going where they wanted or would have their survival needs better met in the more developed countries willing to take them in—all the more so, as there were ample Jewish agencies and rabbinical associations eager to supervise the process and preserve Jewish identity in the doing.

These ordinary human concerns were swallowed in the "historical reckoning" of Zionism and its totalizing logic. As one functionary said of the orphaned children whose fate hung in the balance: "Only immigration to Palestine will guarantee their existence and their future as Jews and human beings. . . ." In other words, there was only one way of being a Jew and one way of being fully human—the Zionist way; all others need not apply, and hence Jews who preferred a different way were no longer Jewish or even human. This trope is usually associated with the radical Orthodox but here becomes the province of Labor Zionists, another one of whom said of the children that "Only this land can absorb them, heal them, turn them into citizens and restore their national and human balance—no other place or land will do so, except our *Yishuv* and country."[20] In this way, several thousand orphans recently rescued from the extremity of judaeophobic evil were forbidden to leave the camps after all arrangements had been made, and were thereby denied a Jewish haven in England and France that many had expressly asked for.

Later, as the war that was to launch the Jewish state loomed, another use was found for refugee "human material." By 1947, Haganah operatives began working in the camps, often clandestinely. Their presence signalled the coming to fruition of a common assumption, one first articulated by Jabotinsky and later installed within Labor Zionism by Arlosoroff—that it would some day come to armed warfare with the Arabs. There is no doubt that the Zionists had long been preparing for this and that the die became cast with the UN Partition of 1947, after which the only questions were the timing of combat and who would win it. Nor is there any question that Zionist organization of the war was brilliantly carried out, a wonder of boldness, foresight, detailed planning and coordination.

One consideration was manpower for the nascent Israel Defense Force. There was great anxiety lest the Yishuv be unable to summon up enough troops for the challenges ahead. Thoughts turned immediately toward the refugee camps in the American Zone, swollen with suffering Jewish bodies brought over from the East. A strenuous effort was made to recruit volunteers for the cause. And when this failed, for easily understandable reasons—for how many Jews, newly rescued from the horrors of the Holocaust, would be enthusiastic for military duty in a strange land?—the Zionist apparatus moved rapidly into a higher gear, and proceeded to forcibly recruit some ten thousand soldiers and ship them to fight for a country that none of them knew or belonged to. The force was chiefly exerted through the administrative control Zionists had gained over the camps, each of them a more or less total institution. Summary loss of employment for recalicitrants, followed by summary denial of food rations, usually did the trick, though quite often beatings and other forms of violence had to be used.

By treating its "human material" in this way, Zionism revealed just how advanced its "identification with the aggressor" had become. As the Advisor on Jewish Affairs to the American Supreme Commander in Europe wrote a week after the proclamation of the new state, "the pressure exerted on the people [who had resisted the draft] was crude, at times reflecting the techniques they had learned from their own oppressors." Or as an editorial in the Paris-based Bundist journal *Unser Shtime* (our voice) stated, it was "unbelievable that Jews, the standard victims of Fascism and terrorism, would be capable of the kinds of violence Zionists in the camps exercise toward their Bundist and other non-Zionist political rivals."[21]

Though it is beyond dispute that many Jewish survivors of the Holocaust successfully ended up in Israel,[22] it is impossible to avoid the conclusion that, taken as a whole, there are many dubious features of the relationship between Zionism and the Shoah. Certainly, we cannot take as axiomatic the reflexive claim that somehow the founding of the Jewish state was necessary for the survival of the refugees. FDR's plan of early 1945 estimated 500,000 refugees, and that the US would take 150,000 of them. In the event, there proved to be 330,000 refugees and the US ended up with some 120,000. The remainder could well have been worked into the provisions of the plan using countries other than Israel, especially given unified cooperation from the Jewish community, needless to say, a very big "if," but still a real possibility, and indeed a certainty were Zionism not a factor.

In any event, though Zionism was not necessary for recuperation from and prevention of, the Holocaust, the Holocaust definitely became a necessity for Zionism, which has processed it right through the present day as a kind of ur-event to certify its inner absolutism. The forbidding of children's immgration to Europe, the forced recruitment of DP's, the vilification and abuse of Jewish refugees who failed to see the wisdom of the Zionist program—all this showed how tragedy could become folded into aggression and used to legitimate the Zionist way.

How has this state, the Jewish state, fared in fulfilling its promise to provide a better, safer life for all Jews? We may summarize:

- Today, more than a half-century after its founding, Israel is by far the most dangerous place on earth for Jews, simply because it has been set up to be perpetually at war.

- The behavior of the Jewish state has provoked both a worldwide outpouring of rational condemnation and a resurgence of judaeophobia. Zionists tend to claim, first, that there is no such thing as rational condemnnation of Israel, hence that all criticism is antisemitic; and second, that antisemitism, as ever, is a virus that springs from the twisted heart of the *goyim* irrespective of what Jews, or Israel, may do. We must reject this grosssly ideological view once again, which flies in the face of the elementary facts of human agency and interconnectedness. If an imperial power invades, occupies, and destabilizes another society, denying its people normal and autonomous means of self-expression, then it can expect with the certitude of a law of nature that the whole spectrum of human responses will be evoked, ranging from emancipatory and nonviolent expression to crude atavisms including racist belief, and in the case when the invader is set up as a Jewish state, antisemitism. Needless to say, what begins in one place can readily spread around the world if the conflict in question is of sufficient general interest. It is an intellectual barbarism to remove such phenomena from their historical context, to single out the less rational elements of the spectrum from the rest and to absolutize them under the rubric of antisemitism. This is to abstract from the various manifestations of hostility to Israel an essence of judaeophobia that arose under vastly different circumstances. It draws from a time when Jews were, if not blameless, at least powerless, and were made to pay the debts demanded by the anti-communism of the fascist state and by Christendom's bad conscience.

- Despite the enormous aid given to it by its American protector and the benefits of the international Jewish community, Israel remains a society in grave social and economic crisis, with rampant unemployment, pockets of outright hunger, and many signs of social disintegration. As we shall take up further in Chapter 5, it now has the greatest gap between rich and poor in the whole industrialized world. More than half of Israeli families cannot meet their monthly bills, and 14 percent cannot buy an adequate diet. In a 2004 *Ha'aretz* op-ed, Michael Melchior, a member of the Knesset, observed that: "We live in a society in which a million and a quarter people—40 percent of them working people—are below the poverty line. This is a society that abandons 366,000 of its children-at-risk and throws them into the street; a society that treats its foreign workers like animals; a society that despises its elderly and sends them to rummage through the garbage. It is a society, according to information given the Knesset Committee for Children's Rights, where in the absence of standards, a social worker has to devote an average of two minutes to a family in distress. It is a society among the leaders in the world trafficking in women."[23] The immediate cause is a fierce neoliberal assault on the poor and public sector led by Finance Minister Binyamin Netanyahu. This is no accident but the result of the drift to the right inherent in the dynamics of the Zionist project.

- Israel provides the worst primary and lower secondary education in the Western world, despite having budgeted adequate funds. It also scores below many poorer countries, for example, Malaysia, Thailand and Romania, which provide it with cheap textiles and labor.[24]

- All this has left the original socialist ideal in ruins. Today, extreme right-wing religious fundamentalism plays a far larger role in Israel than the enlightened socialism that was to have been the emblem of the new Jewish society.

- As an immediate result of these woes, and comprising a
  tremendous threat to the ever-precarious demographic question,
  a serious degree of outmigration of Jews from Israel is taking
  place. As of mid 2004, some 760,000 Israeli Jews were living
  abroad, an increase of 40 percent since the Second Intifada
  began in 2000. Those with a taste for irony may contemplate
  the following: the preferred destination of Jews leaving the
  former Soviet Union is no longer Israel but ... Germany! This
  has prompted another round of Zionist attacks on the fiendish
  Germans, now for "enticing" Jews to settle there.[25]

What kind of a state has Zionism wrought?

Part Two
The Jewish State

4

The Only Democracy in the Middle East

Erect a Jewish state at once, even if it is not in the whole land. The rest
will come in the course of time. It must come ...
David Ben-Gurion, 1937[1]

"We take the land first and the law comes after"[2]

THE AFFECTION OF JEWS for a strong state is deeply
rooted. The Bible recounts brief episodes of state power
punctuating long periods of drifting and subjugation.
These burned in collective memory and became a template for
what was promised to be a glorious restoration. During the
whole sweep of the Diaspora, though the state was not theirs,
its rulers often served as a kind of protector and a relatively
reliable ally against hostile masses beset with judaeophobia.
Indeed, throughout the Middle Ages, Jews owed much of their
livelihood and loyalty to service to monarch and nobility. As
the state became absolute, beginning in 1492 with Spain, it
also became increasingly intolerant of the unassimilable Jews
in its midst, and began persecuting them and forcing them out.
But states were also repositories of an advancing liberalism,
and as such offered hopes for emancipation. On this basis, the
Jewish enlightenment thinkers of the eighteenth century, the
maskilim, postulated, like Spinoza and later Hegel, the state
as the bearer of the highest aspirations.[3]

Bitter history has greatly corrected this judgment, including to be sure, the history of that absolute mid-twentieth century state that slaughtered Jews in unprecedented numbers. But the political Zionists who were hell-bent on conquering Palestine did not have the luxury of reflecting on these matters. As Ben-Gurion wrote to his son—in 1937, when the malignancies of Nazism and Stalinism were already on full display—obtaining state power held the highest priority. He and the other Zionist leaders knew quite well that the state was fashioned by, and owed its being to, the necessity of getting something done in this world, for states are by definition repositories of organized force, with, as Max Weber famously put it, a monopoly of legitimate violence. So even if a state could be set going on only part of the territory it would have the dynamism to propagate itself across the entirety of the Promised Land.

No doubt, being Zionists, they reassured themselves that a *Jewish* state would be different from the ordinary run of states. It would be *exceptional* and also *highly ethical*, such being Jewish racial qualities, thus, a new and superior kind of democracy. That things have not quite worked out according to plan has quite a bit to do with the fact, not that the Jews are really exceptional and highly ethical, but that they are compelled to think of themselves as such. In any case, what is wrong with the Jewish state is the fact of being a Jewish state.

States are bodies that stand over societies and organize them. They have internal tendencies of their own, which operate independently of the people's will, and even, to a degree, of the will of their leaders. Each and every state solidifies a society among the gathering of other states and so creates a new fictive body. In this respect states are like gigantic persons, though their organization precludes the moral logic to which actual persons are subject. They define what really matters to them as "interests," and make this a zone within which considerations of morality function mainly for propagandistic purposes.

We have observed that states marshall violent force. This is a key to their being, but by no means the whole picture, for states also need legitimacy, desperately at times. This is not a matter of intrinsic morality. It arises because the state must secure, as Gramsci put it,[4] internal *consent* to, and external acceptance of its rule. The more consent is secured, the less force is needed, and the smoother things go. Ideally, the exercise of force will be ideologically blessed, as by the invocation of "enemies of the state," like barbarous terrorists, or other states that want to annihilate it. The whole Zionist propaganda apparatus may be viewed in this light, which tells us that states are dependent upon their enemies. If these functions break down and consent withers, then the application of violence becomes openly repressive and can have the unwanted effect of further delegitimising the order of things. This in turn may lead into a downward spiral, which can presage the ruin of the state. Thus an intricate dance arises between these functions, the steps of which we will try to outline for the State of Israel.

But what are these "things" that consent and force secures? The great secret mystified in every state's propaganda system is that irreducible transgression known as *class*—that every state is falling away from universal dignity inasmuch as it is built upon and secures an arrangement whereby one group owns and controls wealth and the apparatus to generate wealth, while another, far larger, group consists of those whose labor is exploited by the former. There is no state without a class system, and no class system without a state, even though many other powerful determinants enter the picture. Securing the generation of wealth for a dominant class is the prime function of the state. And since in the capitalist era wealth is defined as "money in motion," securing money in motion becomes the prime requirement of the state in capitalist society, which we call *accumulation.*[5]

CONSTITUTIONAL BLUES

As a state, Israel must obey the general law of states, and secure accumulation for its ruling class. However, what this story is all about is that Israel is no ordinary state but a *Jewish state*, a state primarily of, by and for the Jewish people, for whom it provides a homeland. It is also held to be a *democratic-Jewish* state, such being its great banner of legitimation, routinely used to compare Israel favorably to the other states of the region.

It is scarcely acknowledged that the self-proclaimed Jewish democracy has never been able to draw up a constitution. Needless to say, a constitution does not in itself guarantee democracy: consider only the case of Stalin's USSR, which had a magnificent constitution, cynically disregarded. Nevertheless, as there can be no democracy without an overarching principle of Law to assure universal human right, and as there can be no such principle in a society absent a constitutional foundation, the absence of a constitution leaves society open to the arbitrary will to power.

Israel has used a body of common law and an independent judiciary to set the standard of legality and justice. This is certainly better than nothing at all. However, the independence of a judiciary is a relative thing, and without a constitutional foundation, and especially a Bill of Rights that installs respect for basic human rights, the legal system of any society is bound to sway in the winds of one kind of pressure or another. Zionist propaganda exults in the virtues of the Israeli judiciary, as if to reassure that the lack of a constitution has had no corrupting effect on the rule of law. Norman Finkelstein does a very effective job of rebutting this in his polemic against Alan Dershowitz, one of the main cheerleaders for the sanctity of Israel's legal system.[6]

Meanwhile, supporters of Israel tell us not to worry, as the democratic bona fides of the Jewish state are buttressed by Judaism's ethical superiority. As Bernard Avishai has written in an influential study of Zionism, the lack of a constitution should not "suggest that Israel failed to become a democracy in essential respects." The country does have a parliament and Arab citizens can vote. Despite the lack of a Bill of Rights, Israel does have a fairly robust tradition of freedom of speech and the press (often superior to that within the United States), as well as the right to worship as one wants. Avishai admits this, however, is not the be-all and end-all of a democratic society. "[F]rom the first, the Arab community as a whole was governed by the military and Arab nationalist political parties were banned"; nor of course, can one imagine an Arab playing any kind of leading role in Israel, with its Jewish state. Faced with these contradictions, Avishai falls back on the principle that the real key to democracy is the virtue of the people: "Besides, democratic life cannot be reduced to this or that network of law, but depends on widespread support among a country's citizens for liberal values and tolerant attitudes."[7]

I find this to be vague, circular, and tendentious. What are the "essentials" of a democracy that it cannot be reduced to "this or that network of law?" Democracy is not founded on one or another type, or network, of law, but on the recognition of Law as a principle over and above the will of any individual (as in dictatorship) or ethnic group (as in Israel), no matter how highly ethical. We should not trust a dictator because he seems to be a nice guy; so why should we entrust Israeli democracy to the Jews because they are ethical? Does not this claim affirm the Jews to be *Übermenschen*, that is, as racially superior, which is scarcely a democratic notion? Are liberal values and tolerant attitudes racially inherent to a people and therefore permanent, or a more or less fickle variable that conflict and fear can sweep aside—as the history of Israel does tend to reveal? Finally, if as Avishai says, "[m]ost veterans of the Yishuv were consciously democratic," then why were they not able to put together a constitutional framework such as might have guided Israeli democracy? Why did they have to set up a state that, more than a half-century later, is still unable to define itself or its borders, that still lives on the fly in a permanent state of emergency, claiming itself as above the law of nations and awaiting a peace that never comes?

We may track the story of Israel's failure to enact a constitution through Avishai's eyes, as his account is widely admired[8] and, while fundamentally animated by loyalty to the Zionist project, quite a bit more critical of Israel than the standard view. As he tells it, the founders of the Jewish state were manifestly eager to build a democracy, and David Ben-Gurion, the George Washington of the nation, promised to convene a constitutional convention as soon as possible—a step that would have left Zionism "enshrined as Israel's heroic *prelude*. ... [Its] principles of action, however, would have been *rightly judged as having had a historically limited purpose; having been realized, Zionism would have been superseded by Israeli law.*" [italics added]

There has never yet been a state that did not crack down on democratic right when engaged in war. Thus under pressure from the hostilities of 1948, Ben-Gurion "worked to establish a firm hold on state power without any further concessions to constitutional principles," consolidating the military and passing emergency decrees, a number of which remained in effect long afterwards. Finally, in January 1949, with victory at hand, a constituent assembly was elected whose chief function (like that of the fledgling United States in 1787 or, ironically, of Iraq in 2005) was to draft a constitution. It failed to do so, and the sticking point was the role to be held by religion in the new society.

The ingathering of Jews from across the Diaspora and the still-raging impact of the Holocaust deeply affected the convention. As an official expressed the mood: if the "institutional forms and civic conceptions" of modern societies were "to have more than a transient meaning, they must strike in the deeper recesses of the soul of the people ... by infusion of the Hebrew spiritual tradition into their functional framework."[9] Consequently, the preamble to the draft constitution gave thanks "to Almighty God for having delivered us from the burden of exile and brought us back to our ancient land." The phrase bears comparison to the "in order to form a more perfect union" of the preamble to the United States Constitution. Where the American document, imbued with Enlightenment hope, looks toward the future, the fledgling Israeli state looks back, across the desolation imposed by Nazism and the centuries of dispersion and marginalization, towards a society whose perfection had been conferred by separation of Jews from the remainder of humanity, and whose union is with their own God. In short, it had been pulled in a tribal rather than a universal direction.

In the event, Mapam, the modernist liberal-left party, objected to the lack of separation between religion and the state, as did its right-wing mirror image, Herut, founded by Jabotinsky. The combination would have provided a majority allowing Ben-Gurion to install a modern, secular constitution. The price, however, was admitting right wingers into the government, and this Ben-Gurion found unacceptable. Instead, he chose an alliance with the Orthodox, reasoning that the rabbinate were passive and other-worldly ("compliant and Torah-bound," Avishai describes them; indeed, one faction had held that it would be enough to declare the Torah as Israel's constitution) and would not get in the way so long as thrown the sop of being allowed to conduct marriages and other civil ceremonies. A half-century on, the idea evokes Shakespeare's *Lear*:

> The gods are just, and of our pleasant vices
> Make instruments to plague us
> Act V Scene iii line 171

Because the rabbinate and the 10 percent of the population they represented would never consent to the establishment of a modern democratic form of governance, the constitution had to be deferred—and deferred, and deferred, until forgotten. It bears emphasis that Ben-Gurion and the Mapam leadership could have achieved constitutional legality in this moment had they wanted it badly enough . . . and Israel could have gone forward to become a normal state in which, as Avishai quite correctly puts it, Zionism "would have been rightly judged as having had a historically limited purpose; having been realized, Zionism would have been superseded by Israeli law." But constitutional legality was not the prime value. Thus it took its back seat to the institutional perpetuation of Zionism, with its guarantee of Jewish dominance—and since one would scarcely expect Ben-Gurion to admit that this was what he wanted, the negation of democratic legality became a badge of fundamentalist power. Both were fated to grow with every expansive act of the Zionist state.

The constitutional assembly became the Knesset, or parliament, which declared itself sovereign and proceeded to define the Israeli state as a pastiche of advanced democratic principles and the ways of the Yishuv. The irreconcilable contradiction at the heart of Zionism between tribalism and universality was finessed, and both elements were allowed to coexist within the state under the emblem of Zionist liberation, where universality was the fig leaf and tribalism the driving force in the form of ethnic cleansing. Thus an effort to exclude the secular right from government set into motion the chain of events that would lead to a permanent right-wing government in thrall to a tribalist religious orthodoxy. So much for the fidelity to democratic value of the Israeli left.

Among the laws ratified by the first Knesset was the "Law of Lands of Israel," adapted from the Yishuv's Jewish National Fund. One of its prime principles had been that lands acquired by Zionist purchase would be leased in perpetuity on the condition that these would never be alienated to non-Jews. In practice, writes Avishai, this "once ... defensible principle of Zionist revolutionary struggle ... now ... became the basis to deny about 200,000 Israeli citizens [almost entirely of Arab extraction] (and their descendants) access to 95 percent of Israel's land."[10] Whatever the revolutionary bona fides of Zionist struggle, the fact remains that this obscure measure, snuck into place as a transitional device, would become a foundation-stone of the permanent dispossession of the Palestinian people—a dispossession that would never have withstood the light of constitutional governance according to human rights.

There were other conveniences brought about by non-constitutional governance on the fly. Various emergency regulations set up by the British to deal with Zionist insurgents—for example, preventive detention, censorship, and the rights of search and seizure—were simply grandfathered as prerogatives of a strong state facing an unending emergency, to be used down the line against other "terrorists." Other measures were prospective, such as the Law of Return, passed in July 1950, that gave stateless Jewish immigrants an open path to citizenship upon landing in Israel—the same law that, turned on its head, denies the same right to Palestinians dispossessed by Israel's expansion. The fate of these stateless people was sealed by another law that would never have withstood constitutional scrutiny, that of confiscating property allegedly abandoned by Arabs. Thus arose the ghost-littered landscape of modern Israel, a nation built on stolen land.

To this grim story Avishai adopts an ambivalent attitude, combining forthright rendition with plaintive exoneration. What else could have been done, he asks? The Orthodox—not just the 10 percent of the fundamentalist faithful but great numbers of those (especially the immigrants) who would not vote for religious parties yet remained "sentimentally attached to Orthodox Law"—would never have tolerated a secular constitution, nor was there time to bring them around given the constant danger of Arab attack. The state was forged under conditions of emergency, and faced a huge influx of

immigration, to whose European base had been added many
from Arab nations who needed housing and basic services.
"Israelis asked themselves," Avishai reminds us, "to what bill
of rights could 120,000 expropriated Iraqi Jews appeal?"

Such questions demand responses at a number of levels.

- Yes, many Jews were—and still are—sentimentally
  attached to Orthodox law, even if they do not practice
  the religious codes. But not all Jews are this way, and
  why should the wishes of those who wanted Judaism
  to be redefined on universalising principles be set aside?
  The only coherent answer is that the state was operating
  under a Zionist compulsion for which the universal was
  anathema because it would have opened Israel to reconciliation with the Arabs and prevented it from becoming a
  Jewish state. Hence the alliance with Orthodox archaisms.
  At any point in its trajectory Zionism could have been
  renounced. Had Israel chosen to do so, the Orthodox,
  who at the time of the founding of the state were indeed
  an other-worldly faction in contrast to one that includes
  today's well-armed fanatics, could have chosen reconciliation, a path that would have included complete freedom
  to worship in its own way, without the needless, and
  destructive, state-granted religious monopoly.
- Second, we should avoid the definition of Israel imposed
  by Zionism—that it, and it alone—provides the haven
  for Jews uprooted by history. According to this circular
  reasoning, only Israel could have been entrusted with the
  fate of Jewish refugees. We have shown in the previous
  chapter that not only was this ideologically imposed, but
  that certain devious measures taken by Zionism toward
  the question of European refugees were significantly
  motivated by the demographic imperative of squeezing
  as many Jews as possible into Palestine. Note that the
  "demographic" imperative belongs to the notion of

"democracy," but at its lowest level only, as ensuring a majority for the Jewish state. Of course, if one believes the Zionist line, then all measures taken to ensure a Jewish state through a Jewish majority are justified. This means, however, that it is the idea of the Jewish state itself that runs against the notion of constitutionality, and *pari passu*, runs with that of lawlessness.

- Finally, we need to consider the actual measures taken by the Jewish state.

Take the matter of the Iraqi Jews, the oldest continuous Jewish community in the world (going back to Nebuchadnezzar in the seventh century BCE). Mesopotamia was Judaism's lifeline, the place that secured the faith after the fall of the Second Temple to Titus in 70 CE, and the world center for Judaism long before Europe had any cities. Indeed, Abraham is said to have come from what is now Iraq.

Yes, there was a great emigration of Jews, some 120,000, from Iraq in the wake of the events of 1948. "Expropriated," Avishai calls them, conveniently linking the story to immemorial suffering at the hands of the Jew-haters, in which Arabs are now to play the role of expropriators. History, however, does not oblige this version of events. For the Jews left Iraq not because their land was being taken away, nor under pressure from the Iraqi government to dissociate themselves from Zionism, but because they had been put into a panic as the result of a series of three bomb blasts in 1950–51. To this day, it is not certain who set off those bombs. One has to take into account a well-documented suspicion that they were planted by Israeli agents to foment fears of a pogrom.[11] To not even suggest the possibility of such shenanigans is quite delinquent, given what is known of the robust Israeli tradition of covert operations, and its perennial interest in addressing the demographic problem by manipulating fears of antisemitism.[12] To round off this story, it should also be pointed out that

Iraqi Jews suffered a serious downfall when they fled what had been a prosperous and highly respected role in an ancient society for the harsh inequalities that awaited the so-called "Oriental Jews" in Israel, where, as Ilan Pappe has written, "a monolithic culture of memory [had] developed that repressed the experiences of marginalized groups within society."[13]

When the principle of Law is shot through with holes by the lack of a constitution and continually battered by evocation of the apocalyptic threat posed by hordes of terrorist antisemites, and, moreover, when the state is set up to fulfill a divinely promised process of expansion, then we are in for a very rough ride, and it is only a matter of time before original emancipatory goals are swallowed up, digested and turned into a hard and acquisitive entity. Beneath all the proclamations about Arab terrorism and the ethical nobility of the Jewish state, expropriation by any means necessary is the master narrative necessary to comprehend the history of Israel/Palestine. And so we arrive at a land-grab state that, under the protective wing of its superpower patron, continues the annihilation of Palestinian society, the conversion of the Occupied Territories into a gigantic prison, and the steady expropriation of its land.

There is an answer, then, to the question why Israel has not put into effect a real constitution with a Bill of Rights. It is, bluntly, that to do so would mean being forced to introduce considerations of human rights, which would make the expropriation of Palestinians, and the Jewish state itself, illegal. Constitutionality would demand radical and even revolutionary change for Israel. The state as it has existed for more than a half-century has formed itself around extra-constitutionality; it could not go on otherwise, therefore, a real constitution would require the Israeli state to abolish itself.

In the meantime, we should recognize that what has been depicted here is no true democracy, and certainly not the only such creation in the Middle East. Are there elements of democracy in Israel? Obviously; as has been said already, quite a bit more open dissent is tolerated there than in the United States. Are the other countries in the region models of democracy? Of course not, they are mainly disasters—though neighboring Lebanon, now ruined by Israeli ordnance, has had fairly vigorous democratic mechanisms in place roughly as long as Israel.

Better, then, to make a firm distinction between the *mechanisms* of democracy, which are various instrumental means, and the *truth* of democracy, which is the end to which those means are directed. What, then, is this truth the appropriation of which is the real standard of democracy? Actually, it is rather simple. A society may be said to be truly democratic to the degree that it puts into practice the principle that all human beings have the same intrinsic worth, or dignity, and that they are given the opportunity to realize who they are. The translation requires implementation of matters like full equality before the law, including universal suffrage, the common right of self-determination—not as individuals, since humans are nothing as individuals, but as freely constituted members of a community—and, since human beings define themselves in the act of production, collective ownership of the means of production. From this it can be seen that all the so-called bourgeois democracies are pale reflections of what democracy can be; while the failings of socialism in the last century to become democratic represented a terrible blow to humanity from which the world has not nearly begun to recover. In all cases, then, the basic human right of equivalent dignity wanders far away. Nevertheless, there are greater or lesser degrees of distance from democratic realization, on the basis of which we can say useful things about various societies. But doing so requires us to pass judgment on how the wealth of a society is accumulated.

5
Facts on the Ground

ON THE POLITICAL ECONOMY OF ISRAEL

IMMERSION IN THE INTERNAL dynamics of Zionism and the tremendous moral issues it poses can cause one to lose sight of the fact that Israel, being a state, also presides over an economy and is an important though peculiar part of a world system for which the paramount goal is accumulation of capital. That the Jewish state and the economy over which it presides is an integral part of global capitalism is easy to minimize, given Israel's diminutive stature among the world economies, the ostensibly socialist character of classical political Zionism, and its utopian reputation. Reflections along these lines are predictably met with accusations of being recycled versions of the Protocols of the Elders of Zion and other antisemitic fantasies of Jewish economic conspiracy. Notwithstanding, Zionist involvement in the world economy and empire is very real, and the common tendency to think of Zionism as simply a wrestling with the fate of the Jews is very shortsighted.

As we have already observed, Herzl's great success was to link the impulse of Zionist utopianism with the worldly sources that could provide it with a material foundation and enable it to purchase alienable Ottoman lands in Palestine and hold them for Jewish settlers. Thus the fracas caused today by the expansion of settlements in Arab Israel and the Occupied

Territories, or in 1948 by the ethnic cleansing of Palestinians from their mandated lands, is continuous with the original campaign to buy up Ottoman Palestine. If that process was legal and the present one illegal, this only poses the need to understand how Zionism has grown more unlawful as it has acquired power.

In their *The Global Political Economy of Israel*, Jonathan Nitzan and Shimson Bichler describe how, as the Jewish settlement in Palestine took shape in the 1920s, it was comprised of three "pluralistic" blocs: the "national sector," a network of internationally founded financial organizations that arose intercurrently with the Herzlian movement and provided its capital; the "Histadrut sector," comprising the direct economic activity of the powerful labor movement in Palestine (including the kibbutzim); and the private, or "civil sector," a loose conglomerate of small economic interests. In addition, there were various foreign investors and multinational corporations, and, conveniently forgotten, the fact that, up until 1948, "the whole process was embedded in a vibrant Palestinian society that was itself starting to industrialize."[1]

That was then. What happened, if we may briefly summarize an elaborate process that developed fitfully through the various phases of Israeli history, was the destruction of the Palestinian economy as the threshold event for the annihilation of its society; and the rearrangement and consolidation of the three sectors into one Israeli economy increasingly integrated into international capital flows, with a rapid acceleration of this process in the 1990s. In the process, the "national" (in fact, international) bloc became the foundation of Israel finance—thus the Jewish [sic] Colonial Trust, founded in 1889, developed a subsidiary, the Anglo-Palestine Company, in 1902, for the purpose of "land redemption" for the settlers.[2] This eventually turned into Bank Leumi, branches of which can now be seen in Manhattan and many other parts of the world.[3] Meanwhile the Histadrut, under Ben-Gurion's direction (helped by Chaim Arlosoroff) staked its claim on the labor embodied in the immigrants streaming in from across the Diaspora, and worked to build this into a comprehensive economic foundation for the new society. This included its own Bank Hapoalim (Worker's Bank), which was founded in 1921, and which by the 1990s, had "tentacles [which] reached everywhere."[4] In the event, and especially as the civil sector chimed in both competitively and through the forming of various joint enterprises, the national-socialist Histadrut suffered a common fate of cooperative enterprises who try to survive in capitalist society: the adoption of the ethos of the dominant system, the consolidation of a ruling class across the various components of the economy and hierarchically separated from its own labor force, and an integration with global capital. The process was accelerated by the dynamic inherent to Zionist nation-building and its powerful military component, which forged the various factions into a common body and added the economic stimulus that comes with militarization, along with the boons accruing from being a client of empire. The post-1948 state acclerated the process in every way, acting, as Nitzan and Bichler usefully describe it, as a "cocoon" in which the accumulation process could gestate.

As the economy grew and became more capitalist, so did the demand for labor power. Here, however, the Zionist project encountered a limit that would profoundly compromise its original impulse. What kind of labor was to meet this demand? As a nationalized socialism, Zionism held forth the dream of an economy in equilibrium with and embedded within a Jewish society. In this vision, Jewish labor, flowing into Israel from the far corners of the Diaspora, would build the dreamed-of Jewish society. The first stumbling block was the fact that this Jewish labor was principally defined by the Ashkenazi, or Eurocentric core of the Zionist movement. If the original settlers had had their way, the nation state of Israel would have been a pure culture of European Jewry. This, however, was rendered impossible as the essential character of the economy shifted to one of generalized accumulation under the auspices of capital. For capital does not see labor as exclusively one way or the other; it is, rather, an infinitely fungible substance—labor power—a commodity in itself required for the fabrication of all other commodities under capitalism. In other words, to the degree that capital reigned over the economy, so did the economy come to reign over society; and with this, Jewish labor dissolves into labor power, and a main foundation of the Zionist worldview breaks down. A twofold crisis emerges here: from one side, the irresistible force of capitalist expansion meant that the demand for labor power would exceed the natural limit of Ashkenazi immigration and override its Zionist principle; and from another, the quality of the labor would no longer be directed, so to speak, at producing "use-values" consonant with the utopian side of Zionism, but rather be at the beck of whatever the market demands. And as if this wasn't trouble enough, the very Holocaust whose ghastliness gave the imprimatur of legitimacy to Israel also deprived it, through brute extermination, of the huge reservoir of Jewish labor it had dreamed of including into its utopia.

The direct consequence was to open the gates to African and Asian Jews. Given the essential structures, inferior status and associated racist treatment became their lot. Moreover, the arrangement solidified a class structure of Ashkenazi overlords and Sephardic/Mizrahi (African Jews) proletarians.[5] This sowed immeasurable conflict and demoralized the Zionist consensus. Thus socialist Ben-Gurion called Oriental Jews "human dust," and compared them to the black slaves brought to America. This was, needless to say, not a very good way of building Zionist unity, and it became further complicated down the line when continued demand for exploitable labor led to the use of Palestinian untouchables for the lowest strata of the labor markets; and later, after conflicts with the indigenous made this undesirable, to importation of coolie labor from the global

South. All this was radically discordant with the utopian vision upon which the Jewish state was founded.

In any case, that vision was to collapse under the pressure of nationalism and perpetual war and crisis. Throughout, Israel remained in a state of essential economic dependence. Palestine is rich in history but poor in natural endowments, and these latter have been greatly compromised, as we discuss shortly, by ecological folly. As a result, the dream of the Yishuv, that the land—*Eretz Yisroel*—would be redeemed by Zionist labor has yielded to a rerun, under modern conditions, of the medieval role played by Jews, as clever manipulators of money, now on an international stage. Under the regime of globalization, this has taken shape chiefly in the bizarre relationship with the United States, as discussed in the next chapter.

The theme is conspicuous throughout the history of Zionism, whose "people apart" has been unable to stand on its own as an authentic nation state. Nitzan and Bichler, writing of the humiliation an Israeli politician had to swallow from a rich donor who scolded the country for being too socialist, add: "But then what else could the Israeli politicians do? Their country was totally dependent, from the very beginning, on foreign capital, and if the donors wanted them to bow and suffer a little humiliation, so be it." These inflows, from individuals, organizations (which include, in the United States, large labor unions), and foreign governments (chiefly the United States and Germany) have financed, on average since the 1950s, an astounding 18 percent of GDP.[7]

A great deal of wealth passes through Israel, but the country in itself is scarcely productive in the essential sense of transforming nature into objects of utility. This judgment is scarcely ameliorated by the fact that the "use values" Israel does manage to produce for global commerce are largely used to kill people and to lay waste cities and landscapes. In any event, Israel has no resource base to speak of, and its national pride as the transformer of the desert into a garden has succumbed to its ecological fecklessness. Much of the Israeli economy has moved to the shadowy terrain where value is pumped up, gets transferred here and there, becomes chips in casino capitalism, and disappears into the mists of mergers and acquisitions. Notable in this respect is the fact that the country has no laws prohibiting money laundering. This has something to do with a large element of gangsterism in the Israeli economy, which the domestic press persistently uncovers, honest accounts like that of Nitzan and Bichler analyze, and the PR machine keeps hidden. This passes over, as such things will, into the political dimension, and it is possible to find in Nitzan and Bichler's study information about the prices charged for their services by one or another of the notable politicians who figure in the story of the Only Democracy in the Middle East. It is amusing to read about these exploits, unless one has a sentimental attachment to Zionism or stops to ponder the larger picture. A notable convergence has occurred with the Russian gangster-capitalists who sprung up after the collapse of the Soviet regime and the wholesale looting of its assets. There is definitely an affinity between the Jewish state and the oligarchs of the new Russian economy, one reflected in the fact that more than a million Russians, a good number non-Jewish, have come to settle in the Holy Land, so that the Russian language is coming to displace English as the second tongue of Israel.[8]

Zionist propaganda would have it that the State of Israel relies upon an innumerable host of humanitarians and seekers of justice for the immemorially persecuted Jews. No doubt, a lot of small donors are out there who feel comfort and pride in Zion—I knew quite a few in my own family circle. But the effective donations are those of mega-rich individuals and powerful institutions, including, needless to say, the most powerful of all, the United States government. "Rich" and "powerful" are words with a definite political vector in the real world, where one usually does not become so except at the expense of others. As the money-power has grown in the

world at large with capital's expansion, so has it grown in
the affairs of Zionism, with increasingly wealthy individuals
bankrolling the state and exacting a matching ideological toll.
And when one says, "the state," it is also increasingly unclear
as to which state, America or Israel, is meant, indeed, the point
is that where Zionism is concerned, it can matter little.

The extensive presence in Israel of United States expatriates
and family members of Jews who live in America gives some
idea of the bond between the two countries. But the personal
network, while important enough, is less than half the story.
The more interesting portion lies in Israel's abiding hunger for
foreign capital. To return to the account of Nitzan and Bichler,
capital, which is never pure liquidity but always invested in a
set of relationships and demands (hence "economy" is better
understood as "political economy"), has undergone a major
restructuring over the lifespan of the Jewish state. In essence
this has consisted of the breakdown of economic forms that
were originally relatively compatible with Zionism, and their
intermittent, fitful, but inexorable replacement, especially after
1975, when the world economy became restructured in the
neoliberal mold. These recent influences are usefully called
"globalized," insofar as they are "deterritorialized," and highly
fluid; and they are also very much under the tutelage of United
States corporations and associated state structures, like the
Treasury Department and Pentagon.

Capital dissolved the organic connections of Zionism, chiefly
the integration between capital and labor, and permitted an
ever deepening American influence to take hold. Over the
years the infusions weakened the cohesive structure of Israel's
economy and dissolved the power of labor—and of the party
of Labor, which yielded to Likud in the late 1970s and has
been a hollow shell since, no more faithful to its founding
principles than the Democratic Party in the United States.[9] The
glitzy, intoxicating, and ultimately ruinous impact of "high-
tech" under the tutelage of giant American firms has catalyzed

the disintegration of Israeli society, leaving it increasingly vulnerable to jolts such as the collapse of the dot.com bubble at the turn of the century. Even so, it comes as a shock to learn that Israel has over the brief period of its life gone from being one of the most egalitarian countries in the world to the one with the greatest structural inequality of any industrialized nation, indeed, twice so in comparison to its patron.[10] This is the chief cause of the social deterioration observed (see end of Chapter 3).

The impact on the politics of Zionism has been complex. It was foreign capital and its representatives like Clinton that imposed the public relations stunt known as the "Peace Process" upon Israel/Palestine. This is because global capital craves comity between nations as a precondition to successful investment. Too bad that global capital fails to provide the essential condition for comity, which would be a just society. Palestinians were forced under this regime to accept the administration of the Palestine Authority as a handout designed to bind them to the global system as permanent coolies, with the hopeless hope of a statelet under Israeli-American terms dangled before them. It has been a recipe for corruption and futility. The Jewish state, meanwhile, under Rabin, Barak, Netanyahu, Sharon and Olmert, went along with the peace process, but shifted the bulk of its strategic thinking to the "peaceful" expansion, under the Oslo Accords, of the settlements in the Occupied Territories. And the Godfather winked at the charade. This deeper shade of deception has meant a radically enhanced role for the ultra-Orthodox, and it led also to Sharon's provocation of the Second Intifada. Characteristically, it is the social toxicity of advancing capital that by destroying community, prepares the way for and ignites outbursts of fundamentalism. In the Jewish state, this takes on the additional dimension of being an instrument of ethnic cleansing.

The epoch of globalization has ushered in a radical deterioration of our civilization's ecological foundation.[11]

Israeli society is no exception, though the process has been accelerated by Zionism and bears its stamp.

MAKING THE DESERT DESOLATE

The annals of Zionism are replete with reverence and love for the actual terrain of Palestine, which was regarded as the salvation for many centuries of landlessness. Indeed, the creation of a Zionist nation depended upon a deeply emotional bonding with the actual "Eretz" of Israel and the imperative to recreate it, variously, as a garden, a forest, a perfected simulacrum of the European landscape, in sum, as a redeemed and bountiful utopia. As Allon Tal—to whom we are indebted for a definitive account of Israel's environmental history—has written, "The Jewish immigrants saw the treeless land as more than ugly; they saw it as abandoned and awaiting a redeemer."[12] Now a mystic, now a sun-burnished farmer, now an ecologist, and increasingly as a technical expert and bureaucrat, this redeemer was to superintend the "making the desert bloom" that became one of Zionism's most enduring mottos. The history of Zionism was well underway before the ecological crisis, which today dominates world history, began to occupy consciousness. Yet, having planted hundreds of millions of trees and developed one of the world's most efficient agricultural systems (particularly through the implementation of drip irrigation), Israel entered this era with a sturdy reputation as an ecologically advanced society. And thanks to its superior public relations apparatus, the average person still thinks of Zion as a place where the desert blooms.

Notwithstanding, Israel, or to take into account the entity that Zionism now controls, Israel/Palestine, is an environmental nightmare, all the more so in relation to its ideals, level of wealth, and technological expertise.[13] The facts are compelling and can be found in Tal's book, among other sources. All of Israel's rivers are seriously polluted except for the Upper

Jordan, and some have been polluted to literally lethal levels;[14] the Lower Jordan is "little more than a drainage ditch for polluted runoff";[15] 88 percent of Tel Aviv's wells contain persistent organic pollutants; as for the air, a quadrupling of nitrous oxide emissions has been observed since 1980; asthma rates among children have gone from 5.6 percent in 1980 to 11.2 percent in 1989 and 17 percent in 2002; Israel has one of the highest breast cancer incidences in the world, with a 32 percent increase in the 1990s; in the 1970s the breast milk of Israel women contained some 800 times the concentration of benzene hexachloride as American women ...

The list can be extended indefinitely, but its mere iteration tells us little about what we need to know, which is the relationship between the ecological crisis of Israel and the Zionism that animates the Jewish state. In other words, separating out the Israeli contribution to environmental degradation from those of other nations (as by setting aside the Jordanian contribution to the pollution of the Lower Jordan River), and bracketing for the moment the forces of capital accumulation that degrade ecologies in all nations,[16] we arrive at certain factors intrinsic to Zionism itself and can regard the Israeli ecological crisis in this light. We will then address in a concluding chapter what difference the overcoming of Zionism can make in resolving the ecological crisis of Israel/Palestine.

Certain tendencies of Zionism are already familiar to us; and we may now look at their ecological implications:

Zionism's obsession has been to preserve the Jewishness of its state at all costs. Well, one of those costs needs now to be taken into account, namely, the incessant pressure to fill Israel with Jews in order to keep a step ahead of the Palestinians—and to preserve and reinforce the myth that Israel is the supreme haven for all Jews, everywhere, in their perpetual struggle against antisemitic exterminism. This so-called demographic imperative has made Israel the only state and certainly the only state along Western industrial lines, hellbent to augment its population. Hellbent indeed. What country would not experience environmental woes with a *sixfold* population increase in half a century in a context of rapid industrialization?

There is a rough rubric in environmental circles according to which the overall burden on ecosystems in a given nation may be formulaically represented as Population + Affluence + Technological impact—that is, the more people, and the more money they have for purposes of consumption, and the more does their economy rely upon earth-disrupting industrial technology, then the worse the environmental impact. It is generally appreciated that a kind of reciprocal relationship exists between the first term and the second plus the third, according to the principle that as a nation becomes wealthier so does it tend to limit its population. Thus the grouping of the teeming poor nations, or "South," on one side, and the less populous rich industrial ones, or "North," on the other, as different kinds of contributors to ecological breakdown. Malthusians hold that the South is the big problem, whereas in fact much the greater contribution to the ecological crisis is made by the North. But all would agree that a country that aggravates all three factors is an environmental bandit. Thus the world worries about China, the colossus of ecological degeneration owing to its huge population and runaway economy, and now also India, playing catch-up along the same lines. Israel is much too small to pose a problem in itself to the global ecology, though it is certainly a big problem to its neighbors;[17] in fact, its diminutive size, roughly equal to that of New Jersey, adds a factor of concentration that aggravates the internal dilemma. But the Jewish state is most certainly an environmental bandit, even more so than the Asian giants. For China and India by and large consider their immense populations to be a problem and have made various efforts to bring it into line. Not so Israel, which only exists on the basis of cramming more and more Zionistic people into its tiny territory, and bends every will to the task of ingathering Jews. This includes taking in Russian immigrants who aren't even Jewish, but will reliably go along with the Zionist program; and it also includes the necessity of promising affluence as a stimulus to immigration and a deterrent to the ever-present threat of emigration to more tranquil and stable lands. This latter part of the demographic imperative has resulted, as Tal documents, in numerous instances when authorities simply failed to take essential environmental measures that might put a crimp in the Israeli lifestyle.

The most serious of the environmental dilemmas and the most compromised by the demographic imperative is that of water. After all, the air may stink, but there is plenty more available, and breezes to sweep away the pollutants. Not so for water, given the naturally arid condition of Eretz Israel and the fact that pollutants largely tend to migrate to the underground aquifers that supply a major portion of the water. Great attention has been given to Israel's arrogation of regional water supplies, a process which reached a zenith in the 1967 war, whose prime motivation is widely recognized to have been control over water.[18] It is less often appreciated that this boon proved insufficient to slake Zion's thirst, unsurprisingly in view of the stimulus to Israel's sense of entitlement provided by effective control over the Jordan River. Presently, the Jewish state faces both an absolute shortage of water owing to persistent overconsumption, as well as persistent contamination of the existing water thanks to rampant "development" and industrialization. Characteristically, the problem is being dealt with through denial—as by lowering the hypothetical "red line" below which water shortages are deemed dangerous (because of incursion of water from the sea, and also because of the threat to the great pumping system necessary to lift the water to the cities, which stands to be wrecked once the pumps are

exposed). Grandiose plans are on the books to annually return
to the aquifers the two billion cubic meters of pure water
necessary to stave off collapse of the system. The desalination
and recovery plants necessary to do this are phenomenally
expensive both to build and operate (the latter includes the
petroleum costs, especially problematic in an epoch of global
warming and peak oil); but there is always Israel's Godfather
to be approached for another handout.

The other, linked obsession of Zionism is of course to get rid
of Palestinians. If these accursed creatures didn't exist, why
then, the Chosen People could settle down and rationally build
their utopia. It was only logical, then, to regard the indigenous
people as another, devalued part of the landscape that had to be
conquered. Had not the revered Chaim Weizmann, President of
the World Zionist Organization called the Palestinian people,
"the rocks of Judea ... obstacles that had to be cleared on
a difficult path?"[19] Note that this remark also devalues the
landscape and undercuts Zionism's romanticisation of the
Palestinian earth, tipping the balance toward the domination
of nature, with ominous environmental implications. Fear and
loathing of the Arab translates readily to an augmentation of
that characteristic Western attitude that the Zionists brought
along with them to their Promised Land, namely that nature
was inherently menacing in its "wild" state,[20] and had to be
"tamed" if civilization was to survive. In 1944, at a moment
when the mounting horrors of the Holocaust were inflaming
the Zionist consciousness, Ben-Gurion put it in grander terms
still in a famous speech to a gathering of youth leaders: "The
tasks that lie ahead will require pioneering efforts the likes
of which we have never known, for we must conquer and
fructify the waste places ... and we must prepare the way
for new immigrants ... from every country in which some
remnant is still alive. ... First of all, we must conquer the sea
and the desert, for these will provide us with room for new

settlers and will serve as a laboratory for the development of new forms of economic and agricultural endeavor."[21] Under these circumstances—which are those of the permanent state of emergency normal to Israel—the sense of nature's intrinsic value essential for an ecologically rational approach collapses into mere instrumentality.

For the ultra-Orthodox who comprise the most problematic portion of the settlers, these tendencies are exaggerated, first, because, they do not share in the romanticization of nature to begin with, and second, because of their abiding disposition to see Jews as the only real humans on the planet, with Palestinians toward the lower end of the Chain of Being, functionally equivalent to inanimate nature that stands in the way. Thus settlers can shit upon them as one does on the ground. And so conquest of Palestine and conquest of Palestinians became two sides of the same figure.

The two sides of the Zionist impulse come together in the notion of adding Jews whose function it is to displace Palestinians. So it was that triumph in 1967 was turned toward Occupation of the West Bank and Gaza, and the Occupation toward ethnic cleansing, chiefly carried out through the instrument of the settlements. This has led to an ecological situation unique in history, and one that precipitously hurtles toward environmental ruin. Human communities are ecosystems, too, and their capacity to fit into the great regulatory patterns of nature depends upon their internal integrity, manifest in mutual recognition and coherent communication. Estrangement, or alienation, is the human form taken by ecological breakdown; it is a failure of recognition between human agents, which makes cooperative action impossible and splits humanity from nature as well as itself. It follows that the most severely estranged society will also be the most subject to eco-disintegration. This more or less describes the State of Israel, and certainly its Occupied Territories, which comprise one of the most bizarre social formations ever planted upon this earth. Here, on a tiny plot of ground, dwell two people with two radically different legal and social systems, one the beneficiary of a powerful state and living in comfort while it works to terrorize and strangle the other, who is stateless and bent upon surviving; the two are therefore as radically denied any cooperative arrangement as can be imagined, and primed to be an eco-destructive accelerant to the State of Israel as a whole.

Why an accelerant? Generally speaking, the ecological crisis is the unfolding of unintended consequences. That is, nobody set out to bring about global warming; it just happened that way as a result of the inability of the capitalist industrial system to control its gaseous emissions. Similarly, the vast majority of species extinctions are the result of habitat loss produced by incursions of the human cancer such as urban sprawl, or overharvesting a resource; that is, nobody plans to get rid of whole species of fish, they just overfish, and become overtaken by the remorseless laws of population dynamics. It is different in the case of ethnic cleansing in general and the disposition of the Palestinians in particular. Here we find deliberate actions taken to destroy the filaments of human ecosystems, by legal and extralegal means of expulsion, by removing, violently if necessary, the grounds of another's communal existence, and by introducing physical means of disrupting the other's relation to nature. This is all speeded along and facilitated insofar as the other is himself regarded as subhuman and an unwanted natural obstacle, like a rock in the way to be dumped upon or bulldozed aside. All of this has been done, and continues to be done, to Palestinians in the Occupied Territories, using instruments of the state such as the IDF and other parts of the bureaucratic apparatus; and also of civil society, notably the settlers. Whether or not these are armed fanatics or just ordinary citizens taking advantage of extremely generous economic subsidies, they serve as the marauders of Zionist expansion. In the Occupied Territories, then, the process of eco-destabilization is accelerated through being conscious, even though the exposure of Israel/Palestine to the world's scrutiny requires constant denial and the usual tropes of blaming the vicitm.

This is what makes the Occupied Territories bizarre. After all, situations of ethnic cleansing have been rife over time; but never have they occurred with quite this mixture, of administrative and military measures from the one side, and from the other, by the unrelenting contiguous invasion by a parallel society, illegal in the eyes of the world but legalized by Zionism and its friends in high places. Settlement society, looking for all the world like poster-perfect suburbia with its serried ranks of orange-tiled roofs, grows like an invasive parasite in the interstices of an existing but subjugated polity— generally on the hills, so that effluents flow down and perfuse the indigenous towns with the settler's wastes. The parasitic order builds parallel systems, of roads, water and sewage, electrical networks, etc; and these both colonize and destroy the land of the Palestinians, while creating, necessarily, a myriad of spaces, set in the interstices and pores of the Territories, chaotically thrown up and turning into sites of a proliferating set of ecological degradations. It is dispossession by parallel possession, and for a metaphor from the animal kingdom one can only think of those insects who lay an egg in the interior of the prey's body, whence a new creature hatches as a larva that devours the host from within. What makes this distinct from other instances of ethnic cleansing is that this phase of the dispossession of the other has to be carried out in an extended manner, under the scrutiny of the external world, in a million small acts that succeed in routinizing the crime and spreading eco-catastrophe over time:

- Each of the innumerable humiliations and harrassments at military checkpoint succeeds in "checking" ordinary movements necessary for life as well as "checking" identity, thus impairing the Palestinian ability to take care of one's environment as well as one's self.

- Looming over it all is the segregating and dispossessing presence of the Wall. Scarcely ever has a landscape been so blighted as by this "fact on the ground," which gives Israelis the illusion that their Other does not exist, and divides up the Palestinian polity in innumerable ways, making travel even over short distances unbearable, while adding more territory to Zion.

- Certain settlers, in their "Dr Hyde" role, act as para-militaries, assaulting the Palestinians themselves, as well as destroying their agricultural and pastoral lands by tearing up olive groves and spreading poison pellets that kill indigenous wildlife as well as goats and sheep. In this regime of terror the Jewish state and its settlers work hand in glove, the former scarcely ever doing more than handing out mild rebukes to the latter; one can easily imagine both parts of the machine retiring in the evening to have a good laugh over the day's marauding.

- Garbage is routinely thrown onto Palestinian land; and in 2005 this became formalized into a regular business with plans to dump 10,000 tons of solid waste from the Dan and Sharon regions into a quarry near Nablus, in defiance of international treaties and the advice of environmental experts that it would further pollute water resources. But there was money to be made by taking advantage of lower transfer costs, which also means less environmental care. The waste is of industrial as well as domestic origin, and arises from both within and without the Occupied Territories.

- A rat's nest of Israeli manufacturing firms have seized the opportunities provided by desperate Palestinian labor and the lack of environmental regulations to penetrate these spaces. Usually situated on hilltops, their effluents drain down on Palestinian towns and have blighted them.[22]

- Comprising 10 percent of the population of the Occupied Territories, the settlers generate 25 percent of its untreated sewage, and use five times as much water as the Palestinians (and 15 percent more water than other Israelis). Palestinians are able to consume only about 70 percent of the minimum per capita daily water allotment defined by the World Health Organization, and often end up paying even for that from their virtually non-existent cash reserves. Alongside this, only one-fifth of Palestinian sewage treatment facilities work.[23]

One can extend this list indefinitely, as thousands of human rights violations are documented in the Territories and many are accessible on the internet though routinely ignored by the official media.[24] But as we focus on the environmental side here, what needs emphasis is the ecological impact of these violations. For though the two human groups vying for Israel/Palestine are split apart by the consequences of Zionist conquest, their physical connection is guaranteed by geography and the tiny scale of Eretz Israel. The wastes hurled down by the settlers, then, and even the poisoned pellets of fluoro-acetemide or brodifacoum wrapped in bread and set down to kill the sheep of Palestinians, join with the untreated bodily wastes of the latter and find their way into the groundwater to accelerate the ecological breakdown of Israel itself.

The military poses a special case above and beyond its role in the Occupation. Since the 1930s the regime of force has held the highest place in Zionist society, as a liberator, a shield, and, increasingly, a source of wealth. No propaganda trick is spared, then, to represent the IDF as Israel's pride and joy. But the armed forces are also by far the most ecologically destructive institution of a society. The business of war is to destroy ecosystems, and the army has not yet been found who is fastidious about cleaning up after itself. Images of weeping

Israeli soldiers notwithstanding, the military brutalizes, and it inculcates habits antithetical to caring for the integrity of nature at every level. Simply from a financial standpoint, military expenditures must be seen as a constant drain on resources that could otherwise go toward caring for the environment; and so if Israel gives too little to the latter, it has something to do with the primacy accorded to the former.

But Israel is not only a military power; it is a prime weapons manufacturer, supplying some 10 percent of the world market in instruments of death. This, too, needs to be added into the environmental balance sheet, on a global level and also as the local effect of weapons industries, which tend to be prodigiously toxic. The ever-pressed environmental agencies are still contending, for example, with the clean up of the Israel Military Industries' Magen factory site, five years after this was discovered in the Dan Valley. As published in *Ha'aretz*, "Pollution in the area of the IMI compound is so high that toxic materials created a separate layer in the groundwater. Vaporous and toxic materials were also found to be spreading to basements as well as trees and bushes around the compound." The more the inspectors looked, the more toxic materials they found in the area from past and present factories. "The Dan region has housed hundreds of factories and facilities that use toxic metals and vaporous materials, according to the survey. These include dozens of dry cleaning laundries that make extensive use of the solvent tetrachloroethylene, but only a few of them cleared waste containing that material. Furthermore, many metal coating factories habitually directed toxic metals into the sewage system, and these trickled down into the soil and groundwater."[25]

The problem, as they say, is systemic. And part of the system is a certain attitude endemic to Zionism and its Jewish state, which appears on countless occasions in Tal's stalwart work on the Israeli environment. Again and again he will recount some environmental infringement or another, observe the remedial action taken by one or another of Israel's ecologically-minded cadre, and then gloomily qualify the result with phrases (these drawn more or less at random from one section of the book) such as: "not one representative showed up for the next meeting he had scheduled" [261]; "ministries that aren't interested in getting advice" [261]; "recycling and composting had missed the boat" [265]; "the Environmental Protection Service tried to play the role of watchdog. But its bark was feeble indeed ...." [267]; "enforcement [is] the weak link in the wide chain of environmental management" [268]; "Israeli authorities seemed to wink at the culture of noncompliance," [278]; "practically no oversight [319]"; and so on.

There is an unmistakable "culture of noncompliance," then, which has to be regarded as a structural ingredient of the Zionist order. "It even appeared sometimes," Tal laments, "that Israelis inculcated environmental irresponsibility to their children from the tenderest of ages." [280] The attitude is complex and resists easy generalization. But many of the features that systematically derive from Zionism and its state—an obsessive preoccupation with security; the never-ending sense of crisis and emergency that enables mere nature to be shoved onto a back burner; a long history of covert operations and shady dealings; a sense of entitlement and exceptionalism that comes from deep within the tradition and has been reinforced over years of flouting one international regulation or another (right of Palestinian return; rules of engagement in the territories; UN Resolution 242 calling for withdrawal from lands seized in 1967; nuclear nonproliferation treaties; the illegality of the Wall, for starters) and being rewarded by the United States for doing so—all drive the Israeli mentality away from the lawfulness and sense of limit essential to an ecologically rational attitude. It is as though the Israeli says: *Respect for nature and a sense of limit—that's for the others. We Zionist Jews are different, a people apart, as it was said in the ancient books. We make our own laws and call them facts on the ground . . . Israel stands apart and will make its own way.*

The ecological crisis exposes vanity as nothing else and is the great leveller of grandiosity. It is one thing to thumb your nose, year after year, at mere UN resolutions, with the Godfather in your corner. It is another to defy the remorseless laws of nature, including the great thermodynamic equalizer. The notion of "sustainability" is problematic but necessary to gauge the viability of societies in face of the ecological crisis. After all, all things must pass; the question is, how soon, and under what conditions. And here it needs be said that a society operating under the terms of Zionism, and engaged in the game of imperial expansion under the tutelage of the great destabilizer that is the United States, neither has nor deserves much of an ecological future. Some day the world will recognize Zionism as a synonym for unsustainability.

6
Partners in Zion

THE STORY OF RACHEL CORRIE

This is not at all what I asked for when I came into this world.[1]

IN THE DAYS WHEN Israel was directly ruling Gaza it became notorious for the demolition of homes that were deemed to stand in the way. The city most afflicted by this process was Rafah, at the southern end of the Strip, which has the awful distinction of being the poorest and most dangerous place in the lands seized in 1967, with 60 percent of its 140,000 inhabitants refugees in 2003. Because Rafah abuts the Egyptian border, Israel placed a wall there, ostensibly to keep arms from being smuggled into Gaza. This one is 50 percent higher than the infamous separation wall with which Israel has surrounded the West Bank—12 meters high and 8 deep, to be exact, with an apron of 100 meters to ensure the free mobility of military vehicles. Since Gaza is one of the most densely populated places on the planet, there are many houses within this perimeter, houses that must be removed according to the iron law of the IDF, which insisted that a network of tunnels runs under them to circumvent the above-ground barriers, even though the majority of the occupants have had nothing to do with the uprising.[2] From the beginning of the Second Intifada in September 2000, until the spring of 2003, some 700 homeowners in Rafah heard the churning of the colossal 60 ton

D9 bulldozers, made in the USA by the Caterpillar corporation
expressly for house demolition and paid for with US taxpayer
dollars, come to destroy their dwellings. Sometimes advance
notice was given, often no more than small arms fire discharged
by Israeli soldiers into houses, sometimes the bulldozer simply
materialized to annihilate a home, and sometimes this took
place with the people still inside, awakening to hear their walls
being knocked down. In mid 2004 Rafah once more seized the
anguished attention of the world when, in the course of the
complicated matter of Ariel Sharon's plan to evacuate Gaza,
Palestinian guerrillas from Rafah succeeded in killing 13 Israeli
soldiers. This unleashed a spasm of revenge as the mighty
IDF, fourth largest army in the world, attacked the town,
killing some 320 Palestinians, of whom more than 200 were
civilians, including 85 children under the age of 18, and 27
women—such being what tends to happen when one has "no
choice" but to suppress "terrorism" by any means necessary,
and has been granted a green light by the United States to do
so. But there was another killing by the IDF a year earlier; and
although no one human life is more important than any other
from the viewpoint of universality, there are some deaths that
focus consciousness in sharper ways than others.

On the bright Sunday of March 16, 2003, Rachel Corrie,
a 23-year-old student from Olympia, Washington who had
been in Rafah for two months, had posted herself as usual
with a group of companions from the International Solidarity
Movement (ISM) to see what they could do to inhibit that day's
devouring of homes. Stricken by the events of September 11,
2001, Rachel had deepened her commitment to reduce the level
of violence in the world and to bear witness to the sufferings of
the invisible. Being of that perilous temperament that pursues
things to their conclusion, her beliefs had brought her to
Rafah, the toughest place in the Occupied Territories—though
as she had reassured her worried parents before she went,
no one was going to harm a freshly scrubbed-looking Euro-

American—and non-Jewish—strawberry blond young woman like her. Indeed, that was the point, to combine wholesomeness with resolution in the well-tested methodology of nonviolent resistance, touching the heart and conscience of the adversary, instilling in him fellow feeling, and moving him toward the recognition of a common humanity.

Once in Rafah, Rachel's mood darkened under the impact of ongoing destruction. She wrote home, "Disbelief and horror is what I feel," and added that she had been having nightmares about tanks and bulldozers. And on another occasion:

> When I come back from Palestine, I probably will have nightmares and constantly feel guilty for not being here, but I can channel that into more work. Coming here is one of the better things I've ever done. So when I sound crazy, or if the Israeli military should break with their racist tendency not to injure white people, please pin the reason squarely on the fact that I am in the midst of a genocide which I am also indirectly supporting, and for which my government is largely responsible.

I know that March 16 was a sunny day in Rafah because I have seen a large expanse of blue sky in a photograph of Rachel standing between a giant bulldozer and the house she is protecting. I also cannot help feeling very strongly that Rachel Corrie was a very beautiful and brave young woman with a radiant soul. How could this have not been apparent to the soldier driving the D9 as he approached another house selected for elimination, that of Rachel's friend, Doctor Samir, the local pharmacist? The camera shows Rachel in plain view of the bulldozer, wearing the bright orange vest of the ISM, waving to him and using a megaphone, and as the giant blade picks her up, they are at the same eye level. Does he look through Rachel as the blade turns her under like a clod of dirt and crushes her? What can he have been thinking as he puts the D9 into reverse and grinds her further into the ground before lifting his blade? What has happened to this man?[3]

I have also read four (of seven) internally consistent accounts by eyewitnesses who were close enough to see every detail and to hope, vainly, that their screams would have an impact on the driver of the D9. They fill out the story with grief-stricken precision. However, and this is to the present point, this extremely well-documented and horrific event had scarcely any impact on the larger world. The mainstream US media hiccoughed for a day or two and then let the story sink like the proverbial stone. The Israeli military refused to look at the photographs and concluded that Rachel was not struck by the bulldozer at all but killed by falling concrete, despite testimony that she was out in the open and under only the sky as the incident unfolded. Later, after two more shootings in early April of ISM volunteers—Brian Avery, of Albuquerque, who had much of his face blown off, and Thomas Hurndell, of London, who was left brain dead by an Israeli sniper while he was trying to help a little girl, and eventually perished ten months later—the IDF reacted by demanding that visitors to the Occupied Territories sign a waiver upon entry absolving Israel in advance for any harm it may do them.

One would think that the brutal murder of one of its citizens by a foreign state, and especially a beautiful young white woman of the privileged classes, would have provoked a considerable reaction from the United States government. Protection of its civilians abroad is, after all, an essential function of the liberal state. The British government actively pursued the killing of Thomas Hurndell and eventually succeeded in getting Israel to punish the sniper who killed him. And America will go to prodigious lengths to protect citizens abroad when victimized by proper enemies. Recall the sensation caused about the same time as Rachel was killed by the injuries to and presumed abduction/rape of Private Jessica Lynch in Iraq. In this case—which was 99 percent pure disinformation and was swiftly thrown into history's dustbin after Jessica changed her story—the nation was roused to a frenzy of adoration for Jessica and

rage at her violators. The president was said to be "full of joy
for Jessica Lynch"; and her home-state Senator, Jay Rockefeller,
told the Senate that the case of Jessica proved that "we take
care of our people."[4]

Not all of "our people," at least when the perpetrator is a
certain privileged state. After the killing, strenuous efforts by
Rachel's family to reach the authorities succeeded in provoking
some lamentation from Washington State's Democratic Senators
Maria Cantwell and Patty Murray. When this liberal duo went
back to the Capitol, however, they must have been informed
about the code of behavior governing relations with Israel,
for nothing further happened beyond a House initiative, HCR
111, which called for an investigation into Rachel's killing,
and mustered all of 51 signatures over the next year. By the
summer of 2003, 401 Congresspeople had been mobilized for
yet another resolution saying in effect that the United States
supported Israel across the board, where—and whenever it
chooses to set its hand against "terrorism."[5] Rachel's murder,
therefore, was made invisible; indeed, by August, a Peace Center
in East Jerusalem dedicated to her (along with a Palestinian
woman also slain by the IDF) was facing demolition by, of all
things, another bulldozer.

Rachel had to be defiled over and over if Israel and the
United States were to escape responsibility for her murder. In
a striking example of Zionist propaganda, there appeared in
June 2003, an op-ed article in the *Los Angeles Times* under
the signature of Martin Peretz, publisher of *The New Republic*
magazine, and among other things, a board member of the
Washington Institute for Near East Policy (WINEP), foreign
policy arm of the powerful lobby, the American Israeli Public
Affairs Committee (AIPAC), of which more below.[6]

Peretz does not attack Rachel head-on. He proceeds instead
to discredit her cause, the International Solidarity Movement.
Exuding *Weltschmerz* for lost dreams, Peretz classifies ISM
among the "deluded ... political pilgrims," the fellow travelers

who followed "every failed revolution in modern times." But since "[o]nly certified kooks are in the business these days of changing the nature of man," our "present-day romantics, who at home typically despise the idea of the nation-state and the realities of national interest, are left with often contrived and almost always murderous nationalisms to adore. The nationalism du jour is Palestinian nationalism."

Now the black hole of Palestinian terrorism yawns, to swallow the deluded fellow-travelers of ISM. Peretz is too circumspect to claim "that all Palestinians are terrorists ..." He will aver, however, that "polls show an overwhelming proportion of them to be supporters of terrorism." Nor does Peretz stop at mere polling data. No, he generously provides a theoretical construction, viz., "terrorism happens to be the defining paradigm of the Palestinian cause," in other words, its *essence*, a construction that trivializes considerations like the fact of stolen land and an unlawful military occupation. Therefore any whiff of sympathy for Palestinians or hint of legitimacy to their cause means that one is objectively supporting the "defining paradigm" of terrorism. It takes a Harvard-trained political scientist to think this way.

There follows a passage accusing the ISM of abetting Arab terrorism by "supporting the Palestinian right to 'legitimate armed struggle'" on its website and helping Hamas terrorists move freely in and out of Israel (an allegation that the group has repudiated),[7] and then the real point, a reference to an unnamed Rachel Corrie. Here is how Peretz puts it, in words of jaw-dropping callousness: "sometimes its own volunteers get hurt—or even killed, as one American was by an Israeli bulldozer. The best you can say of them is that they are gulled. But this is not bravery; it is stupidity."

Peretz finishes dolefully with a lament for the wretched Palestinian cause. He "concedes" that the Arabs do need a state, but blames their own campaign of "unrelenting terror" and the starting of "a bloody insurrection in the midst of negotiations with Israel during the fall of 2000" for its not having come into being. Then he turns to a theme close to the Zionist heart. Why even bother with this miserable people, who have contributed nothing to world civilization and are merely one rather insignificant member of the set of stateless nations? In fact, the only interesting thing about the Palestinians is that the Jews have blessed them by being their neighbors.

> The truth is that no one who has had a real hearing among the Palestinians has ever articulated a vision of Palestine that is premised on an idea of social justice, a new relationship between the classes, among the clans and tribes, between the sexes. Believe me, Palestine will not be a democratic state because Palestine is not a democratic or tolerant society. This is in devastating contrast to the Zionist enterprise that had true ideals about how human beings and political difference were to be treated, ideals that were turned to realities.

The Arabs should be grateful that such fine folk live next door. The tolerant Zionist side is good because it has been able to realize "true ideals about how human beings and political difference were to be treated"; whereas the other side, lacking tolerance and being a pack of inveterate terrorists, must be crushed. It is a splendid object lesson of tolerance at work. A devastating contrast, indeed.

The story goes on. Three years later, a play comprised of Rachel's own words in letters and emails, which had done well in London, was prevented from reaching a New York Off-Broadway theater in the city with the world's largest Jewish population; the producer, James Nicola, saying that as a result of consultation with Jewish groups, "what we heard was that after Ariel Sharon's illness and the election of Hamas, we had a very edgy situation. We found that our plan to present a work of art would be seen as us taking a stand in a political conflict, that we didn't want to take."[8] It is as though the *Diaries of Anne Frank* were to be postponed, or if Picasso had withdrawn *Guernica* because of fascist protest.

Once again the established press gnawed away at Rachel, now in a review of the London engagement that replaced the New York run of the one-woman play based on her writings. Writing of Rachel's "sense of mission," the reviewer, Matt Wolf, commented that this "can, of course, cause very real pain to others: a fascinating program essay ... reveals that Ms Corrie's former boyfriend, Colin Reese, committed suicide in 2004." One wonders how Mr Wolf found out how, a year or so after she was murdered by the D9 bulldozer, that Rachel's sense of mission proved fatal to her boyfriend. But then, Rachel was menacing even as a toddler: "it's hard not to be impressed—and also somewhat frightened—by the description of her as a 2-year old looking across Capitol Lake in Washington State and announcing, 'This is the wide world, and I'm coming to it.'"[9] Pretty scary stuff. This is the first instance I know of when the robust self-assertion of a toddler has been taken as a sign of incipient terrorism. Such is the moral universe of the Great War of Civilizations.

A very odd phenomenon has arisen in the United States where questions about Zionism are concerned, and it is time to examine it here.

THE APPARATUS

It is not that Israel doesn't get an easy ride from other Western states—recall only the indifference throughout the EU to the bombing of Gaza and Lebanon in July 2006, and the customary support given by the UK to its superpower offspring in alliance with the Zionist state. One needs to appreciate the extensive social and institutional networks that interconnect the ruling classes on a global scale, and recognize the degree to which Israel, now snugly within global circuits of capital, is included within these networks as well.[10] But there are differences in degree that become differences in kind, and the relationship between Israel and the United States goes far beyond a bland word like "support." It raises profound questions about the actual interpenetration of the two nation states—and as with the discoveries that certain dinosaurs had two brains, one in the head and one in the tail, just where does the executive thinking arise?

Other countries, one thinks particularly of Germany, may give guilt money to Zion to compensate for past atrocities, but there has never been one sovereign state that so extensively bankrolls another and lends it ideological and military substance as the United States does for Israel. It is impossible to get a precise figure for the amount of funding and military aid poured into the special client over the years, given the number of odd-channels, squirrel holes and creative riffs of bookkeeping that apply. Suffice it to say that the awesomely destructive weaponry employed by Israel in its military escapades, from the bulldozers that crush homes and people like Rachel Corrie, to the F-16 fighters, the Apache helicopters, the guidance systems, the supersophisticated missiles, even the jet fuel for the bombing of places like Lebanon and the intelligence systems that guide the bombs—all either come directly from the superpower, or are bought with funds provided by it, or produced through an intricate interplay of Israeli and American components. This degree of interpenetration of the weapons complexes of the two powers translates directly into political influence. If colossal weapons manufacturers like Lockheed Martin, Boeing and Raytheon are fed from the same trough as Israel, then their power over American foreign policy is automatically transferred into ironclad support for the Zionist state.

I have read estimates of as high as 1.6 trillion dollars in aid to Israel since 1973, when all the hidden costs over the years (like payments on the American debt, or bribes to countries like Egypt and Jordan, even the higher cost of oil as a result of US favoritism to Israel, etc.) are factored in.[11] My own estimate is of the order of $200 billion, while official figures run about half that much.[12] But it comes down to the fact that the United States expends about one-third of its foreign aid budget on a country that has roughly one-thousandth of the world population and has been called by many thoughtful people over the years a liability to American national interest. Behind this ratio stands a very intricate relationship, which implies a certain "zionification" of the United States, a kind of mutual adaptation that enables the support system to function routinely and to a degree automatically according to a cybernetic mechanism in which even the slightest criticism of Israel is met with howling accusations of antisemitism. Thus although the United States has the power to not just put a crimp in Israeli national designs with the flourish of a pen, but to cripple and even eliminate the ever-dependent Jewish state in short order by the same means, it often appears the weaker and less resolute in the common affairs of the partners. To deal with a common conundrum in left circles, we may say that although the prime mover of imperialism in the region remains the American behemoth, with its stupendous military force and highly aggressive brand of capitalism, this behemoth has also taken into itself the qualities of its junior partner, which has gotten under the imperial skin and become able to regulate to a remarkable extent the inner affairs of the host.

The linkage between the partners is the American Jewish community, the most phenomenally successful group of immigrants in world history, and the most politically conscious and focussed. Like Israel itself, American Jewry was long regarded with suspicion by the United States elites as congenitally radical and socialistic in its politics. But in the great cauldron of the post-war era, both the host nation-state and its small but potent Jewish population evolved into highly functional partners. A major instrument was anti-communism, most dramatically evinced in the sensational Rosenberg atom spy case of the early 1950s.[13] This show trial of Jewish loyalty, in which every major participant, from accused, to key witnesses, to lawyers and the judge himself, proved, along with the rest of

the apparatus of repression, a kind of watershed from which
the mainstream of American Jewry emerged strengthened in
its integration into the moral universe of Cold War America.
At the same time it proved able to shape that universe to its
own Zionist ends.

Zionism is Jewish power—worldly and state power: military,
economic, and ideological, too. It is the power, which, to
paraphrase Thomas Hobbes, is the *capacity to give names
and enforce definitions*, including the definition that collapses
the meaning of Jewishness into the support of Israel—a piece
of unreason that became another "fact on the ground" when
in 1956 Webster's *Third New International Dictionary of the
English Language* included along with the customary meaning
of antisemitism, as "hostility toward Jews as a religious or
racial minority group, often accompanied by social, political
or economic discrimination," the following two: "Opposition
to Zionism; Sympathy with opponents of the State of Israel."
A language, a wag once said, is a dialect with an army behind
it. The language of Zionism is a rendering of the dialects of
Judaism into a singular power-form, and with a big army
behind it, an army not just military but also a very large
apparatus within state and civil society, staffed by new Jews
who are not simply Jews, therefore, but *power-Jews*, Jews
whose sincere devotion to Israel is also a sincere attachment
to the pillars of empire.

We have observed that Martin Peretz is an "Advisor" to
the "Washington Institute for Near Eastern Policy." This is
quite an honor. WINEP is an integral part of an apparatus,
which joins together the enterprises of the United States and
Israel, and a sign of the way the client state is now within its
patron as a second brain. One of WINEP's full-time fellows,
Dennis Ross, has been described as America's "point man on
the peace process" in the Clinton and first Bush administration. Another is the "Distinguished Military Fellow," General
Moshe Ya'alon, recently retired Chief of Staff for the IDF

from 2002–05. Ya'alon is also distinguished for having been indicted as a war criminal and mass murderer for his role in the first 1996 bombing of the refugee camp in Qana; and these days, for being one of the principle boosters egging the United States on to war with Iran.[14] The joint presence of Ross and Ya'alon in WINEP speaks volumes about the basic fairness of the "Peace Process" in Israel/Palestine.

Looking at the list of those who sit on the advisory board of WINEP with the publisher of *The New Republic* magazine is proof that Israel is far more than a "client" or "puppet" of the United States. Here we find the elite of the American Security State itself, arrayed in fealty to the Zionist ally: former Secretaries of State Warren Christopher, Lawrence Eagleburger, and Alexander Haig; former National Security Advisors Jeane Kirkpatrick and Robert McFarlane; former CIA Director James Woolsey; and former Secretary of Defense George Shultz. Richard Perle and Paul Wolfowitz, major foreign policy figures in the second Bush administration, have all been on the board, the latter stepping down when he became undersecretary of defense. Wolfowitz, then directing the World Bank, was both an ardent supporter of Israel and perhaps the prime architect of the invasion of Iraq. Israel craved this war unreservedly,[15] whereas in the United States significant countervailing voices to the endeavor were heard from senior officials from the Reagan, first Bush and Clinton administrations, who correctly foresaw the catastrophe that would follow upon the invasion. That this supreme folly was committed, therefore, required the suppression of these old conservative voices by voices inflamed with Zionist dreams. These reveal the degree of influence from the second, implanted brain as embedded in institutions like WINEP and its sponsor, the American Israeli Public Affairs Committee, or AIPAC. Founded in 1953, the year of the Rosenberg executions, AIPAC has been the institutional form taken by the zionisation of America and an enabler of its aggressive lurch under the second Bush administration.

The special relationship is a two-way street. Just as Israeli influence is felt in major United States foreign policy decisions, so have influential American advisors worked for the Israeli state. Of particular note is the fact that Richard Perle served, along with Douglas Feith (who became undersecretary of defense in the second Bush administration) and other leading Zionists as advisors to the Netanyahu administration of Israel in the 1990s, for whom they drafted a major report that called for provoking the Second Intifada, increasing an already aggressive policy toward Iraq, Iran, Syria and Lebanon, and augmenting the degree of neoliberal privatization of the Israel economy. Two days after Perle presented the document to Netanyahu, the Israeli prime minister presented it as his foreign policy initiative before a joint session of the United States Congress.[16] And just as Israel played a role in fomenting America's Iraq war, so has the United States played a role in Israel's Lebanon war, going beyond supplying weaponry and extending to strategic planning.

The people in whom these structural changes have become embodied go under the rubric of "neoconservatives." The neocons are largely Jewish and entirely Zionist, and they have succeeded in translating the original content of Zionism into the argot of foreign policy, which becomes in their hands, messianic, peremptory and tribalized—and thoroughly tooled to the needs of the American security apparatus. Typically, they stem from a failed position of the radical left, as expressed in a faction of "New York Intellectuals" who turned 180 degrees in the 1960s and 1970s from their infatuation with Stalinism and hitched their wagon to the rising star of a newly aggressive US foreign policy under Ronald Reagan.[17] As it acquired members and strength from this opportunistic turn, the group fell into an alliance with Richard Cheney and Donald Rumsfeld, and when these latter took over the United States government through the instrument of George W. Bush, neoconservatives became primed to extend Zionist influence yet more deeply into the national security state. In the neocon promotion of extreme unilateralism, these latter-day messianic Zionists are turning the United States as well as Israel into a "People Apart."

The American Israel Public Affairs Committee, or AIPAC, coordinates some 190 Jewish/Zionist federations in the United States and is the central ganglion in the network advancing the Zionist cause. AIPAC switches back and forth between state and civil society, using each to discipline the other. Its people can freely publish in major media because the major media are run by sharers of Zionism's consensus (among Peretz's co-advisors at WINEP is Mortimer Zuckerman, publisher of *US News and World Report* and the New York *Daily News*). And it uses a phenomenally potent political network to discipline Congress in order to exert considerable muscle on behalf of Israel over all presidents from Truman forward, with the exception of Eisenhower.[18]

AIPAC is a lobby like no other in its ability to intimidate the legislative as well as the executive branches of government. The case of Earl Hilliard will illustrate this, though a number of other examples would do as well. Hilliard served five terms in the House of Representatives from Alabama's seventh district, the first African-American to do so. In 2000, he defeated a black opponent, Artur Davis, in the primaries, by 20 percentage points, both candidates raising about the same amount of money. In 2002, Davis, mounting another challenge, began noticing large numbers of substantial out-of-state contributions bearing Jewish names. He raised nearly ten times the funds this way, without lifting a finger, and Hilliard never caught up. Hilliard again won the primary, but just barely, and in a run-off, went down to defeat, his career ruined. Today, Davis is still the Congressman from the seventh district. He owes his seat to AIPAC, which took a dislike to Hilliard for "pro-Arab" sympathies (he visited Libya), and particularly because on two occasions he refused to sign onto the frequently circulated Congressional petitions pledging eternal and unconditional support to the State of Israel. There is ample evidence that this was a vendetta, as the lobby wanted to use the incident (along with the associated squashing of the rebellious, and similarly African-American, Cynthia McKinney) as a demonstration of its vengeful power. And indeed, there has been nary a hiccough of Congressional doubt since.[19]

Note the "bipartisan" character of AIPAC and WINEP. For some time serious observers of the American scene have observed that the two main political parties, while ostensibly dividing the political universe between them, are in fact no more than Tweedledee and Tweedledum on the deeper issues affecting the economy and state, hence, their unity on questions of empire like the Iraq war and trade agreements. A conventional Marxist approach will point out that such results are chiefly due to the dependence of politicians on lobbyists and campaign contributions, and therefore on the abstracted form of big money-in-motion—capital—whose will is done by politicians and other operatives. There is certainly nothing wrong with this view. But it says nothing, either, about how economic power is translated into political power and back. The actual workings of the great forces of accumulation pass through socially and historically constructed persons and their institutional attachments. Thus just as the "Republocrats" are indifferently subservient to capital, so can they each be manipulated by an especially well-organized group that knows how to make money and use it for political ends.

Imagine a smallish but highly efficient bloc, tremendously sensitive to the winds of capital and skilled in the ways of accumulation, but also tightly organized by a national-redemptive ideology, say, one like Zionism. There is no reason why such a group cannot insert its high degree of consciousness and discipline into the political process in a country like America where Jews have achieved tremendous degrees of success, no reason at all why its national-redemptive goal cannot render it more rather than less effective as an

organizer of politics within the terms of the capitalist state—
especially if its mythos resonates with that of the host. Within
this world, it is quite possible to imagine such a bloc exerting
effective power over each political party according to its own
specifics and essentially contributing to the welding of those
parties into the kind of effective national unit required for the
advancement of the national-capitalist project. There need be
no contradiction, then, between the aims of Zionism and those
of the United States ruling class as these converge in the Middle
East. Both are integrally fitted into the project of accumulation
and empire; both have used Old Testament messianism as an
ideology so that when they invade a country they see it in
redemptive terms; they are truly well-adapted for symbiosis.

It can be said that Zionism conquered the Democratic Party
with the checkbook and the Republicans with their resort to
the sword. This statement, needless to say, is figurative, since
both sides of the American duopoly are amenable to both
checkbook and sword. But it conveys a sense of how this
intricate process has been colored. The Zionist bloc largely
controlled the Democratic Party before it set its sights upon
the Republicans, in large measure because of the historical
affiliation between Jews and progressive issues. The Zionists
got nowhere with Roosevelt but sunk their talons deep into
Truman and never let up since, though it was rough going
for a while with Kennedy, whose father had been a virtual
fascist, and who strenuously but impotently stood against
the Israeli building of nuclear weaponry. They made a cosy
accommodation with Johnson and Humphrey, never liked
Carter too much—because he was the first president to take
the Palestinian cause seriously—but did splendidly with the
Clintons and indeed every neoliberal and liberal Democrat of
modern times, pausing only to stomp on those, like Hilliard
and McKinney, who refused to get with their program.[20]

To say that AIPAC has bought itself a Congress and hence
can get them to dance to its tune is more than metaphor. It has

been observed, for example, that in the 2000 election cycle, of the 400 leading contributors to the Democratic Party, 7 of the top 10, 12 of the top 20, and 125 of the top 250 were Jewish.[21] Undoubtedly, some of these Jewish contributors may not have been interested in advancing Zionism's agenda. But even if only half of them did, an almost certainly low figure, this would comprise a very major degree of influence. And in any case, we know of one such Jewish contributor who definitely had his eye on purchasing the advancement of Israel, the greatest of these, Haim Saban, fourth wealthiest of Israel's tycoons, and whose story we may introduce with two little-observed extracts from the internet:

- [The following item appeared in January 2006 in the *Jewish Journal of Los Angeles* under the heading of "Gala for IDF"]:

  More than 850 people, including many of the most prominent leaders of the Jewish community, gathered at the Regent Beverly Wilshire Hotel in Beverly Hills to honor the brave men and women who serve in the Israel Defense Forces. The Friends of the Israel Defense Forces Western Region held the event to raise funds for an auditorium, library and synagogue at the soon to be built new REIM Base in the Negev.

  The gala dinner was co-chaired by Cheryl and Haim Saban and included a live satellite hook-up with soldiers stationed near Gaza. The evening's special guest speaker was Avi Dichter, who recently retired as head of Shin Bet. By the end of the evening, the gala dinner had raised nearly $4 million with many additional pledges and commitments under discussion.

  Even in Beverly Hills, it's not every day that someone gets up to pledge $1 million to a good cause, to say nothing of two successive million-dollar donors.

Dichter, a rising star in Kadima, warned that the "terror states" of Iran, Syria and Lebanon had not given up on their hopes to destroy the Jewish state.[22]

- [From the website of CCR] On December 8, 2005, the Center for Constitutional Rights and the Palestinian Center for Human Rights brought a class action lawsuit against Avi Dichter, the former Director of Israel's General Security Service, on behalf of the Palestinians who were killed or injured in a 2002 air strike in Gaza. The attack occurred just before midnight on July 22, 2002, when the Israeli Defense Forces (IDF) dropped a one-ton bomb on al-Daraj, a residential neighborhood in Gaza City in the Occupied Palestinian Territory.

  The attack killed seven adults and eight children, including plaintiff Ra'ed Matar's wife and their three young children and plaintiff Mahmoud Al Huweiti's wife and two of their young sons. It injured over 150 others, including plaintiff Marwan Zeino, whose spinal vertebrae were crushed. The attack was widely condemned by the international community, including the U.S. government, at the time. On July 23, 2002, White House Press Secretary Ari Fleischer stated that President Bush condemned this "deliberate attack against a building in which civilians were known to be located." These attacks on civilians, however, are ongoing, with the IDF carrying out regular air strikes on residential neighborhoods in the Occupied Palestinian Territory to this day.

  The case charges Avi Dichter, then Director of Israel's General Security Service (GSS), with war crimes and other gross human rights violations for his participation in the decision to drop the bomb on the residential neighborhood, and charges that GSS provided the necessary intelligence and final approval to implement the attack. Dichter was served papers in New York at 10:30 pm on the night of December 7, 2005. He retired from the GSS earlier this

year and has been a fellow at the Brookings Institution
in Washington, D.C.[23]

Haim Saban, who co-chaired the celebration of Avi Dichter
and the Israeli soldiers patrolling Gaza—the same territory
onto which Dichter directed bombs that killed 15 Palestinian
civilians and injured 150 others, was born in Egypt and raised
in Israel, coming to America as a young man. Saban is what
is known as a "self-made man," chiefly through his skill at
conquering the culture industries. He is now a media mogul,
a regent of the University of California, and has the honor
of being the 245th richest person in the world (worth either
$1.7 or $2.8 billion, depending on who you read—but why
quibble?). Saban's contributions to civilization include the
"Mighty Morphin Power Ranger" TV series, and, in alliance
with that bellwether of the ultra-right, Rupert Murdoch, the
presidency of the Fox Family Network. Note well: Saban is no
reactionary, but a mover and shaker in the Democratic Party,
who counts among his friends Howard Dean, John Kerry,
and especially Bill Clinton, on whose administration's Export
Council he served, with whom he vacations, and whom he
from time to time trots out like a show dog to impress clients.
Saban provided $600,000 in 2005 so that Clinton could
travel in style to Israel to be honored at the annual dinner
of the Saban Center for Middle East Policy (of the centrist
Brookings Institution, where Avi Dichter hangs out when he
is not being served subpoenas for crimes against humanity,
and made possible by a $13 million donation; there is also the
Saban Institute for the Study of the American Political System
at the University of Tel Aviv), $250,001 to the Democratic
Congressional Campaign Committee (the extra dollar given so
that he would be the year's largest contributor), and perhaps
most notable of all, $13 million toward the construction of
Democratic Party Headquarters in Washington. All this from a
man who has said, "I'm a one-issue guy and my issue is Israel,"

and who has claimed that he "regularly spends hours at a time on the phone with Ariel Sharon." Recently, Saban bought up Germany's largest commercial television system, ProSieben, consummating the deal on cellphone while visiting the Dachau concentration camp.[24] He has since acquired Univision, putting Spanish-American media also comfortably within the Zionist sphere of influence.

Now just as modern Democrats move smoothly through the neoliberal world, so does the "liberal" Saban mesh nicely with ultrareactionary Rupert Murdoch. But he goes well beyond that, to mesh, however uncomfortably, with the Christian right. The remarkable convergence between the American Christian right and Zionism has often been noted. Less often observed is that the Christian right speaks to something very basic in American society, which is homologous with what Jewish fundamentalists say in Israel.[25] America, the "redeemer-nation," and Israel, the Chosen one, are set upon tracks that remarkably parallel each other, and their respective national mythologies, derived from messianic readings of the Old Testament, provide many switching points as well as a kind of lingua franca for their elites, even as they shape the worldview of many ordinary people.[26] A society bobs up and down on a magma of shared texts, which have been processed into innumerable cultural forms and internalized in the psyche; it is this, in fact, which gives the psyche a unifying, collective force across society. Hence the rigidity of such beliefs, no matter how irrational they may be. To tamper with them by introducing the truth would dissolve powerful social bonds.

In the United States, Christian fundamentalism sustains the bizarre presidency of George W. Bush, and the "zionification" of the state as well. The Pew Research Center has found a formidable level of support for Israel at the base of American Christianity. In a 2003 poll, 44 percent of respondents averred that God gave the Land of Israel to the Jewish people, while 36 percent believed that creation of the state of Israel is a step toward the Second Coming of Jesus, that is, Armageddon followed by the "rapture" of true believers.[27] This belief is compatible with severe antisemitism of the nativist kind, a fact that fails to inhibit its usefulness as a common link between the security elites of the partners in Western expansion. In any case, the people who actually direct capital and empire also have to believe in something; and their beliefs have to be congruent with the processes they direct. No Gandhian, liberation theologist, or anarchist is going to be found directing Israel or its lobby. A deep believer in Old Testament eschatology and the Book of Revelation, however, can fit in quite well. I make no claim to fully understand the motivations of a man like Haim Saban. But his reason for supporting Israel with all his heart, given in an interview in *The New York Times*, deserves to be pondered:

> "I hate quoting Tom DeLay, I really do," Mr. Saban said. "If you're going to quote me quoting Tom DeLay, say I hate quoting him." He continued, apparently quoting Mr. DeLay, the House Republican leader: "He said: 'It is the right thing for us to do to be supportive of Israel. The reasons go back to the beginning of time.'"[28]

The now-fallen ultra-reactionary Christian fundamentalist DeLay addressed Israel's Knesset, in the Summer of 2003, during his salad days when he was the most important man in Congress. He was the first foreigner accorded this honor. DeLay gave a speech of 2884 words, which contained 46 references to "terrorism," and whose meaning can be succinctly rendered as: Israel and America stand as one, now and forever under God, in the never-ending war against evil. To have such people in your corner may arouse a twinge of ambivalence in the sensitive Zionist. But Zionism is also that fraction of the Jewish heritage that, for all the furor about wanting to put Christian Europe behind it, has also been driven by the desire to join hands with the West, and to be forgiven by the *goyim* for the blood-curses of killing Christ and dipping their hands in all-corrupting usury. There must be a profound gratification at finally being included in the inner circles of *goyische* power.

Jewish skill in handling money helped define the path to capitalism, which from a subjective standpoint can be interpreted as the causing of money to grow by itself. Capitalists often need assuagment of a spiritual kind for the devastation inherent to this phenomenon. Hence the "Gospel of Wealth," which grew in nineteenth century America, and used Calvinist predeterminism to assert that making a lot of money was a sign of God's grace; hence also the usefulness of Judaism's Day of Atonement, Yom Kippur, which gives the Jewish bourgeoisie a once-a-year opportunity to wipe the slate clean before they begin transgressing anew. The big Jewish capitalists who bankroll the Zionist project also experience this need. Saban's reaching for "reasons [that] go back to the beginning of time" is not mere posturing, therefore, since at the beginning of time there was no money. However spurious it may be by any rational standard, the Zionist claim of divine entitlement to Palestine is a definite spiritual force, which first directed the Zionists to Palestine, now exonerates them for its conquest, and is widely shared by Americans who might be antisemitic but nonetheless see Israel as a dynamic element in their Christian fundamentalism. These are notions with which the national security elites of the United States are quite at home, and have served to bring those from the conservative/Republican side of the political landscape into the Zionist consensus.

It took a while. For some time sensible voices in the American foreign policy establishment saw little use for Israel, given the need to avoid trouble with the Arab world. However, under the steady political pressure applied by Zionist groups and the overarching priority of global confrontation with the USSR a reorientation took place, which became cemented into a strategic partnership after the 1967 war.[29] In exchange for superpower protection and active assistance, Israel was to serve as a regional gendarme destabilizing the potential for uprisings among the Arab masses, who were seen as objectively pro-Soviet; and also to render such services to its patron as it was able to carry out because of its lack of concern for constitutionality as well as many of the public relations matters that were staying the United States' hand.[30]

Through the 1970s and 1980s Israel helped its partner to crush popular insurgencies in places as far removed from the Middle East as Latin America and Southern Africa. Israel sold arms and gave training to counter-revolutionary United States client states like El Salvador, Guatemala, and Nicaragua (when Somoza's dictatorship was in power, and to the CIA's Contra army after the Sandinistas took over and became Public Enemy Number One); it did the same with Chile under Pinochet, and Argentina under its murderous junta. Elsewhere it was deeply embedded with the apartheid state of South Africa (a very important relation to which we turn below) and Iran under the second Shah, whose deadly secret police, Savak, it helped train, thereby hastening the coming of political Islam. These escapades evolved in synchrony with the Occupation of Gaza and the West Bank, and doubtlessly provided a kind of laboratory for state terror in the lands conquered in 1967; just so has Israeli expertise in the arts of torture provided useful lessons for the second Bush administration as it followed its friend in the flouting of international human rights statutes in its "War on Terror."[31]

As remarkable as it is, the special relationship has definitely not been without conflict. States are too complex and irrational for that, especially the State of Israel, which is set up to not get along smoothly with anyone. The identity of "a people apart" cannot be overestimated where Israel is concerned, often taking shape in some variation or other on the theme that a people who had suffered so and faced so much hatred need not play by ordinary rules of behavior. This was seen time and time again in the story of Israel's acquisition of its nuclear arsenal, in which sheer stubbornness and nihilistic desperation combined with manipulation of Holocaust guilt and financial muscle to wear down the Americans'pathetic efforts to stop the deadly process. The title of Seymour Hersh's _The Samson Option,_ where a lot of this is spelled out, expresses the widely held identification with the Biblical hero who sacrificed himself in order to bring down the temple on his enemies. Thus the culture of ancient Israel produced the first suicide bomber, something that ought to be pondered by Zionist ideologues today when they rant about Muslims resorting to this expedient.[32] A similar theme is expressed by the deep, though spurious, identification with the holdouts at Masada, who allegedly committed mass suicide rather than submit to the Roman legions in 70 CE.[33]

Over the years, a number of outrageous incidents have confirmed that the Jewish state is anything but a compliant stooge of the superpower.

- The attack on the _USS Liberty,_ a supersophisticated surveillance vessel, on June 8, 1967, the fourth day of the Six Day War, by Israeli planes and boats, resulting in the death of 34 sailors and the wounding of 173 others. Israel has claimed this to be an accident in which the vessel was mistaken for an Egyptian craft, and every president since Johnson has agreed, along with any number of official bodies and, to be sure, Zionist watchdog agencies as well as authors in one degree or another of association with Israel. On the other hand, the surviving crewmen, and various investigative reporters, along with an ex-chairman of the Joint Chiefs of Staff, the Secretary of State, the CIA director—in short, non-politicians less likely to be under immediate AIPAC supervision—insist that the assault was deliberate and undertaken, so says one theory, to hide certain atrocities committed in course of war. The reader may infer the likelihood of some tendentiousness here; in any case, the incident has been fought to a standstill and, to Israel's comfort, buried under a mountain of obfuscation.[34]

- The scandalous Pollard spy case of the 1980s, perhaps the greatest breach of security in the whole post-war period. CIA employee Jonathan Pollard passed virtually a ton of documents to Israel, which proceeded to claim that this was a mere peccadillo, virtually an accident. However, Israeli PM Yitzhak Shamir decided to pass a lot of it on to the USSR, chiefly because he didn't want to be too dependent upon the United States, resulting in the ruin of much of Washington's spy apparatus in Russia and the executions of several agents.[35]

- Behavior most strange on and around September 11, 2001 in the United States. All this has been steadily pushed down the memory hole, but there is commentary throughout the international, including the Israeli, press, and extensive coverage by off-center journalists in the United States about the hundreds of Israeli "art students" keeping close tabs on the highjackers, and various United States law enforcement agencies throughout 2001. Then there is the New Jersey "Urban Movers" cell whose members were seen laughing and taking pictures of the burning towers from across the river, became arrested, and disappeared from view. Given the high likelihood that these were Mossad agents, the entire affair suggests Israeli knowledge of the impending attack, and that nothing was done to notify the United States government. Some have argued that the marked improvement in an already strong position for Israel after the September 11 attacks constitutes the ground of a motive. All that can be said here is that this much smoke demands a search for fire.[36]

- Finally, the case of Pentagon analyst Larry Franklin (who worked under Donald Rumsfeld and Douglas Feith) who passed information to AIPAC officials Steven Rosen and Keith Weissman (who have since been fired). In January 2006 Franklin was sentenced to 12 years; the trial of Rosen and Weissman, which is potentially explosive for AIPAC, remains suspended as of this writing.[37]

These are peaks in a fractious range. Like the murder of Rachel Corrie, they manifest a self-reinforcing circuit, which begins with wanton disregard for the ordinary principles of humanity and ends with the granting of impunity for the "special" state, which, emboldened, commences the circuit anew. The same pattern obtains throughout the entire pattern of Israeli history, most notably in the flouting of scores of UN resolutions pertaining to the Occupation of Palestine. There is a kind of exception in the Pollard case, where the extreme degree of damage to the CIA caused the intelligence community to put its back up and successfully insist on maintaining Pollard's incarceration for life despite massive Zionist pressure to commute it. This, along with the bitterness over the *Liberty* incident and like matters, indicates a smoldering hostility to Israel within the "permanent government" of the United States that may some day come back to haunt Zion.

It is not only the transgressions of the Israeli-American apparatus that must be denied, but also its very existence. And so when two high-profile political scientists from Harvard and the University of Chicago published a long and scholarly essay early in 2006 calling into question the activities of an "Israel lobby" as deleterious to both the United States and Israel, AIPAC and its attack dog-intellectuals sprang into action, baying accusations of antisemitism and every possible calumny in its direction and in the process proving the article's thesis, that there is a potent thought police patrolling the question of Zionism and impeding a minimally honest debate on Israel in the United States.[38]

No part of American political culture has been more harmed by the suppression of such a debate than the left, which is crippled to an extent scarcely appreciated by unacknowledged Zionism. The feebleness and lack of clarity, even confusion, evinced by the left in the United States on innumerable occasions cannot be simply laid at the doorstep of Zionism, to be sure. But a defect of this kind weighs very heavily. Acceptance of the "special" nature of Israel, often manifest in an appeal to just how horribly Jews have suffered, goes hand in hand with devaluation of Israel's victims and minimization of its crimes. Given the indisputable fact that Israel's conquest of Palestine radiates across the world and sets into motion so much hatred and disorder, the inability of progressives in the global superpower to come to grips with Zionism drags down everything they do, and makes it impossible to deal effectively with war and peace alike.

One thing that is truly special about Israel is continual moral embattlement. A seemingly eternal struggle over wrongdoing and justification dogs its every step. This has inner ramifications that cut to the heart of the Zionist project.

7
Bad Conscience and State Racism

IT IS A REMARKABLE phenomenon, specific, I should think, to the State of Israel, that its obsession with being the victim of terrorism goes hand in hand with the fact that no fewer than three of its prime ministers have been world-class terrorists, in the sense of having commanded major military and paramilitary operations whose purpose was to sow a climate of fear and panic through the targeting of civilians. Thus we have:

Menachem Begin, PM from May 1977 to August 1983. Begin first appeared as a disciple of Jabotinsky. The loss of his parents and brother in the Holocaust further hardened his attitudes and led him to conflate Arab hostility with the antisemitism that spurred Nazism. Thus he became the chief translator of the Holocaust into a text of imperial Zionism. After Jabotinsky's death in 1940 Begin assumed control of the underground arm of the revisionists, *Irgun,* and it was in this capacity that he engineered the dynamiting of the British headquarters in Jerusalem's most famous hotel, the King David, on July 22, 1946, killing 88 people, including 15 Jews. In 1948 he commanded the most spectacular terrorist act of the Zionist era, leading an expedition against the Arab village of Deir Yassin on the outskirts of Jerusalem whose 400 inhabitants had been known until then for their peaceable relations with their Jewish neighbors, never complaining, working with the Jewish Agency at times and even said by a Jewish newspaper to have driven out Arab militants. Perhaps because this good behavior made the village a specially tempting example for terror, at 4.30 am on April 9, a force of 132 *Irgun* and *Stern* militants under Begin's command, acting in collaboration with the official Zionist leadership and with tactical support of the *Palmach*, the Haganah's elite force, descended on the village and systematically set about to slaughter its people, disemboweling a pregnant woman, raping others, taking prisoners and then shooting them, and not stopping until noon the next day when 93 villagers lay dead. The purpose of the atrocity, and what made it the purest kind of terror, lay in its impact on the indigenous people. As Benny Morris writes of the massacre, it "had a profoundly demoralizing effect on the Palestinian Arabs and was a major factor in their massive flight during the following weeks and months. The IDF Intelligence Service called Deir Yassin 'a decisive accelerating factor' in the general Arab exodus."[1] This is ethnic cleansing by any standards—and for the Arabs, it became the centerpiece of their notion of *Nakhba*, or catastrophe, which has been emblazoned on collective memory as a symbol of dispossession. The massacre was condemned by many Jews within Israel and prompted outrage around the world, including from leading Jewish intellectuals in the United States such as Albert Einstein, Hannah Arendt and Sidney Hook, who protested Begin's visit to the United States. Yet less than thirty years later the perpetrator of the slaughter at Deir Yassin was to become prime minister of the State of Israel.

Begin entered the government as head of the ultra-nationalist party, Herut, in 1967 during the frantic build-up to the war with Egypt and Syria. As prime minister he presided over the invasion of Lebanon. This was consistent with the fact that he was the first to bring the notion of "Greater Israel" from the margins of Zionist discourse into the realm of statecraft. Begin's tenure in office was also notable for state sponsorship of the religious right. He supported the ultra-Orthodox Gush Emunim as they spear-headed the growth of settlements in the Occupied Territories; and also made the first formal overture to the United States religious right immediately after his election, capping this off by awarding Israel's Jabotinsky Prize to Jerry Falwell in 1981 in exchange for the latter's endorsement of the bombing of the Iraqi nuclear reactor at Osirak.[2]

It should be added that Begin, in contrast to the hardliners who followed him, was capable of introspection and candor. Thus in *The New York Times* of August 21, 1982 he was quoted as saying in the course of defending the invasion of Lebanon, that "In June of 1967 we again had a choice. The Egyptian army concentrations in the Sinai did not prove that Nasser was really about to attack us. We must be honest with ourselves. We decided to attack him." He was also prone to the suffering that comes from inwardness, and this proved devastating in his case. Consumed by guilt and depression, in part over the horrors of the Lebanon invasion, where he blamed himself for letting Ariel Sharon get away with mayhem (see below), and in part over the death of his wife, for which he also blamed himself,[3] Begin withdrew from public life and relinquished his office.

Yitzhak Shamir, a man incapable of qualms, assumed the post upon Begin's resignation and remained (except for 1984–86, when Shimon Peres was PM) until defeat by Yitzhak Rabin in June 1992. After arriving in Palestine in 1935, Shamir gravitated quickly to the Stern Gang, the farthest-right element of revisionist Zionism, whose lineage was not only terrorist but frankly fascist, even pro-Nazi. Avraham Stern believed ardently in Greater Israel and in the necessity for forceful expulsion of the entire Palestinian-Arab population; and in 1941 his organization made overtures to the Third Reich, in which they offered to "actively take part in the war on Germany's side ... [in the interests of] a positive-radical solution of the European Jewish problem in conformity with the ... national aspirations of the Jewish people."[4] After Stern was killed by British police, Shamir, at the time imprisoned, escaped and eventually became operations commander of the organization. In this capacity, he played a major role in the assassination of Churchill's Middle East envoy, Lord Moyne, and of Count Folke Bernadotte, the UN envoy and humanitarian, and was also active in the massacre at Deir Yassin. In 1955, Shamir was recruited into the Mossad by the Labor government that had once reviled him as Israel's worst terrorist. Then, in 1970, he joined Begin's Herut Party and rapidly rose to the top. As foreign minister in 1982, he received a slap on the wrist for the Sabra and Shatila massacre (see below). Shamir's views about force and toward Arabs while prime minister may be judged by the following remark, made in reaction to the nonviolent Palestinian resistance of the First Intifada: "The Palestinians would be crushed [by Israeli forces] like grasshoppers ... heads smashed against the boulders and walls."

Ariel Sharon, who before his tenure as PM was deemed guilty of terroristic war crimes by Israel's own judiciary as well as the world for permitting the Sabra and Shatila massacre in 1982, in which he bore responsibility for the fact that Christian Phalangist thugs bent on revenge murdered 700–800 (other estimates went as high as 3000) Palestinian refugees in a Lebanese camp, the vast majority of them innocents. This dreadful act, which in a morally rational country would have finished Sharon's career or led to his imprisonment, was by no means the first of his terrorist exploits. He had established his reputation in the early 1950s as the swashbuckling leader of Unit 101, an unorthodox commando company of the IDF created to deal with Arab incursions across the borders from

which they had recently been expelled. On the orders of Pinhas
Lavon, the acting defense minister, and Chief of Staff Moshe
Dayan, Sharon led a cross-border raid on the Jordanian village
of Qibya on October 14–15, 1953, in which the community
was reduced to rubble, with 45 houses blown up and 69 people
killed, the majority women and children. This was only the
most dashing of the future prime minister's accomplishments as
commander of Unit 101, but it established an enduring pattern:
first, it furthered the terror-convergence between the IDF and
the rogue organizations that emerged after 1929 and had been
cemented at Deir Yassin, thus gave terror an official stamp
deriving from the state; second, it laid down a gray area between
the commands received by Sharon and the atrocities carried
out by him, the former having some sheen of rationality ("we
need to show the Arabs that they can't cross our borders and
harm our people and communities"), the latter being wanton
exercises in bloodlust and ritual humiliation; and third, it was
received with a great deal of enthusiasm by the Israeli public
and Jews in general. Joel Beinin has written: "The members
of Unit 101 became Israel's new culture heroes, and the unit's
'successes' encouraged a reckless mentality in military circles."[5]
This sort of behavior afforded an exhilarating throwback to
imagined Biblical days, and it became extolled in literature,
drama and film. The most notorious example was Leon Uris'
1958 novel *Exodus*, a celebration of Zionist paramilitaries
inspired in part by Sharon's exploits (and chiefly by Yitzak
Rabin). Of non-existent literary merit, Uris' work exceeded
the influence of *Gone With the Wind* as a romantic defense of
ethnic aggrandizement. With 20 million copies printed in 50
languages, it became the definitive representation of a heroic,
rambunctious Zionism to the Western world.

That a terrorist would ascend to national leadership on three
occasions, and moreover, that those three occasions would be
recent and therefore the sign of a tendency as well as a fact, is

a truly remarkable occurrence. Just as remarkable is the fact that scarcely anybody has bothered to ponder its meaning. The reason, of course, is that to look in depth at the Israeli relation to terror does tend to vitiate the obsessive harping on Palestinian terror. And it also brings us up against the wildly contradictory fact that this record is combined with obsessive claims of democratic virtue and appeals to the ancient sufferings endured by Jews and their high ethical standards. The discourses of realpolitik cannot account for this, given the relentlessness with which these moral claims are made. The ordinary rogue government resorts to instrumental lies with a yawn in order to deny its criminality. But for the Jewish state this is a veritably cosmic matter.

The ex-terrorist statesman lives in a milieu where his adaptations have become normalized through a matching set of compartments and codes that deal with harsh moral contradiction. Luminaries of Israeli history, notable leaders and generals like Ben-Gurion, Moshe Dayan, Shimon Peres, Yitzhak Rabin or Ehud Barak, along with innumerable lesser-knowns who commanded the state and/or its armies, may have been more "moderate" and disapproving of "extremism" than the terror-trio; yet they engaged in actions and policies, often clandestine, that have been essentially continuous.[6] There is a kind of transmission belt between terrorism waged on an individual level and that form of legitimated state violence that demands to be called *state terrorism* because it, too, engages in acts in which civilians are targeted and the purpose of which is to sow a climate of fear and panic—as was blatantly the case in the attacks on Gaza and Lebanon in 2006.

As for the physiology of this creature, we have called attention numerous times in this study to certain fundamental contradictions that interact about Zionism's foundations and drive it onward. We have metaphorically called these, "compartments." Extending the term a bit, let us think about them as kinds of *splitting*, that is, facets of being that

radically exclude one another, yet coexist, because they are
each necessary and driven by powerful forces. Broadly, we see
on the one side, the powerful ethical component to Judaism,
and on the other, the commission of dreadful crimes and the
honoring of those who have done so. These incompatible
elements need to be arranged so that the national project
can go forward, which means, to extend the metaphor, that
the splits within the Zionist project need to be patched over.
They cannot be resolved within the terms of Zionism, whose
national identity requires a self-image of ethical superiority in
endless conflict with the aggression necessary to expropriate
Arab lands. Hence the "patchworks" are needed to build a
kind of solidity. The essential features remain, in that there
is no mutual recognition, no practical consciousness of the
conjunction of opposed states of being—and crucially, no
reconciliation and no forgiveness. Yet at the same time the
mutually contradictory elements are able to be yoked together
for the pursuit of power. Their fundamental estrangement
endures; but under conditions conducive to worldly success,
chiefly by the construction of a fierce militarism, a hardened
vindictiveness, and a shield of virtuousness.

Since we are talking about the moral dimension here, it is
important to identify this patchwork as a species of collective
conscience, that is to say, a device to define, organize and guide
the morality of a nation state, with its needs for legitimacy.
When Zionism was a pitifully weak movement of outcasts and
dreamers it did not need such a collective conscience, for it
then had the real presence of antisemitism as the means around
which the shield of Jewish suffering and the endowment of
ethical virtue could be constructed. But as it grew into a state
and achieved a kind of empire, the conscience needs of Zionism
grew with the state's need for legitimation and became more
complex and internally riven.

If I refer to the product as a *Bad Conscience,* this is not
meant to cast aspersion—though it is scarcely necessary to

point out that I take a dim view of the moral universe put forward by Zionism. But other meanings of "bad" are more germane. I mean also a conscience in which a kind of *badness*, a sense that something is noxiously wrong, persists within the social body. And I mean also a conscience that works *badly*, impeding internal development and the ripeness that comes to those who can comprehend some aspect of the wholeness of things and thereby achieve the capacity of forgiveness. Badly, too, in that it brings evil and suffering into the world and propagates them.

One of our oddest words, this "Bad."[7] At the earliest level of individual development, it means what is spit out, then shit out, in other words, the rejected parts of the primary universe, or what is refused by the "purified pleasure Ego," to use a valuable term coined by Freud. Psychologically, what is deemed bad is met by the affect of hate; conceptually, it becomes associated with excrement, dirt and filth; while in the spiritual/religious dimension, ritual cleanliness is its negation and the dividing point of the traditional community. Jewish exceptionalism is customarily expressed in terms of the Covenant, as Yahweh's beneficent endowment of the Abrahamic tribe and eventually the Israeli nation. But in the centuries intervening between these historical termini, ritual *un*cleanliness came to define the special position of the Jews within Christendom, much as it did untouchables within Hinduism and blacks within United States racism and South African apartheid—though in the case of Jews it was elaborated in terms of Ghetto existence and their special relation to money and usury: "filthy lucre."[8]

Monotheistic religions can become factories of splitting, in which the categories of goodness and badness are rendered into heavens, hells, and regimes of sin and accusation, almost always along patriarchal lines. State formation adds the dimension of legitimated violence, which in the case of Israel means the processing of the deep strata of archaic desire necessary for the forming of the Zionist nation as well as the aggression inherent to setting forth a Jewish state in the midst of hundreds of millions of Muslims and Arabs. All this hardens matters further by enforcing and codifying what is bad and burdens Israel with a special quotient of hate and its vengeful sequelae. The result is a more or less permanent regime of paranoia, felt by visitors at Ben-Gurion airport, by those who would criticize Israel, and principally, Arabs and Muslims, for it is these whom Zionism must actually dispossess.

The elements of bad conscience are played out across various dimensions, especially that of guilt, the feelings of which become intolerable to the degree it is fed by archaic streams of hatred and revenge. The resulting feelings become projected and turn into the blaming of others—whether these be expropriated Palestinians or critics of Israel, who become either antisemites and/or that curious entity, the "self-hating Jew." All this is entailed with the fact that Jewish culture has been since the days of the Pentatuech a guilt culture par excellence, regulated by a harsh conscience and dominated by feelings along the spectrum of what can describe wrongdoing, or its negation, ethical virtue. The rising of the Jewish state transformed a normally harsh conscience into a full-blown bad conscience. Now the permanent, because institutionalized, transgression of lofty Jewish ethical ideals is locked into place by material exigencies such as the demands of an Occupation or the need to lick the boots of global capital, that is, what are colloquially called "facts on the ground." Thus what is "bad" about the bad conscience is the walling off within, the splitting introduced by the irreconcilability of a collective will whose guiding principle had once been ethical superiority and is now shaped by an aggressive, militarized and vindictive state.

It is an essential feature of the bad conscience to drive toward greater transgression. We have observed that recognition of common humanity and acceptance of moral responsibility leads to reconciliation and forgiveness. However, the bad conscience of Zionism moves in the opposite direction, to join the cycle of vengeance that stains human history. It is possible to see this emerging in the early period of the state, when Israel was, despite the terror campaign of 1948, still able to command a healthy dose of world approval. But who could have foretold back then just how cruel and coldly malevolent would be the direction given to Israeli state aggression by the bad conscience?

We are fortunate to have a primary source that prefigures this with painful clarity: the diaries of the anti-terrorist Prime Minister, Moshe Sharett, who succeeded Ben-Gurion in December 1953 and remained in power until 1955. Sharett is one of the forgotten men of Israeli history. Because he stood against the tendencies outlined here, Sharett today tends to be regarded as weak and foolish, a vacillating throwback to Jewish submission. Avi Shlaim is judicious enough to dispute this. He sees in Sharett not weakness but wisdom, grounded in the fact that, virtually alone among the Zionist leadership, he grew up amongst Arabs, could speak Arabic and knew Arabs to be fellow human beings and not blank screens upon which diabolizing images could be projected.[9] It was not weakness that led Sharett to speak out in internal Zionist debates against the burgeoning terror strategy. Nor was it foolishness that led him to write in his diary after the Qibya massacre led by Sharon:

> In the thirties we restrained the emotions of revenge and we educated the public to consider revenge as an absolutely negative impulse. Now on the contrary, we justify the system of reprisal out of pragmatic considerations ... we have eliminated the mental and moral brakes on this instinct and made it possible ... to uphold revenge as a moral value. This notion is held by large parts of the public in general, the masses of youth in particular, but it has crystallized and reached *the value of a sacred principle* in [Sharon's] batallion which becomes the revenge instrument of the State. ...[10]

We may rephrase: Revenge is the recycling of terror, and terror is the instrument of revenge. The deadly complex is an inherent potential of nationhood informed by principles such as those of Zionism, and follows from the fact that to forge the disparate and scattered Jews into a compact nation requires scrapping the universalizing ideals acquired from the Enlightenment during the Diaspora and replacing them by the retributive Old Testament ethos that was the common root of Jewish history. It took statehood—with its legitimated violence—to allow this to harden ("crystallize" as Sharett says) into a *structure*, a "revenge instrument." Thus does the state insert itself into the ancient circuits, making revenge not just morally desirable but, with its Old Testament fountainhead, actually sacred. Sharett identifies here that conduit for godhead that states have immemorially exploited. The state drains away the spiritual content of prophetic Judaism, turns Zionism into a state religion of archaic yet instrumental blood revenge, and hardens what had once been the province of dreamers and romantics into a regime of vengeance and moral splitting.

It is tempting to regard the case of Sharett as a "what might have been," and to see him as the Good Zionist whose counsel, if heeded, would have led the next half-century in a better direction. I would see Sharett, however, as fundamentally tragic and deluded. He is one of those worthy yet agonized souls who get trapped between good instincts and axiomatic belief. Such folk, often quite leftist, still occupy the "progressive" pole of the debate about Zionism; they essentially want it to be, in the words of the Bushes, "kinder and gentler," or "compassionate." Meanwhile they share, with Sharett, the same Zionist ends as Ben-Gurion, differing only in means. In other words, Sharett, as a proper Zionist, still wanted his Jewish state. Now if said state is to be Jewish, and if it must use electoral means of reproducing itself according to the indispensable ethos of democracy, then a permanent Jewish majority in Israel must be guaranteed.[11] But for this it is necessary that the Palestinian right of return to the lands from which they have been expelled need to be shelved indefinitely, which is to say, that a regime

of ethnic cleansing needs to be preserved. Is it really better to
do so by legalized, even "compassionate" means as against
terrorism? Is it really different to do so?

The liberal Zionist tries to solve the riddles of bad
conscience by squaring the circle. He returns to the same
starting point, of Jewish ethnocracy, only he has provided it
with a more enduring and less episodic basis than the state
terrorist. A moment's reflection will reveal that these two
strategies can readily coexist within the same polity, as indeed
they have in Eretz Israel. Neither escapes the strictures of the
bad conscience, and each helps the other get along: the state
terrorist can point toward preserving the "only democracy
in the Middle East" as justifying his extreme measures; the
liberal Zionist can salve some of the bad conscience by chiding
his violent compatriot. Having established his virtue, he can
then sit back and go no further.

STATE RACISM

The settler-colonial has two strategies for contending with
the moral pressures stemming from his aggression against
indigenous people, and their unruliness: he may elevate his
conquest with some surpassing virtue, such as claiming God's
blessing or by invoking the sufferings of his kind—and/or,
from the other side, he can undertake to degrade and debase
the troublesome victims so that they are not considered
equivalently human. Once this happens they are no longer
within the discourses of morality. The second line is mapped
in various ways according to circumstance and history; and the
result, measured in systematized difference between over- and
under-people, becomes a species of what we know as *racism*.
Thus the core racist judgment is denial of equivalent humanity.
It will do equally well to denigrate the culture of the lesser
people as to call them animals, or even vermin or bacteria,
or to regard them as incapable of civilization, or, particularly

apt these days, to consider them as congenital terrorists, in contrast to one's own terrorists who act in a higher, that is, more human cause.

The racism of Israel is the specific outcome of settler-colonialism. Colonizing invasions with settlement of another's territory are of course rife throughout history. But a certain type of such invasions conducive to racism has arisen in the modern era, for four main reasons: first, it emerges from the clash of peoples with radically different cultures; second, it occurs in the context of a modernizing capitalism and uses various capitalist means; third, it has to contend with and break loose from a mother country, for example, England; and four, it eventuates in the establishment of a modern state that incorporates the notion of universal human right as a basic regulating principle. This latter is what makes racism systematic in the modern world, as it forces the conquerer to rationalize and elevate his domination in order to secure legitimacy. This is done through the state, which mobilizes various myths and turns them into the ideological fabric of its racism.[12]

Settler-colonialism is not the only path to racism. Outright conquest can also produce this result, as can other forms of internal social disintegration such as befell Nazi Germany. But it is the mode of interest in the case of Israel, as well as two other societies of significance here, the United States and South Africa. In all these cases we need to carefully attend to the distinction between the systematic or *structural* character of racism and the innumerable individual manifestations of racist or prejudicial behavior that occur when a social field becomes polarized along racist lines.

The underlings can and often do develop contrary racist attitudes, as Jews did against antisemites in old Europe, blacks against whites in America or South Africa, and Arabs against Jews in the contemporary Middle East. These can have major consequences, but their presence should not be allowed to mystify the basic power arrangements that undergird racism. Mutual hatreds abound in a divided society, indeed structure it, but do not in themselves change the power structure that ultimately gives rise to hate between peoples. Jewish hatred of gentiles during the centuries of Christendom's judaeophobia did not constitute a racism distinct from antisemitism. It was only the negative part of antisemitism, albeit one that left traces on Judaism that took on a malignant character once Israel became an expansive state and Jews were in power. These traces include internal racist hierarchies within both master and subaltern groups, witness the Ashkenazi-Sephardim polarity within Israel, or, to recur to other examples, the way Zulus and Xhosa have been set against each other in South Africa, or blacks of direct African as against West Indian background in the United States. Overlooking the distinction between the structure that generates racism and particular racist manifestations leads to a hopeless muddle in which the perpetrator and his victim are placed on the same moral level.

It is, finally, the state (or an equivalent, such as a chartered trading company in the early modern epoch of imperialism) that provides the structure that sets racism into motion. And the structure provides the scale by which we evaluate a racism's heft and decide what is to be done about it. We would hold in this regard that Zionism became profoundly racist once it achieved its state, nor can it ever cease being racist so long as the Jewish state is its necessary expression; that the basic structure of Zionist racism is set forth by the bad conscience; and that the racist character of Israel constitutes its most basic indictment, that it is *state-structured racism*.

One reason we invoke the bad conscience in the structure of Israeli racism is the vociferous degree to which racism is denied where Israel is concerned. It is truly amazing. Here is a country where top generals of the IDF have called Palestinians "drugged cockroaches in a bottle"; where the ultra-Orthodox speak openly about Arab subhumanity and are rewarded with settlements in the Occupied Territories; where soccer fans curse and attack Arab members of the national team; where in a poll taken early in 2006, more than two-thirds of Israelis would refuse to live in the same building as Arabs; where, in the 2006 national election that was supposed to "resolve" the nation's boundaries, the far-right Yisrael Beiteinu Party won ten seats on a platform calling frankly for "transfer" of Israeli Arabs out of the country where they are putatively citizens with voting rights; and where, as we have seen over and over, the entire society is structured around ethnic cleansing.[13] And yet, to raise the question of racism in polite, official or other Zionistically influenced circles is to be met with the most vehement assertion of Israel's non-racist bona fides, often accompanied by literal shrieking, furious denunciations, storming out of the room, and so forth. I recall attending a conference in Paris, of Marxists no less, held shortly after the 2001 Conference on Racism in Durban, where it virtually came to calling in the police to quiet down raging members of the audience who were screaming at the speaker for daring to suggest that the efforts of the World Conference Against Racism to reopen the matter of Zionism as a form of racism, were worthy of serious attention.[14]

There is a very important practical reason for this, as exposing the structurally racist character of Israel would put it in the same category as apartheid South Africa, with dire implications for Zionism. But there are also formidable subjective barriers to acknowledgment of the obvious, as anyone who has tried to discuss this matter in depth with a person under the influence of Zionism can attest. These stem directly from bad conscience, which acts as a permanent burr in the soul, causing the suitably jumpy to storm out of a room where Israel is being criticized, and triggering the persecutions by the Zionist lobby, which are carried out with a vindictive zeal that cannot simply be reduced to the very successful defense of Israel from criticism— although it contributes mightily to Israel's sense of impunity. For these reasons, both practical and subjective, Zionism has woven an amazing web of deception to conceal its racism and evade the linkage with South African apartheid.

This can fool only the suitably disposed or those bemused by the propaganda system—which is to say, a very large number of people. But it can never remove the stain. It is as simple as this: if you sign on to the idea of a Jewish state, you are taking the particularism that is the potential bane of any state, mixing it with the exceptionalism that is the actual bane of Judaism, and giving racism an objective, enduring, institutionalized, and obdurate character. You accept, in that one moment, a state that systematically denies basic human rights to a fraction of its people and systematically grants another set of people superior right over them. Thus racism is set into motion, and remains so, grounded in an exclusion based not on what the Other does but entirely on what the Other *is*, or to be more exact, *is not*, namely, Jewish. By this one gesture, no matter how one rationalizes a Jewish state as owed to the Jews by virtue of their sufferings, or ethical superiority, or promises made to ancestors, or generations of landlessness, or a Covenant with God, or cultural genius, or just because it feels good to have a state for one's own kind—one violates the whole law by which humanity has risen above the muck of narrow self-interest and cyclical vengeance. And you cannot overcome that violation unless you undo the compact that locks it into place. For you have set going an objective racism that inevitably brings along its subjective side in train. It is a self-made trap, of fourfold dimension:

The mark of bestiality. We have already observed that a divide exists between pre-modern and modern racism defined by the emergence of the notion of universal human right. This frames a value which, no matter how disregarded in practice, stands forth as a criterion of judgment against which all political formations must be measured. Before this notion arose, each place had its own deity and law, and so the exclusions characteristic of flawed societies were themselves dispersed and polymorphous. The rise of a notion of human right means, however, that *systematic* exclusion is necessary to rationalize the system, and that means proving the Other to be subhuman. In other words, it requires racism for legitimation. At the same time, each and every racism is now confronted with a benchmark by means of which it can be judged.[15] Thus racism arises out of the need to legitimate, and then becomes a fresh source of illegitimacy. The workings out of this dialectic have placed racism front and center in modern politics.

If only we can convince the world—and, crucially, ourselves—of the bestiality of these insect-like people, argues Zionism, then we can march forward on the path of Jewish redemption. The primary decision of the state, to simply accord inferior rights to non-Jews, can take place without immediate racist affect. But the abstraction necessary for legalisms also creates the space upon which the tropes of racist ideology can be written. These use as raw material the behavior of the oppressed. Each racism contains a template of the adaptations and struggles of the underlings, especially as these have been rendered irrational and self-destructive by circumstance and social definition. Shylock is a vicious, conniving, vengeful fellow, so sharply drawn that the mirror Shakespeare holds up to the world of generalized avarice from which he arises is often clouded by audiences who cannot bear to see the truth that an *oppressed* group is also *impressed* with the badness imposed by the overlord. African slaves torn from their home, who were deliberately shorn of culture, community, and family in order to render their labor more fully exploitable, could suffer the consequences of broken family patterns and being held in contempt. Some rose above this, others succumbed, and often, deeply wounded self-images would arise that impaired functioning. Racism saw to it that all, the strong and weak alike, were caught in the trap. Hence the blacks were regarded as incapable of "civilization," that is, as a kind of beast. When they rebelled passively by sabotaging their work, they were considered congenitally lazy; when they rebelled actively but indirectly they were considered innately criminal; and when they rebelled actively and directly they were considered violent by nature, as befitted their animal status. Similarly, when the desperation to which Palestinians are routinely driven erupts in one form of violence or another, the Zionist ideologue greedily pounces on the fact and blares it over his well-functioning network: Aha! The TERRORIST returns!

Aversion and denial. Since racial epithets require the expenditure of energy and bring down upon themselves a fresh cycle of accusation, a more parsimonious solution to the dilemmas of overlordship is to ignore the underling and simply deny his existence. Sharon's apartheid wall, along with being part of the land grab, is a pure culture of removing what is unpleasant from view and by all indications, quite popular with the citizens of Israel, who are said to cherish every opportunity to not think of those whom they have displaced. This is an instance of a structural tendency inherent to all racisms of the world.[16] It is routinely reinforced by pseudo-scholarship. The most notable example in the case of Zionism was the flap over Joan Peters' *From Time Immemorial*, which put the imprimatur of social science on the canard that Palestine was a "land without people" for a "people without land."[17]

The racist code. A legalized web of prejudice is also serviceable to racism, impersonally worsening the status of the underlings while removing them from view. In their construction of a Jewish state the founders of Israel drew upon centuries of experience in rabbinical obfuscation. In contrast to apartheid South Africa, which attempted to clothe its racism with utopian rhetoric, the Zionist state devised regulations to show that it was not racist at all. This was especially related to its need to present itself to the UN, which had passed the highly controversial resolution partitioning the country, as a bastion of democratic right.

Thus it is not that purchasing property across some 92 percent of the country is forbidden to Arab ownership, not at all. For the land is simply held by the Jewish National Fund for the benefit of Jews. *Tant pis* that Palestinians, poor things, somehow fail to meet this criterion. The labyrinthine legalisms set forth by the non-constitutional state would take a book to describe. Fortunately we have such a book, *Apartheid Israel*, meticulously assembled by Uri Davis, who calls himself a Palestinian Jew and lives in the Galilee Arab town of Sakhnin, which is in the process of being swallowed by Zionist confiscation and other forms of land-grabbing.[18] The reader may follow the details through Davis' eyes, from the mystifying Covenant root (it's God's will that we take this land); to the four classes of citizenship: Class A Jews, who have full rights; Class B Non-Jews, who lack equal access to material resources meted out by the state; Class C Non-Jews, the grotesquely named "present-absentees," who held property prior to 1948 and are now denied, as are their descendents, all rights to same as well as suffering the restrictions of Class B; and Class D Non-Jews, that is, any refugee or descendant of same, whose right as a citizen is to never be a citizen, whatever the UN or anybody else says. Thus Israel has a substantial group of people who dwell within its boundaries yet are "stateless in their own homeland."[19] The labyrinth extends to the maze of regulations governing who is allowed to return and who is not, birth and death certificates (a Jewish-born baby is registered as *Israeli* at birth, while an Arab-born baby is registered as *indefinite*), identity cards, and the network of regulations surrounding categories such as citizenship, nationality and religion. The *coup de grâce*, administered to deal with the endless irrationalities of this arrangement, is the establishment of a kind of shell game by which the state finesses the imperative of ministering to human rights by transferring crucial authority to non-governmental organizations or religious bodies, which—surprise!—are Zionist to the core. This has been a main avenue for the growth of the religious right in Israel, as it requires empowering the rabbinate in order to disguise state racism, and in the same gesture, legitimating their astounding bigotry and giving them a platform from which to spout racist propaganda worthy of the worst Nazi.

As Davis summarizes the technique:

> In other words, in the critical areas of immigration, settlement and land development the Israeli sovereign, the Knesset, which is formally accountable to all its citizens, Jews and non-Jews alike, has formulated and passed legislation ceding state sovereignty (including taxation) and entered into Covenants vesting its responsibilities with organizations such as the [World Zionist Organization, the Jewish Agency, and the Jewish National Fund] which are constitutionally committed to serving and promoting the interests of Jews and Jews alone. It is through this procedure . . . that legal apartheid is regulated in Israel. ... The same procedure has been applied by the Knesset in order to veil the reality of clerical legislation in Israel. Israel is a theocracy in that all domains pertaining to the registration of marriage, divorce and death are regulated under Israeli law by *religious courts* [which have been ceded to the Rabbinate since 1953].[20]

The result is that although in contrast to apartheid South Africa and the Jim-Crow US South, Israel does not have segregated public areas like beaches and buses, it envelopes its people in a dense web that defines groups as so rigidly split apart that it is only a short, inevitable step to see one group as fully human, the other as subhuman.

"*Normal racism.*" This mingles with the state-structured anti-Palestinian kind, both drawing from it and undergirding it. As with every society that has been subjected to imperialism, numerous racist scars persist in Israel. The oft-noted tensions between Ashkenazi and Sephardic Jews are vicissitudes of the

innumerable identities adopted by Jews over the centuries of
Diaspora. If there is an overriding fracture line between these
two "super-identities," it is that Ashkenazi signifies a "Jew of
the West," and Sephardim, a "Jew of the Orient," hence that
the great conflict between Europe and the East is overwritten
onto the interior of Israeli society. Since this conflict is no
abstraction to Israelis but the very sign of their struggle to
overwrite the West upon the East that is Palestine, it can be
no surprise to find outbursts of florid anti-Sephardic racism
within Israel. Still, it comes as a distinct shock to learn of the
dreadful "ringworm" experiment carried out in 1951, when
the state, then under the guidance of the great Ben-Gurion,
accepted 300 million Israeli lira from the United States (at a
time when the whole health budget was 60 million lira) to
test the effects of extreme radiation upon children. Under the
guise of treating "ringworm," some 100,000 youngsters, *all
Sephardic*, were given some 35,000 times the safe dose of X-
Rays to the head. At least 6000 died within a few days, and
innumerable cancers, birth defects, etc., followed. This was
the first instance of the "special relationship" between the
partners—occurring 16 years before the special relationship
is recognized to have taken hold—and was evidently the
result, on America's part, of the need to hide its ghoulish
nuclear radiation studies by finding a compliant stooge, and
on Israel's part, of the extreme penury of those days. But
nobody told the Ashkenazi bureaucracy to carry out the
experiment exclusively on Sephardic schoolchildren; that just
came spontaneously out of the racist matrix itself. We might
also point out that in its cold willingness to sacrifice innocents
to death by advanced technology, the fledgling state certainly
proved its bona fides as a representative of Western progress;
nor is it out of line to speculate that this, too, represents one
of those episodes of "identification with the aggressor" by
means of which Zionism has worked out its relationship with

the Nazis, who set the standard for ghoulish experiments on helpless victims.[21]

Efforts to defend the systematic inequalities of Israeli society usually take the form that this is necessary to give the Jews a homeland, such as every people deserves. However, whether or not we all deserve a "homeland," one has to face the fact that under certain conditions this achievement is simply impossible. No matter what Zionism does or says, there can be no homeland on stolen land, all the more so when the expropriated other remains an everyday presence. The same goes for the risible argument that, for example, "the French have their state. Why can't the Jews have their state?"[22] Well, needless to say, the Jews do have a state. But that doesn't put it in the same category as the state of France. After all, as Jehudith Harel has put it: "A Jew can be a Frenchman, but a Frenchman can't be a Jew"—unless he is one already or undergoes an arduous process of giving up his former identity.[23] Failure to acknowledge this distinction opens the way for the ravages of racism.

8
Slouching Toward Jerusalem

Dear Friends ... I was put under arrest today for "obstructing the work of soldiers" and though I didn't go to prison, I'd like to ask a few minutes of your time to tell you about what happened today, and the larger prison that all Palestinians in the Occupied Palestinian Territories are in. ... The soldiers kept telling me to leave the area, as I was in a closed military zone and preventing them from doing their job—really annoying them. I refused, telling them that there was no way I was going to leave these guys when it was obvious the soldiers were being very abusive, and even if they considered serving the occupation as their "job" there was no reason not to treat the people as human beings. ...

By 3.30 pm, more pushing, yelling, loosening and tightening of cuffs, Ramsy (the sick one) was released. One of the soldiers kept saying to us in English, "I want to kill him today." I asked why he couldn't realize that we're all human beings like he was. He replied, "*I'm not a human being, I'm a beast. I'm a beast, OK, and I want to kill him.*" He came up behind Rashed, grabbed [his] arms and tightened his plastic cuffs until they couldn't be tightened any more. When I protested, he yanked Rashed away and threw him behind an area of cinder blocks telling him to kneel so that he was out of sight. Rashed tried to stand up a few times, "my hands, my hands!" ... Nael, still cuffed, ordered from a young boy vendor, three colas, for me, Rick and himself. He urged me to leave, assuring me that he would be OK.
Email from a Palestinian woman[1]

THE TWINNED DEMONS OF the State of Israel, bad conscience and state racism, interact with its political economy and geostrategic position to produce an unmistakable breakdown of the moral fabric of the nation. This plays itself out in various configurations, which we may take up briefly here in the Israeli fractions comprised, first, by the Gush Emunim Religious-National Jews,[2] and then the liberal intelligentsia.

WE'RE LIKE JUDAEA, MAN

When I was a boy growing up in Brooklyn, I would often observe the "strange Jews" on the streets. Their rejection of what seemed the self-evident virtues of modernity and their embrace of marginalization were radically alien to an assimilationist youngster like me, whose chief ambitions were to root for the Dodgers, learn to swing a bat like their centerfielder Duke Snider, and grow up to become a famous scientist. Although Baruch Goldstein, the most notorious of this type, was not to be born in Brooklyn until eight years after my family left for the suburban purgatory of Baldwin, Long Island, it could have been that I passed members of his family, descendents of the founder of the Chabad Lubavitcher sect, as I walked about Coney Island Avenue and environs. Many years later I must have crossed paths with Baruch himself in the halls of the Albert Einstein College of Medicine, where he was a student during the period I was on the faculty of Psychiatry.

We have mentioned Goldstein before, whose infamy as the mass murderer of 29 Arabs at prayer in Hebron on February 25, 1994, was preceded a decade before by a public controversy for not treating Arabs (mainly Druse) during his stint as a doctor in the IDF. The reader will recall Goldstein's remarkable claim at the time that there were only two authorities whose teachings he followed: Moses Maimonides, the sainted medieval philosopher and physician to the Caliph of Alexandria; and Meir Kahane, the ultra-right founder of the Jewish Defense League and advocate of violence, who was assassinated in 1990.

This bizarre synchronization tells us much about the inner workings of Zionism. Maimonides was the flower of medieval Jewry, while Kahane is an extreme and strictly modern example of the type of "tough Jew" who sprang into action in the wake of Zionism's successes. The former epitomized the canon of a vast array of theocratic communities under the dominion of a rabbinate, as these became scattered over Europe and the Mediterranean basin and took hold in the interstices of Christendom and Islam. Contrary to the sentimentalized "Fiddler on the Roof" version of Jewish history, which has become reflexively accepted today, there were many rough edges to the internal lives of these communities; and some of this appears in the teachings of the great physician-philosopher, who along with his more sublime writings would proclaim, with the force of law, the desirability of not treating sick Gentiles and the killing of Gentile women who had sexual relations with Jews. Such hatreds are the product of powerlessness as played out in submission to patriarchal authority such as was represented by the rabbinate in the classical period.

Maimonides also counseled a kind of prudent opportunism. Jews were not to do anything that got them into trouble with the authorities—like not treating the Caliph, or a millennium later, getting in trouble with the IDF by not treating Druse personnel. And he never counseled wantonly slaying Muslims at prayer following which one is beaten to death by the survivors, which is about as much trouble as can be imagined. In fact, Goldstein himself did prudently treat injured Arabs on occasion, turning them over to another physician as soon as possible but nonetheless following Maimonidean principles. That he would have flagrantly violated the law in 1984 and gone way beyond a decade later means that we need invoke another set of influences overriding the great doctor's writings. Here one needs to recognize Kahane as Goldstein's true guide.

Kahane himself idolized Vladimir Jabotinsky, who was close to his parents and often visited the family home during Meir's boyhood. He grew up to carry forth Jabotinsky's legacy within Zionism, which was to express the actual implications of building a Jewish state, regardless of the niceties of conscience or the demands of diplomacy. Kahane's message was a simple one: *get rid of the Arabs*, by forced transfer if necessary, despite the uncomfortable resemblance to the behavior of a certain Central European state only a generation or so before. Maimonides would not have approved. Nor did the US State Department, which eventually designated his American-based organization, the Jewish Defense League, as terrorist. More interestingly still, the Israeli government arrived at the same position and banned Kahane's Kach ["Only This"] Party in 1985 from the Knesset for, of all things, being *racist*.

Kahane had finally won a seat for himself in the Knesset and Kach was poised to become Israel's third party, with substantial power to sway votes. At the same time Israel was embroiled in the opprobrium following the massacres in Lebanon and a drawn-out struggle to remove the stain of the UN resolution declaring *it* to be racist. Let us quote the source for what happened, the website of the Information Service of the Israeli Foreign Ministry:

> The Kach movement thus ran for election in 1984, winning 26,000 votes, and Kahane became a member of Knesset. He announced that Kach would not support any government that did not advocate the expulsion of the Arabs from Israel.
>
> In August 1985, the Knesset passed an amendment to the Basic Law: [sic] The Knesset, in accordance with the High Court's comment in the Kach case. The amendment added incitement to racism as grounds for barring a party from participating in elections. The law now states as follows:
>
> "A candidates' list shall not participate in elections to the Knesset if its objects or actions, expressly or by implication, include one of the following:
>
> 1) negation of the existence of the State of Israel as the state of the Jewish people; 2) negation of the democratic character of the State; 3) incitement to racism."
>
> Accordingly, in 1988, prior to the elections to the 12th Knesset, the Central Elections Committee disqualified the Kach list, basing its decision on the above amendment. In his appeal to the High Court of Justice, Kahane claimed that security needs justify severe measures of discrimination against Arabs. The Court rejected the

claim and the appeal, stating that the aims and actions of Kach
are manifestly racist.[3]

By 1991, with Kahane eliminated from the picture and
with the help of John Bolton and the neoconservative forces
in the United States, Israel finally got the racism resolution
set down, and no doubt breathed a collective sigh of relief.
Consider, however, the implications of the fourth paragraph
of the above extract. They are still in effect, and dictate that
the path to true democracy is indeed negated within the terms
of the "Only democracy in the Middle East," which continues
to do what Kahane declared to be the will of Zionism, namely,
get rid of Arabs, which certainly comes under the heading of
"incit[ing] to racism." For so long as Israel is to be a Jewish
state set down amidst hundreds of millions of Arabs that is
what it has to do.

The views toward Arabs of a Meir Kahane or a Baruch
Goldstein, or countless other Orthodox Jewish nationalists
now active in Israel, may have points of origin in the medieval
community; and it is understandable that a man like Goldstein
would have wanted to connect himself with so great a figure as
Maimonides. But the race hatred evinced here far surpasses the
medieval model on which it is based. The racism characteristic
of the premodern period (which included the Inquisition) never
went so deep as this. It was hate-filled, to be sure, and often
eventuated in cruelty and gruesome punishment; but it was
also basically tied to what might be called the predicates of a
person—what he professedly believed and practiced—and not
to the very subjective center of the other's being. Both Christian
and Muslim authorities (the former tending to be harsher than
the latter) had in mind the conversion of the victim and/or his
usefulness to their order of things. By contrast, the modern
racist, and here the figure of the Nazi needs be brought into
the frame, had with few exceptions a primary interest in what
the other *was*, rather than what he *did*. The other was an
affront to existence itself, and elimination from the face of

the earth was engrained in the very categories with which he was regarded.

The tough Jews in the Kahane-Goldstein lineage belong firmly to the modern style of racism. As Teddy Preuss wrote about the Goldstein affair soon after the deed in Hebron:

> Whenever an infidel was ready to convert to either Christianity or Islam, an inquisitor or Muslim Jihad fighter would, as a rule, spare his life. Goldstein and his admirers are not interested in converting Arabs to Judaism. As their statements abundantly testify, they see the Arabs as nothing more than disease-spreading rats, lice, or other loathsome creatures; this is exactly how the Nazis believed that the Aryan race alone had laudable qualities that were inheritable but that could become polluted by sheer contact with dirty and morbid Jews. Kahane, who learned nothing from the Nuremberg Laws, had exactly the same notion about the Arabs.[4]

The reaction of Rabbi Moshe Levenger to Goldstein's atrocity was extreme but nonetheless characteristic. Levenger, a leading figure in Gush Emunim, was asked the day after the Hebron massacre how he felt about the deaths of so many Palestinians, and replied: "I am sorry not only about those dead Arabs but also about dead flies."[5] The extremity here comprises an edge of a massive reef of ethnocentricity built upon hatred of the Other. Anyone who looks at Israeli society with an open eye will be impressed at the astonishing degree to which all attention is focussed upon the Jews and the Jews alone. It is not that the Arabs are treated with indifference, far from it. But not being Jewish they are not recognized as fellow human beings. And when they are seen as transgressing on Jewish ground they are unforgiven and set upon with vengeance. No longer capable of being ignored, they turn into lower and malignant beings: *beasts*.

The history of religious fanaticism may be as old as the history of religion. But the present cannot be explained as a linear extrapolation from the past; it must be seen, rather, in terms of its concrete context. The peculiarities of medieval

Judaism are to be grasped in relation to what was agitating that community at that time; this we have neither competence to do nor intention of doing. But part of every moment of historical time is the way its own past is internalized; and what is at issue here is the way Zionism incorporates its own representations of the Jewish past. Therefore what is wrong with Israel and Zionism is not the insertion of religious fanaticism into a secular-liberal state, implying that it is the crazy fundamentalists who prevent the state from rationally carrying out its "peace process."

Zionism had no use for fundamentalism until it became a state, since when its quotient of religious fanaticism has continually risen. Nor is there any convenient mapping of a religious tendency onto a political ideology. The assumption that Orthodox Judaism, for example, conduces to support for the State of Israel ignores not only those extreme religious Orthodox who continue to reject Israel because it is insufficiently Jewish (in not allowing for the accession of the Messiah before occupying the Holy Land); it also sets aside Orthodox groups who oppose Zionism on political grounds, like Neturei Karta, who can be seen marching in traditional religious dress alongside Palestinians and other anti-Zionist activists in demonstrations.[6]

Put properly, the question is, how and under what circumstances are the various shards of religious practice, which lie about in the storerooms of any faith, brought together and reassembled as fanaticism? For what reason does the liberal Zionist state require a dose of religious fanaticism? Here I should think that the notion of bad conscience offers a useful way of looking at things. Perhaps an excerpt from an email I received in 2004 from an intellectually sophisticated rabbi, whom I will call "C," will help clarify this. C had read the article in which I first advanced the notion of bad conscience in relation to Zionism,[7] and wished to comment upon it. He lost no time in affirming that his "theo-political worldview is the very right-wing religious zionism that you are so much opposed to," but that, nevertheless, he agreed with the crux of my argument, specifically, that "Zionism and democracy are incompatible." "Indeed," C went on,

> you are correct that this incompatibility causes a bad conscience in otherwise liberal Jews. *However, I am not a liberal Jew, and I have no guilt feelings in this regard.* [italics added] What divides us [that is, C and myself], essentially, is much more axiomatic than historical. The argument between us is the ancient argument between Athens and Jerusalem. That is to say, what is to be the source of our values, man or G-d? ... fundamentally, the worldviews of the West have been shaped by Greek thinking for almost three centuries. The Jewish idea, as opposed to the Greek one, is that man is certainly not the measure of all things, rather God is. Why do I believe that Eretz Yisrael belongs to [sic] Clal Yisrael? Is it because of Herzl, or Balfour, or the U.N.? By no means! I believe that the G-d of Israel gave us this Land as an eternal possession.

C goes on to challenge my "humanist" value system as afflicted with a fatal relativism, and concludes:

> In order for you to state that Zionism is morally wrong, you must disprove it axiomatically. If you cannot, then you are forced to admit that your argument against Zionism is subjective, and that you will advocate the deconstruction of the Jewish State by force of arms, and world opinion, rather than Truth. I pray that Hashem will guide you along the right path, and open your eyes through the words of His Torah.

Setting aside the issue of ultimates, about which we certainly disagree,[8] and simply looking at the working logic of Zionism, C and I are on the same page: Zionism can only be legitimated on the basis of the Covenant; yet it is forced to legitimate itself on the grounds of being a liberal-democratic state and hence slips into an implacable, guilt-generating contradiction and the bad conscience that ensues. Why forced? For two reasons: because the people who affirm its ideal are inextricably bound to modernity; and because of brutal necessity deriving from Israel's absolute dependence on the world capitalist system, which recognizes only one legitimate political economy. If it had a gazillion barrels of oil under its sands, like Saudi Arabia, then it could finesse the point and freely impose its ethnocracy. But, ah, the cruelty of geostrategic fate! Israel is only a poor little sister in the world system, forced to trade on its "unique" Jewish virtues and history of Jewish suffering, do the will of its Godfather, and receive its reward. Zionism *knows* this, that it cannot form a democratic state as an ethnocracy, but it cannot face itself and therefore falls into the grip of bad conscience.

Playing the card of the virtuous "only democracy," with its weeping soldiers, has taken Israel far and made it a major military power, but at a huge and growing cost. One calculus of this is in the economy of guilt. The Chosen path forces that guilt inward yet forbids its transmutation into conscientious-ness, so that all the screaming at critics or demonization of Palestinians cannot resolve the dilemma, but only seals the guilt inwardly. Guilt so constructed takes on a bestial character as it becomes conscious; rarely but tellingly will it implode and inundate the self—as the IDF soldier manifested in the epigraph with which this chapter begins: "*I'm not a human being, I'm a beast. I'm a beast, OK, and I want to kill him.*" One imagines that the insight was swiftly covered over and the soldier went about his business—but without transcendence, and still pursued by his demon.

It is logical, then, that a fraction of Jewry would rise in influence that can equably exteriorize the will of the state as divine and, guilt-free, think of Palestinians as no better than flies, or in some other bestial guise. For as C correctly understands but erroneously values, the most efficient way to evade the bugbear of bad conscience within the Zionist world is to embrace a medieval moral construction in which the internal-ization of guilt is short circuited through divine means. For the Orthodox nationalist, G-d's will trumps Man's conscience. This lifts the burden of guilt, or more often, keeps it from arising in the first place. The land is ours because G-d said so: all is justified; case closed. The codicil attached to this is barely stressed though it is strenuously lived out: that the fact of "G-d telling us so" means in practice the submission to Rabbi this or that telling us so on the authority of the Halakhah. These Jews wish to live like their medieval forebears, in rabbinically supervised communities within a larger state—which, as it turns out, finds them quite convenient for its purposes.

This is an escape without transcendence, even if one is never going to convince a religious nationalist, engorged with the feeling of spiritual power, of the fact. Escaping the onerous strictures of bad conscience is to remove the restraints upon the will except for those legislated from within the tribe through its rabbinical chiefs. It is to set up a downhill path at the end of which stand Meir Kahane and Baruch Goldstein. For such people, conscience is directly turned into enmity, and its judgmental quality turns into paranoia. This nasty complex turns against the victims of Israeli expansion, against other Jews, and even against the Zionist state as this tries to contend with reality while manipulating its attack dog settlers. A similar paranoia obtains for the mere remainder of humanity.

> Kfar Tappuach, a settlement near Yitzhar which is populated by followers of Meir Kahane, is home to an organization called the Jewish Legion. Its stated goals include training dogs to guard settlements in case of an Israeli Army pullout. One of its activists, Lenny Goldberg, who is originally from Queens, told me, "We've got to do this for ourselves. It's the new thing. The Israeli government doesn't want to help us, fine, so we're going to do our own self-defense. We're ready. We're ready to build a true Jewish state up here in the mountains. You remember when the Kingdom of Judaea split from the Kingdom of Israel?" he asked, referring to an event that occurred three thousand years ago. "It's like that. We're ready to go our own way. We're like Judaea, man."
>
> I asked if it was realistic to expect that several thousand settlers could hold off millions of Arabs, as well as the Israeli Army. "Realism? Forget realism," he said. "We're the nation that dwells alone. We can take care of our own Jewish state." Besides, he said, the dogs were very well trained.[9]

Back to basics, as they say.

"EXTERMINATE THE BRUTES!"

The reader will recognize "We're the nation that dwells alone" as a reprise of the Biblical identity of the ancient Israelites. But the Orthodox nationalist in the settlement is also a kind of dog, well-trained and kept on a tight leash for all his ferocity. The settler-fanatics not only do not have a state, but they use their statelessness to create legitimacy as the "true Jews," contrasted to the false compromisers and sell-outs comprised by the State of Israel and its satraps. They remain dependent upon the state they despise, however, which gives them scraps of power but no more, and periodically whacks them across the snout to show them who's boss. Like good guard dogs, the settler-fanatics can be tied up when the master determines, as may be the case in the next phase of Zionist expansion if Israel decides that it has gone as far in the Occupied Territories as the world will tolerate. This is not to say that there will not be some havoc in the process, because they are also not dogs, but stubborn and prideful people who will have revenge. But there will be no more than that. Israel is too deeply rooted in the institutions of the West to permit its transformation into a theocracy; indeed, those roots tell us just what is wrong with it, which is better represented by the liberals who run the state apparatus than the Orthodox fanatic.

In any system so marked by contradictions as that presided over by Zionism, one is bound to get dyads of this kind, partners in mutual loathing such as marks a bad but enduring marriage. So it is with the State of Israel and its fundamentalists, and between the latter and the liberal faction, who eschew religion as a vital force, adhere to the rules of the state, and take refuge in its aura of rationalized power. The term, liberal, must be seen in the full complexity of its two chief political meanings: as the mark of modern bourgeois democracy that realizes capital; and also as the "progressive" edge of that order. The "liberal" within politics, then, is attached to the modern, "liberal" state, and wishes to reform this—a project that would be feasible if only the Dark Forces can be eliminated. There are many liberal Zionists who don't approve of what Israel does but remain very attached to what Israel *is*, and hasten to remind everybody at every opportunity that "of course I support Israel's right to exist." Their goal, accordingly, is to normalize Israel, reform it, and bring it into the community of nation states. Sometimes they are satisfied with the notion of a "peace process" and the goal of a Two-State resolution to Israel/Palestine.

In contemporary Israel, no one fits into this role better, albeit by revealing its own dark side, than the eminent historian Benny Morris. We have frequently used Morris' work in this study, for his broad and synoptic view of the history of the relations between Zionists in Israel and the Palestinians and his contribution to unmasking the terroristic violence that spurred the Nakhba. As for his liberal credentials, we may turn to his own words, drawn from a famous interview he gave to *Ha'aretz* in January, 2004: "I always voted Labor or Meretz or Sheli [a dovish party of the late 1970s], and in 1988 I refused to serve in the territories and was jailed for it. ... I still think of myself as left-wing. I still support in principle two states for two peoples."[10]

The interview has two major themes: the first announces some new historical findings that were to appear in his latest book, and the second—the part that sent shock waves through the intellectual world—gives his evaluation of these. As for the history, Morris has learned that "there were far more Israeli acts of massacre than I had previously thought. To my surprise, there were also many cases of rape ... [also] we have to assume that the dozen cases of rape that were reported, which I found, are not the whole story. They are just the tip of the iceberg." As for the massacres, by which Morris means an explicit set of marching orders "to uproot the villagers, expel them and destroy the villages themselves," that is, to commit "ethnic cleansing" in its most violent form, the orders came from Ben-Gurion himself, who implicitly condoned wanton violence, as shown by the fact "that no one was punished for these acts of murder. Ben-Gurion silenced the matter. He covered up for the officers who did the massacres." The worst in terms of body count was the massacre at Lod, which (along with others) exceeded the death toll at Deir Yassin by more than a hundred. In a word, Ben-Gurion, like Jabotinsky and later, Kahane, was a "transferist": the Arabs had to be removed at all costs so that Israel would arise. All in all, claims Morris, [Palestinian sources give a higher figure, as does Ilan Pappe] some 800 people were killed in 24 massacres, a terror incentive for the "cleansing" of some 700,000 Palestinians and the destruction of over 500 villages: The Nakhba.[11]

And what does Morris think of such a thing? He is frank, and shocks the interviewer: "Ben-Gurion was right. If he had not done what he did, a state would not have come into being. That has to be clear. It is impossible to evade it." And Morris sees why quite clearly: Ben-Gurion "understood that there could be no Jewish state with a large and hostile Arab minority in its midst. There would be no such state."

"Right" here admits of two meanings: First, that Ben-Gurion was *correct* in this judgment, that is, he saw the practical situation for what it was; and second, that he was *justified* in deciding to unleash the Nakhba, given the larger meaning of a Jewish state. We must also be quite clear: we agree that Ben-Gurion was correct in his practical assessment. Given the context, anybody who thinks that the kind of state envisioned by Zionists could have emerged with the ghost of a chance of survival without the Palestinians substantially cleared from the land, is hopelessly naïve.

But morally *justified*? That is another story, which depends upon one's grasp of the whole and the history to which one has committed. If one has made the compact with Zionism, which herds together its various forms into a single conquering force stretching in an unbroken chain from Herzl to Ben-Gurion and now Morris, well, then, one cannot hold back at this moment, or the whole immense effort is lost. Had not Arlosoroff the moderate (see Chapter 2) said the same—and that was before the Holocaust put the seal of destiny on Zionism? And so Morris states what is existentially compelling: that if one believes in Zionism, then the Jewish state is necessary, and what has to be done to get it, in this case, the violent ethnic cleansing of 700,000 Palestinians, is also necessary.

He says so freely, ostentatiously denying remorse and guilt: "If you expected me to burst into tears, I'm sorry to disappoint you. I will not do that." Has Morris freed himself from the chains of bad conscience and achieved some kind of serenity through self-recognition? Well, no, not at all. For the liberal intellectual does not have the luxury granted the Orthodox believer. G-d's word, short circuiting the need for justification, is not heard by him. Instead, Morris must *prove* his point. His conscience and his reason must function together—but the conscience is *bad*, and as the argument reaches down into it, he cracks under the pressure of justification and goes haywire. Instead of tears Morris gives us a wild dithyramb in which the fear and loathing that lie at the dark side of Zionist existence spill forth. Like Conrad's Kurtz, the Ur-Colonialist on the banks of the River Congo surrounded by those the empire has annihilated, his reason succumbs to hatred and he hatches dreams of extermination:

- Morris commits outrageous category errors: "the Arab people gained a large slice of the planet. Not thanks to its skills or its great virtues, but because it conquered and murdered and forced those it conquered to convert during many generations. But in the end the Arabs have 22 states. The Jewish people did not have even one state. There was no reason in the world why it should not have one state. Therefore, from my point of view, the need to

establish this state in this place overcame the injustice that
was done to the Palestinians by uprooting them." This is
to be sure, standard Zionist fare, and amazingly shabby
reasoning for a prominent historian: the poor little Jews
against the whole of Arabia, as though the property of
being "Arab" defines an undifferentiated unity in which
the Palestinians are just a fungible part, like a bank deposit
that can be moved from here to there, not a vast and
variegated set of cultures, nor people who have a claim to
land—in this case because of the elementary fact that they
happen to have lived there for a very long time. Then, in
the middle portion of the interview, he increasingly links
Jews with the West, and by the end sinks into the rhetoric
of War of Civilizations. Now Israel has become not just
the persecuted Jewish people who need their "even one
state," but an outpost of a higher social order. He goes
where even George W. Bush fears to tread in making this
claim: "I think that the war between the civilizations
is the main characteristic of the 21st century. I think
President Bush is wrong when he denies the very existence
of that war. It's not only a matter of bin Laden. This is
a struggle against a whole world that espouses different
values. And we are on the front line. Exactly like the
Crusaders, we are the vulnerable branch of Europe in
this place." Europe, Morris seems to have overlooked,
has quite a bit of conquest, murder and forced conversion
in its own background, which the Zionists were only too
eager to condemn when it suited their purposes. Now,
however, the eminent historian identifies the Zionists with
one of the worst episodes of European aggression, the
Crusades, a particularly dreadful episode for the Jewish
people, untold thousands of whom were massacred in
the process. Morris would have us feel sorry for the poor
Crusaders, made "vulnerable" by their invasion. This is
truly deranged thinking.

- He pours down upon the Palestinians a torrent of racist abuse, beginning with the above slur on the murderous Arabs (which tramples all over the actual history of Arabia) and proceeding to prodigies of invective that justify the direst recommendations. Forget the Crusades: this problem is even more basic: "the West today resembles the Roman Empire of the fourth, fifth and sixth centuries: The barbarians are attacking it and they may also destroy it." Being barbarians, the Arabs have barbarian values. "There is a deep problem in Islam.[12] It's a world whose values are different. A world in which human life doesn't have the same value as it does in the West, in which freedom, democracy, openness and creativity are alien. ... Revenge is also important here. Revenge plays a central part in the Arab tribal culture." Morris then turns to what the poor besieged West can do "to repulse this wave of hatred. The phenomenon of the mass Muslim penetration into the West and their settlement there is creating a dangerous internal threat. A similar process took place in Rome. They let the barbarians in and they toppled the empire from within." An astounding reading of history—has not the man read Gibbon?

- It gets worse. "Palestinian society is in the state of being a serial killer. It is a very sick society. It should be treated the way we treat individuals who are serial killers." And how should that be done, Doctor? Do you recommend legal-juridical means such as society uses to correct human malefactors? No, because the Palestinians are not human. Once more, the Beast returns: "Something like a cage has to be built for them. I know that sounds terrible. It is really cruel. But there is no choice. There is a wild animal there that has to be locked up in one way or another." Would a wall do? Well, one would suppose so; any effort to enclose the Palestinians would likely meet with Morris' approval. But it wouldn't, so to speak, be the final solution. That was given earlier in the interview when Morris criticizes Ben-Gurion, not for ethnic cleansing but for not going all the way: "If he was already engaged in expulsion, maybe he should have done a complete job. I know that this stuns the Arabs and the liberals and the politically correct types. But my feeling is that this place would be quieter and know less suffering if the matter had been resolved once and for all. If Ben-Gurion had carried out a large expulsion and cleansed the whole country—the whole Land of Israel, as far as the Jordan River."

Ben-Gurion was not the sole "transferist" then. Morris, too, is a transferist, more so than Israel's Founding Father. He's just as much a transferist as Meir Kahane, though he tries to temper the upwelling of Zionist desire with *weltschmerz*, rather than use it for demagogic purpose. That's a distinction but not a real difference between the religious nationalist and the tormented liberal-Zionist, who goes beyond the ordinary limits of the liberal vision into the dark truth about Israel. Morris realizes that the Jewish state would not have arisen without committing massive terrorism, but he is stunned and falls into the black hole of race hatred to justify the deed, and calls for its repetition on a larger scale.

There are many patterns through which the bad conscience is played out. In the course of his interview, Morris twice reveals what loyalty to the West means:

- Seeking to minimize the scale of Zionist criminality during the Nakhba, he plays the numbers game. "You have to put things in proportion. These are small war crimes." Only 800 dead, that's "peanuts" compared to Bosnia; and then he gratuitously adds, "In comparison to the massacres the Russians perpetrated against the Germans at Stalingrad, that's chicken feed." Here is a novel reading of history in which the *Wehrmacht*, having launched the most violent war of all time, becomes the victim of violence. Is Morris saying that the Soviets weren't properly grateful to the invaders who had caused tens of millions of deaths and more destruction than had ever been meted out in human history?[13] That the Communists, being barbarians, were insufficiently appreciative of the Western values of "freedom, democracy, openness and creativity" represented by Nazism? Can it be that the victimized invaders, whether Christian Crusaders or Nazis, are standing in for the IDF?

- Employing another well-worn trope of justification, that the ethnic cleansing of Palestinians was justifiable because done in a great cause, Morris says, "Even the great American democracy could not have been created without the annihilation of the Indians. There are cases in which the overall, final good justifies harsh and cruel acts that are committed in the course of history." This "you can't make an omelette without breaking eggs" argument is a well-known rationalization for aggression. It is a dull, heartless and mechanical view of history, which in this instance opens upon some reflections.

The annihilation of the American Indians can truly be called a kind of Holocaust, differing from what Nazi Germany did to the Jews chiefly in the extended way it unfolded and in the markedly different prior histories of perpetrator and victim.[14] It is certainly the case that the United States *as it exists today* would not have arisen without annihilating the Indians, just as it would not have arisen as we know it without chattel slavery of Africans. But the United States as it exists and what Morris calls the "great American democracy" should not be conflated. There have been contributions made by the United States to democracy; but these may be reckoned as having arisen *despite* the atrocious record of Indian-killing, either as the product of innumerable struggles from below to democratize the conditions of life, or more pointedly, from various appropriations of Indian ways. These latter would include the lessons the framers of United States democracy learned from the egalitarian Indian societies, especially of the Iroquois nations, and also the countless examples of the free intermingling of common peoples—the "going native" on the part of whites (especially women), as well as communal arrangements between Indians, escaped slaves and poor whites, at times of a frankly utopian character.[15]

The "American democracy" would have turned out much better had such processes prevailed instead of the genocide against the indigenous. This could have happened; that it didn't happen is a matter of having the wrong class forces ending up on top, from which place they could impose their economic dominion and systematic racism, according to the ethos of Puritan elites. It was these who carried out the extermination of Indians, often co-opting the lower classes into their project. And it is to a very great extent this annihilation—along with slavery, indentured servitude, and the violent suppression of workers—that made America a racist society and eventuated in a nation state whose democratic facade has accompanied and helped to conceal an endlessly repeated record of blood, fire, and lawless intervention.[16] Benny Morris puts on rose-colored glasses when looking at Israel's great protector. But the country of which Simon Bolivar said back in 1828 that it was destined to plague the world in the name of democracy, and which entered the twenty-first century with a man of the calibre of George W. Bush as its president and a population riddled with Christian fundamentalism, has a lot to answer for—including, to be sure, its partnership with Israel.

There are few generalizations that hold up across the historical spectrum. One of these is the necessity of coming to grips with one's national past in order not to repeat its crimes. The United States has a dreadful record of not accepting responsibility for its history, and so it constantly repeats its crimes. Think of how much better the "great American democracy" would be if it were to begin to confront its murderous past—one sign of which would be to build a great museum about the annihilation of indigenous cultures, and another one on the slave trade and its consequences, alongside, or even, heaven forfend, instead of the Holocaust museum, which deflects attention from America's lost history. Because what the United States did to its Indians and black slaves is at the center of its existence and demands priority.

And the Holocaust museum in Jerusalem should be accompanied by a museum along the lines of the great museum in Johannesburg that gives witness to the crimes of a racist regime—and to their overcoming—because the racist expropriation and oppression of an indigenous people is at the center of the existence of Israel as it was of apartheid South Africa, and will not begin to be overcome unless it is recognized and reflected upon.[17]

One might imagine a series of exhibition rooms in such a museum, dedicated to the various transgressions spawned by Zionism from its inner being, inexorable deductions from the "bad idea":

- From its beginnings, Israel has been internally compelled to annihilate an existing indigenous society; once it achieved statehood, and especially as it became the occupier of what Palestinian land was left over from 1948, it turned itself into a machine for the manufacture of human rights abuses;
- These latter necessarily and normally configure about an all-pervading ethnocentricity that readily turns racist and is sown throughout society;
- The culmination is a system as structurally racist as apartheid South Africa, however distinct many of the external forms may be;

- It produces militarism with its associated disregard for life in every corner of society and spreads this around the region and beyond, attacking its neighbors in an incessant drumbeat of aggression;
- It has perverted the memory of the greatest calamity ever to befall the Jewish people, the Shoah, or Holocaust, in order to aggrandize itself;
- Alongside this it has degraded a great world religion, Judaism, and fostered the rise within it of a narrow fundamentalism and stifling orthodoxy tooled to the needs of the state;
- It has severely undercut the principle of lawfulness through its flouting of innumerable UN resolutions designed to check its behavior; most seriously, it has actively contributed to the deadly spread of nuclear weapons by withholding its own arsenal, built clandestinely with the disgraceful collusion of the United States, from any international covenant;
- It has further, and bizarrely, entangled itself with the United States, doing the latter's dirty work, in a relationship that has deeply corrupted American politics, and driven American Jewry into a moral abyss;
- Said dirty work has included material support for a great many vicious regimes whose chief stock in trade has been violent repression, for example, apartheid South Africa, with whose weapons industries Israel worked hand in glove and to whom Israel smuggled automatic weapons and other antipersonnel devices, disregarding the will of the international community; this culminated in working hand-in-glove with the apartheid regime to help it build nuclear weapons.[18]
- It has hastened the environmental destruction endemic to capitalist society, by its demographic pressure, its oppression of Palestinians, its militarism, and its lawlessness;

- It has been the greatest single instigator in the rise of political Islam, the hinge around which much of our history turns. It is one of the great ironies that dog Zionism that, arising as a reaction against the persecutory tendencies of the West, it should have become the spearhead of Western persecution, with dreadful consequences. Nobody has put this better than Edward Herman:

> The situation in Palestine is also very important because hundreds of millions of Arabs and a billion or more people of the Islamic faith, and billions beyond that, interpret the West's treatment of the Palestinians as a reflection of a racist and colonialist attitude toward Arabs, Islamists, and Third World people more broadly. It is a producer of anti-Western terrorism, but also and even more importantly a deep anger, hatred and distrust of the West and its motives. It is a cancer that bodes ill for the future of the human condition.[19]

To all of these charges, the Zionist will respond: It's not our fault, but that of Arab barbarism, terrorism, and the antisemitism that is built into the human genome and persecutes the Jews down through the ages. This is the intellectual surface of the above-mentioned moral abyss. Hopefully the arguments advanced in this work will have helped put to rest this shameful line of reasoning by exposing the roots of the problem in the Jewish state and the Zionism that animates it. Put most directly, the fateful—and ultimately fatal—decision for Zionism brings on all these abuses in train.

Having demonstrated so much, however, only takes us to the threshold of what matters. What can be done about this state? How can a just peace arise in the tormented land of Israel/Palestine?

Part Three

Zionism Overcome

9

Beyond the Two-state Solution

I should much rather see Jews living together with the Arabs on the basis of living together in peace than the creation of a Jewish state ... [M]y awareness of the essential nature of Judaism resists the idea of a Jewish state, with borders, an army, and a measure of temporal power, no matter how modest. I am afraid of the inner damage Judaism will sustain—especially from the development of a narrow nationalism within our own ranks ... We are no longer the Jews of the Maccabee period. A return to a nation in the political sense of the word, would be equivalent to turning away from the spiritualization of our community which we owe to the genius of our prophets.
Albert Einstein in *Ideas and Opinions*, 1954.

I think what came out [of my work as a historian] is something which I think many, many Palestinians before me realized, but for me it took this individual journey into the past to understand that. I was taught as an Israeli academic that there is a very complex story there, and in fact what you find out is that this is a very simple story, a story of dispossession, of colonization, of occupation, of expulsion. And the more I go into it, the clearer the story becomes, even it becomes simpler, and it also brought me to think of the state of Israel, and the Jewish majority in it, in very much the same terms that I used to think about places such as South Africa, and the white supremacy regime there. So I think this is the natural, main conclusion.
Ilan Pappe[1]

THESES ON ANTI-ZIONISM

IN A FIELD CONFIGURED by chains of vengeance and retribution, tracking down "who started it" never can get to the root of the problem. This applies to the riots of 1929, the wars of 1948 and 1967, the collapse of the Oslo Accords, the Second Intifada, as well as each and every act of aggression within the whole history of Israel/Palestine. Each of these is a story, and for each story there is a counter-story, with "another side." What matters, however, is to get beyond the level of "sides." We need to grasp the whole of things, and its basic historical movement and form. This cannot be determined by any merely empirical study. It needs concern for underlying structure and inner relationships, that is, basic principles. The nature of these principles cannot be given in advance as a simple set of rules. They unfold in the course of an inquiry, the object of which is not to determine "who started it," or who has the better claim according to the rationalizations of imperial states, the "Word of G-d", or some conjured-up legalism. The question is, what is this all about according to the standards of justice and the well-being of the human community?

1.   *The most basic principle is respect for the inherent dignity of each and every person.*
     The precondition of all human rights is the inherent and integral dignity of each human being, determined by respect for that individual's value as a freely constituted person. This applies as well to the extension of human right into doctrines such as democracy, anarchism, and socialism. Integral dignity does not arise from any particular belief or merit. It can only be grounded in the affirmation that we all belong to the same species in relation to the universe; thus it becomes a true universal. To this way of thinking, humanity is not separate from nature, nor to be sure, are we over nature. We are, rather, that part of nature granted imagination, creativity, and the capacity for freedom. When we affirm the inherent dignity of each and every person, we affirm those powers and beyond them, nature's formative power. This may be known under the various names given

to god, the divine principle, and so forth. Therefore when we separate ourselves from nature, or equivalently, from other people, we diminish nature and "god." The core spiritual beliefs of "first" or aboriginal peoples frequently contain this insight; thus did the American Indians often welcome the Europeans with generosity, much to their rue. The whole history of estrangement, or, what comes to the same thing, the whole estrangement of history, is the falling away from this realization. The struggle for what is called a better world is a struggle to regain it. This achievement has never ceased being contested, and never more fiercely than in the subject at hand. But its basic truth should not be denied, else we fall into the abyss that happens to be our fragmented, hate-filled, that is, existing world.

2. *"Basic principles" incorporate the categories of responsibility and justice.*
The responsible agent is a human being with the capacity to choose and the power to make a difference—to do and undo, including the admission of mistakes—and to become self-conscious of this power. Justice is grounded in the sustenance of the inherent dignity of every person. This extends naturally to his or her right to not be denied the necessities of life; such necessities include the physical conditions of life, and also the opportunity to fully express one's humanity, including spiritually. Justice pertains to the connection between people; and it can only be fully realized when those connections are fully affirmed. Therefore justice is unitary and indissoluble across all humanity, though each of us lives it concretely according to our situation. The responsible person recognizes the injustices she brings about and accepts the necessity for undoing or overcoming them according to the power she

wields. When we speak about "people of good will," we mean those who recognize the primacy of this goal.

The victim of injustice is not without responsibility, and the domain of his responsibility, like that of the perpetrator, includes the undoing of injustice. But since injustice has been done to him, and includes the deprivation of those things necessary for life, he is obliged to fight to restore them. Therefore invaded and occupied people have the right to defend themselves, defense being the preservation of integrity and dignity. When defense turns into revenge, however, then it enters a new cycle of injustice. No "normal" (in the sense of being shaped by the actual, fallen world) human being is immune from the temptation to vengeance; and all have the obligation to fight this temptation.

With these basics in mind we can examine the matter at hand more closely.

3. *No group of people is inherently better than any other, or "special" in any way.*
    All humans are equivalently unique; and anybody who fancies himself chosen by God is by that measure fallen. It is impossible to ground the notion of exceptionalism in any spiritual value inasmuch as the ground of every spiritual value is the universality of our being within nature. For a group to say that they are the Chosen People of the Divine Being, who promised them a certain territory, is unworthy of their humanity, not to mention, intelligence. It is perfectly understandable why certain peoples would have constructed such a belief irrespective of any divine being, as did the ancient Israelites with their Covenant, which bcame incorporated into the notion of being "a people apart." This can be coherently explained as an entirely subjective and instrumental act: it feels better to think of oneself as special in relation to God, especially

in hard times, and the resulting sense of group cohesion can be very useful in a hostile world, as it has been during the course of Judaism and Zionism's ascension to power. But this cannot justify such a notion, or overcome its essential estrangement, which is the particular dilemma of Judaism. The finer minds of the faith have sought to inflect the Covenant so that it meant that Jews are obliged to develop themselves spiritually and ethically. Well and good, but at some point this higher development has to lead to jettisoning the Covenant itself. For once it is fulfilled, the sense of specialness can no longer be maintained without corrupting the Jewish faith. Such has occurred in the widespread effort to authenticate Israel as an exception to the general laws and rules of humankind, one of the most pernicious aspects of the wars of Zion.

4. *No amount of previous suffering can legitimate present injustice.*
    The horrors of the Holocaust understandably reinforced the Zionist resolve for a strong Jewish state. But this was also an instance of exceptionalism, hence unjustifiable. The move commited Zionism to using the Holocaust as a means of legitimation for violence; thus it entered the cycle of revenge and has not only answered evil with evil, but with greater evil because, having achieved state power, it could marshall maximum force in order to legitimate violence. This has betrayed the memory of the victims of the Holocaust. Moreover, since Israel's coming to power has been at the expense of others who understandably resist having their land and homes taken away, and since these others never did the Jews any harm before the arrival of Zionism, a triple injustice was committed by Holocaust-driven state formation in Palestine: perpetuating revenge, accelerating this through the agency of the state, and doing so to people other than the real malefactors.[2] The past

needs to be overcome and not repeated in a recycling of injustice. The only legitimate response to a massive evil like the Holocaust is to step off the wheel of vengeance and work with all one's strength to build a world in which Holocausts cannot happen, which is to say, a just world that respects integral human right.

5. *No state has an absolute right to exist; hence all states are to a degree, illegitimate.*

States come and go across the field of history. They proclaim themselves immortal, hang around, then proceed to crumble away. This represents an acceleration of the ordinary breakdown processes within nature because states are a twofold falling away from our integrity as a species: externally, they set themselves up against other states (or nowadays, against the shadow-states of "terrorists"); and internally, they are set up for the benefit of a ruling class, that is, they perpetuate an unjust division within society. To say, therefore, that any state has an inherent "right to exist" is to deny the power of humanity to become conscious, responsible for history and able to overcome injustice. There is nothing immortal about a state, which is no more than a kind of revocable contract, optimally embedded in a constitution, between society and its governing body. The great achievement of the Enlightenment—remember the American Declaration of Independence—was to see through this and recognize that the state must stand before the bar of a higher law: fidelity to basic human rights. We may say that states need to be made precarious through a reminder of their basic illegitimacy and delusional character. We need to be aware, however, that such precariousness stirs up dangerous degrees of anxiety. Every state sells itself as the provider of "security" against the forces of darkness within and without. In our fallen world, configured by injustice and revenge, a grain of truth is embedded within the propaganda. And the capacity of states to marshall and deploy what they call legitimate violence is quite impressive. One needs therefore to proceed with care in undoing state-sponsored delusions—but undo them we must.

6. *States may either be relatively or absolutely illegitimate.* The chief consideration is this: are there self-corrective mechanisms within the social contract that comprises the legal foundation of the state, or not? In the former instance, which covers a great range of possibilities, the state is *relatively* illegitimate (which is to say, relatively legitimate), in that its violations of human right are at least potentially remediable through the given contract. Most of what passes for "democracy" in this world is of this type, including the "polyarchies" that infest the developing world,[3] as well as the rapidly deteriorating bourgeois democracy of the United States. All these can be said to verge on absolute illegitimacy, in that genuinely popular forces are thwarted by a variety of means from exercising their democratic birthright. Nonetheless, potential pathways exist within the given arrangement of things to at least envision this. For example, in the United States, actual possibilities remain for massive popular pressure to force Bush out of office, to build a serious alternative party, and so forth, however dim the chances may be. However, states can become *absolutely* illegitimate, according to the degree to which political structure seamlessly imposes ruling class hegemony: monarchies like Saudi Arabia, fascist dictatorships like Pinochet's Chile, the rule by military junta as in Myanmar, or one-party states that ruthlessly impose capitalism, like China;[4] along with these we take into account other instances such as often obtain in Africa, where state formation has simply broken down, leading to hellish cases of warlordism and/or civil war.

There are however also certain instances of absolute state illegitimacy in which the forms taken by human rights violation have the peculiar power to radiate across the human community. Apartheid South Africa was one such; Israel, the subject of present concern, is another.

7. *A racist state is absolutely illegitimate.*
Racism is often banally reduced to individual cases of hateful or prejudical behavior. But the truth is that in the category of racial domination lies the leading edge of humanity's fallen condition. This is because racism exposes the violation of essential dignity in the most readily universalizable way. A hundred years ago, two hundred years ago, brutal race oppression was a fact, but there were few categories by means of which humanity could become conscious of this. Today, we have evolved to the point, thanks in part to an emerging global society at the tail end of the break-up of colonial empire, in which racist exclusion can be perceived as intolerable. Therefore it is incumbent upon people of good will to give priority to anti-racist struggle. One does not expect the snug minority atop global society to get this point, nor the considerable numbers of people whose skin color or social position enable them to identify with this minority. But there are billions of the "non-white," including the Arabic and Islamic masses, whose historical being is forged against the dominance of the West, and the racism against whom has ensued from this. In the context of the suppression and potential rise of these masses, structurally produced racist oppression becomes the supreme crime against humanity. It is the imposition of a condition of radical separation simply because of what a person is not. If recognition of the intrinsic dignity of each human being comprises the point at which human ethical development is realized, then systematic suppression of that recognition becomes

the point of barbarism. When this barbarism is imposed by a state that professes membership in the society of Western democracies and comes trailing clouds of utopian glory and carrying a stack of Biblical justifications, why then, the real character of that system, its radical denial of humanity to a non-European people, had better not become open knowledge, or the very right of the racist state to exist can be taken away. This is what happened to apartheid South Africa, and what is poised to happen to Zionist Israel.

8. *Israel, as a Jewish state, is a racist state.*
    The question is often raised: does Zionist Israel practice a form of apartheid? This is useful but can lead to a muddle in which one tries to squeeze the particular features of Israeli society into a mold defined by the particular features of South African society. The better question is: are Zionist Israel and apartheid South Africa both instances of absolutely illegitimate statehood, namely, that which produces racism on an expanding scale and has no internal means of correcting this, for structural reasons? We have developed the theme at considerable length and need not dwell upon the argument here, except to say that the prodigious effort to deny the glaring fact that Israel is a racist state, or even to allow any serious inquiry into it in the great range of Western liberal institutions such as universities, foundations, or the media, is proof positive that this question is worth posing. To say it once more (and considering the resistances, one cannot say it often enough), one cannot build, much less sustain, democracy, whose ground is the provision of universal human rights to human beings, by defining human beings according to what faith or ethnic identity they possess. If racism is the exclusion from universal humanity according to what a person is not, the Jewish state is the imposing of the

definition of *"what a person must be"* that ensures this exclusion along with all the forms of racism that ensue from the imperial consequences of this exclusion. The notion of a "democratic Jewish state" is *ipso facto* racist. Racism and democracy are mutually exclusive; the former haunts the latter in its bad conscience. The racism of Israel resides in its basic social compact (and as we have seen, keeps this compact from becoming a constitution, thus preserving the lawlessness inherent to the Jewish state). Israel is very explicit in declaring that there is no path within Israel's system for challenging the Jewishness of the state. One need only remember the anti-Meir Kahane law of 1985, which says this directly, with the effrontery—I believe the Yiddish equivalent is *Chutzpah*—to add other statutes declaring Israel democratic and non-racist by prohibiting "1) negation of the existence of the State of Israel as the state of the Jewish people; 2) negation of the democratic character of the State; 3) incitement to racism." If one can make sense of this, then *Alice in Wonderland* is Aristotelian logic.

The many human rights offences of Israel, which have been summarized toward the close of the last chapter, are the direct consequences of the contradictions spelled out here. They follow from the basic assumptions of Zionism, and are not mere abuses of those assumptions, the way, for example, giving corporate wealth and power control over democracy in the United States is an abuse. One can imagine the American people rising up and forcing the passage of a law against corporate control over campaign funds; but one cannot imagine Israelis voting the Jewish state out of existence. It's against the law to do so—a "law" unrestrained by constitutionality.

9. *The problem, then, is with Zionism and the Jewish state as such, and not its illegal occupation of the West Bank.*

The horizon of liberal intervention in the affairs of Israel is to end the Occupation of the West Bank, after which Israel is supposed to settle down to become a normal state, and the Palestinians are to get their own state, hence, a "Two-State" outcome. Many well-meaning people adopt this limit, essentially because they are afraid to look further. But it won't work. The Occupation, which undoubtedly needs to be ended, is simply an inevitable manifestation of the fundamental goal of the Jewish state, namely, elimination of Palestinian society. From another angle, getting Israel to relinquish its Occupation—we do not speak of little gestures here and there to tie the package together more neatly, but of removing the python that is squeezing Palestine to death—will require such fundamental changes in Israeli society as to be tantamount to liquidating the Jewish state as it now exists.

10. *Israel does not have the right to exist.*
There, it has been said, nor has the sky fallen. But what does it mean? That Jews will be pushed into the sea?; that the many fine institutions that have been built in Israel will be razed to the ground?; that the Jewish people will be off on another Diaspora, to again become homeless wanderers across the face of the earth? No doubt, these and other florid ideas are still active in the Zionist imaginary. They are constantly whipped up by the propagandists and inflamed by Islamist demagogues like the President of Iran. But stop and recall: Israel, finally, is a state, and a state is a form of the social contract, which can be changed once the will to do so is strong enough. There is nothing that says that a single person has to be harmed in the passage from one form of the state to another, excepting those who might have to stand trial for human rights abuses; nor will these be executed if the constitution of the new state is consonant with human rights. Though in some cases, the worst by far being Nazi Germany and

the American Confederacy, horrific wars were necessary
to usher in a post-racist form of the state, quite a few
countries, including, notably, South Africa, have changed
fundamentally in recent times with remarkably little
harm.[5] Though the ante-bellum South, Nazi Germany and
apartheid South Africa were full of people who saw the
loss of their regime as an annihilation, the vast majority
came to eventually approve of the transformation.

The only thing that will have to go in the transition
to a non-racist, truly democratic state in Israel/Palestine
is the Zionist dream. But what is so terrible about that?
Better to call Zionism a delusion than a dream. Though
it protects itself by labeling all criticism as antisemitism,
a strong case can be made that Zionism itself is a kind of
antisemitism, in that it falsely essentializes Jewish being and
brings Jews into harm's way. Zionism has been a wrong
turn in the history of the Jewish people. It has brought
about spiritual, ethical and intellectual deterioration, and
sowed desolation wherever it sets its tents; it by no means
represents the alpha and omega (to resort to a useful
Hellenism) of Jewishness, and its peaceful demise can
usher in a great renewal of the people and their culture.
Quite unlikely—to be sure—but by no means impossible;
and in this possibility resides the hope that the will to
change the state can become strong enough.

11. *The point, however, is to change it, which is to say, to*
    dissolve the Jewishness of the state. For this, one does not
    smash or trample Zionism; one overcomes it, and frees
    people from its chains.

TWO-STATE, OR NEW STATE?

The horizon of change according to the so-called peace process
in Israel/Palestine is the so-called "Two-State solution," noted

in Thesis 9, in which a new Palestinian state comes to coexist with the Jewish state on the territory of Israel/Palestine. Setting aside the extremes in which one side annihilates the other—Arabs "throwing Jews into the sea," Jews "transferring" Arabs either to Jordan or their collective grave—this is the only alternative to the present state of affairs taken seriously by the great range of opinion. In the view argued here this horizon needs to be extended with a superior vision, as the Two-State solution should be seen as no solution at all, in part because it is not even Two-State.[6]

The Two-State notion stems from the special background to the present struggle, namely, that both sides in the period up until 1948 were stateless, the Zionists by choice, in that they had insisted on throwing off statehoods of the Diaspora and beginning anew; and the Palestinians by necessity, in that they had lived under Ottoman rule for centuries. When this collapsed in the wake of the first Great War, an opportunity arose to achieve some real autonomy from colonialism. When the struggle heated up in the 1930s and 1940s, it therefore took the shape of two competing state claims, and has kept that basic form through all that followed.

This was quite different from the conditions of state-formation in the United States, Germany and South Africa, the three other societies to have sunk into the morass of state-produced racism.[7] In the American model, the settler-colonials had to deal with the mother country and competing empires like that of France, while the aboriginals were scattered tribes who had never lived under anybody's dominion, and had as a result never come together as a nation. Therefore there were no competing state claims between the European-Americans and the American Indians; these latter were crushed under the expanding colossus of the United States and placed on reservations, American bantustans, where they were given shards of autonomy under the tutelage of the master.[8] Meanwhile the dynamics of state-imposed racism became displaced and re-centered upon African chattel slaves, structural discrimination against whom was built into the constitution and deeply anchored in civil society. Except for thwarted attempts to export the "black problem," such as the founding of Liberia and the twentieth century Garvey and Black Power movements, the extended and ongoing conflict over state racism in the United States has never entailed competing state claims for the same territory but rather exclusion of blacks from the polity. The most recent turn has been de facto disenfranchisement in the last two presidential elections, a half-century after the civil rights movement seemed to have put to rest once and for all the demons of state-produced racism. But however the history of racism has scarred the American nation, the changing of the Constitution after the civil war, along with subsequent laws establishing civil rights to the whole population removes the United States from the category of absolute illegitimacy. Condoleezza Rice may be a bad Secretary of State, but this is because, as a black woman in the United States, she has the civil right to choose the wrong political path and to move very far along it, whereas there is no chance at all for an Arab citizen of Israel to achieve high government office. No, the "land of the free" is merely a very bad instance of a relatively illegitimate society.

Germany in the Nazi period, by contrast, was a recently coalesced state formed from an ancient nation, one of the most highly developed and powerful nation states of its day. Carrying the germ of judaeophobia since at least the time of Luther, it also had a splendidly "emancipated" Jewish community prior to its Nazi degeneration. There was no question of any competing state claim, just as there could be no question of settler-colonialism in a society whose tribal origins were the subject of cloudy myths revived in Wagnerian opera and Nazi fantasy. In sum, although from one angle the contribution of Nazi race hatred to the mythos of Zionism places Germany at the epicenter of the formation of the Jewish state, there is no structural resemblance worth speaking of between the two, such as is too facilely brought forward in many critiques of Israel. The points of contact derive, rather, from the fact of being transformed from victim to overlord. Here a psychological mechanism is at play, which has been discussed above as the "identification with the aggressor." But as psychology in itself can form no material base for a society, the immense shadow of the Nazi period is just that: a shadow that can be lifted and overcome, or hardened into Zionist propaganda and ideology and repeated in the everyday oppression of Palestinians.

Not so with South Africa, which provides by far the most salient point of comparison with Israel.[9] Both were settler-colonial formations formed by Europeans obsessed with the Old Testament and under the thumb of British imperialism, and each launched their peculiarly racist state in the same year, 1948. A hint of the profound connection between the two formations goes back at least to 1919, when the esteemed Jan Smuts, in addressing the South African Zionist Federation and the South African Jewish Board of Deputies in Johannesburg, stated that:

> The white people of South Africa, and especially the older Dutch population, has been brought up almost entirely on Jewish tradition ... The Old Testament has been the very marrow of Dutch culture here in South Africa ...
> That is the basis of our culture in South Africa, that is the basis of our white culture, and it is the basis of your Jewish culture; and therefore we are standing together on a common platform, the greatest spiritual platform the world has ever seen. On that platform I want us to build the future South Africa.[10]

From that platform 42 years later, in 1961, the South African Prime Minister Henrik Verwoerd would say, with a degree of candor not vouchsafed to liberal opinion, that the Zionists took Israel from the Arabs after the Arabs had lived there for a thousand years. In that, I agree with them. Israel, like South Africa, is an apartheid state.[11]

This is not to say that Jews always found life in apartheid South Africa easy. The manifest Nazi sympathies of the founders of the racist state, especially Daniel Malan, gave considerable cause for alarm at first. But with time, and the remarkable rapport that developed between South Africa and Israel, things settled down. As Chris McGreal has written, "Within a few years [after 1948], many South African Jews not only came to feel secure under the new order but comfortable with it. Some found echoes of Israel's struggle in the revival of Afrikaner nationalism."[12] After the 1973 war, when most African states broke ties with Israel, the Zionists and Afrikaners drew closer. Prime Minister John Vorster, whom the British had interned for Nazi sympathies, paid Israel a state visit in 1976 and was toasted by Yitzak Rabin for "the ideals shared by Israel and South Africa; the hopes for justice and peaceful coexistence." A few months later, South Africa officially stated that "Israel and South Africa have one thing above all else in common: they are both situated in a predominantly hostile world inhabited by dark peoples." This ushered in a major integration of the military establishments and arms industries of the two countries, including development of nuclear war capability,[13] on-the-ground assistance in the Angola war, and the provision of anti-riot vehicles to use in the suppression of the black townships. In the words of a high Israeli official, "there was a love affair between the security establishments of the two countries and their armies."[14] Many senior Israeli officials came to believe that the Jewish state could not have survived without the support and financial aid of apartheid South Africa—all this during a period when Israel was manifestly opposing apartheid.

There remain numerous points of distinction between racist South Africa and racist Israel, the most salient of which is that although both states have been closely allied with the United States, the character of that relationship is greatly different, first, because of special US interest in the Middle East, and second, because South Africa had no comparable constituency in America compared to the Zionist lobbies and was never remotely able to penetrate the state apparatus to the same degree.

The African victims of apartheid differed from the Palestinian victims of Zionism in having a complex internal history of struggle between different tribal units, and having been under the thumb of the European invaders for hundreds of years (albeit with periods of fierce armed struggle like the Zulu uprisings of the nineteenth century) before the instauration of the modern racist state. The racist state itself was more overtly segregated than Israel inasmuch as its ruling Caucasian class, being ethnically divided between the majority Boer Afrikaners (of the Calvinist Dutch Reformed Church) and the minority English (of the more liberal Anglican Church), had to find common ground in whiteness. As a result, overt segregation was more rigidly enforced than in Israel, where Jewishness, whether as religion or ethnicity, defines social dominance. There were other relevant distinctions. South Africa by the mid twentieth century was already a regional superpower with a formidable industrial base grounded in immense mineral reserves, in contrast to Israel, which has no significant economic base, and is deeply dependent on handouts from global capital.

The blacks (and so-called "coloured people," as well as a sizable Indian population), tribally, ethnically and linguistically divided, approached the emerging Afrikaner state from a position of severe military and political weakness. On the other hand, they came equipped with powerful reserves of class consciousness arising from an advanced proletarianization deriving from labor in the South African mines and mills. This took the form of highly developed trades unions and an active Communist Party. They also had the benefit of the sojourn of Mohandas Gandhi in the country early in the century, from which point (chiefly Durban, where a century. later the international conference on racism would be held) the concepts and tactics of *Satyagraha* were developed and transmitted to the emerging anti-apartheid struggle. These traits were eventually to coalesce into a powerful and compelling . strategy; but they would not for many years add up to a bid for state power.

The conjunction of these factors allowed the South African state to act with a degree of confidence. For one thing, it already controlled its territory, being a mutation, directly influenced by Nazi ideology, of an already existing polity rather than a *de novo* state formation. From this position of strength it could legislate a grandiose project of social engineering that consigned and further divided the blacks into an intricate set of statelets— the infamous Bantustans—while retaining their status as a pool of labor power for the economy, meanwhile maintaining a sheen of utopian legitimation. Thus there was more of a need to provide minimal physical care for the blacks than has been the case for Israel and its Palestinians, where the basic goal has been to get rid of them by all means possible.[15]

A starkly different scenario awaited the Jewish state. Here the future ruling class were johnny-come-latelys in an ancient and relatively unindustrialized land, to which they had no claim except that generated by their ideology. Weak politically as well as economically, the Zionists began their statehood by doing what they could to secure as much land as possible in 1948 beyond the original UN Mandate through a prodigous ethnic cleansing that displaced some 700,000 Palestinians from some 531 villages, the great majority of which have been erased from the land and the memory of the non-Arab world, including, of course, that of the Jewish conquerers. And they took off. from there, playing the hand they had been dealt with skill and determination. Given their original weakness and shaky claim to the land they coveted, the Zionists had no choice but to go along with the two-state plan imposed by the international community. But this was never more than a framework for the achievement of their goals, hence consent by Israel to the Two-State idea was from the beginning grudging and purely tactical, while the objective has remained the eventual possession of the whole of Palestine and dispossession of the remainder of its Arab inhabitants.

Regarding this as a point of origin, the history of the years since 1948 may be read as a complex and subtle dance to gain the goal of a wholly Jewish Israel. Although there are opposing voices within Israeli state and society, as there are within any society, there is an extraordinary consistency to the behavior of the Jewish state, which has been crafted into a machine for expropriation. This is evinced by the entire record, punctuated by wars, occupation, moments of relenting, international maneuvers, expansion of settlements, the building of walls, and the steady application of legal and physical force to continue the ethnic cleansing of Palestinians, directly when necessary, indirectly always, through a constant effort to render Palestinian life unendurable.

With an unending condition of crisis dictated by its internal contradictions, the Jewish state, obsessed with a "security" that will never come, expresses its inner being in the constant, unrelenting devouring of what is not Jewish. Within this context the "Two-State" option becomes for Zionism a necessary idiocy, and has been so from 1947 right through to George W. Bush's "roadmap," the latest flap with Hamas, and the now victorious Kadima Party, which in early 2006 talked about tucking in the borders of the state by lopping off a few impracticable settler communities from the West Bank while retaining IDF presence where they have stood. No doubt many are still talking about foisting the problem off onto Jordan, another euphemism for the transfer option.[16]

The Jewish state does not want another state on territory that it considers its sacred preserve, but goes along with the

game because, when all is said and done, and the F-16 fighter-
bombers and the nuclear arsenal and the super-effective spy
service are weighed in the balance, it still finds itself weak
and will always be weak given its geostrategic and economic
condition. Thus it always remains dependent upon "the
kindness of strangers." Even if these are its ardently Zionist
pals in Bush's neoconservative regime, many of whom are
Jewish themselves, Israel will always be aware that its giant
patron can abandon it as swiftly as it has taken it under its
wing once strategic considerations or internal politics change.
Under this permanent state of insecurity it continues the two-
state façade while reserving for itself the intention of total
expropriation, including the entire "transfer" of the non-Jew,
an option for which as many as 40 percent of the population
has expressed fairly consistent approval. Thus the Two-State
notion is essentially a code word for the maintenance of the
status quo. Within Israeli discourse the notion of "Two-State"
simply means, then, the continued aggrandizement of the
Jewish state along with a more or less negligible "other state"
on an ever shrinking fragment of land. What it does not mean
is an equable sharing of the space of Palestine.

The negligibility of the Palestinian state is exactly what has
happened in reality. More than a half-century of chewing and
gnawing away at Palestinian land has left the latter more a rag-
doll on a stick than the framework for a living social organism.
Down to some 8 percent of the original territory, surrounded
by the IDF, laced with Jews-only roads and peppered with
hundreds of settlements that arrogate the water and best
land, a dumping ground for Israeli waste, its fields and olive
trees destroyed, its land carved up by the "apartheid wall,"
the potential Palestinian state is no more than a bad joke, a
less-than-bantustan (which in the South African version had
coherent and stable borders, and funding from the center),
and is more aptly called a concentration camp than a state-
in-waiting. With no viable economy save handouts, and no

prospect of authentic foreign relations, the proposed Palestinian state is a nullity.

Thus if the basic condition for a Two-State solution is that there be two functional states on the ground, the Two-State solution has been annihilated. Fifty-eight years of aggression and chewing away on the part of Zionism has, simply, eliminated this as a real possibility and reduced it to a script for the posturings of statesmen, the filling of airtime on the networks and column-inches in the press, and the diverting of the mind from coming to grips with what needs be done in Israel/Palestine. It remains only as a false hope and another source of propaganda allowing Israel to be perceived as a bona fides member of the community of nations.

It will be argued that what we need is a *real* Two-State solution, one that gives the Palestinians a viable state. For this, however, the grip of Israel on Palestine must be greatly altered, ending the settlements and allowing Palestinians in their place, expanding the territory and restoring it to a semblance of the integrity observed before 1948.

To this I have objections both subjective and objective. Subjectively, the whole idea of a *volkisch* state for any singular kind of people—whether Jewish, Arab, Muslim, Christian, or any ethnic fraction—is unappealing, simply because life has taught me that people do better when they are mixing and mingling in conditions of a rich diversity. This stricture would apply to any nationalized state, and especially one centered on a religion. I find an Islamist state as objectionable as a Jewish state; and if I care more about transforming the latter, it is only because my people and my country are responsible for Zionism's success, and have not directly built Islamic states. This latter point, however, needs an important qualification, which gets us into the objective side: for the United States–Israel axis has been over the years by far the most powerful *indirect* cause for the rise of political Islam in its theocratic form. And this means that a Westerner who wishes to undercut the power of Islamic fundamentalism cannot do better than work for the overcoming of Zionism. It is hard to imagine anything more futile and counterproductive (except, of course, to the power structure, which thrives on enemy-building) than for the West to rail against Islamism, as though this were a demonstration of superior logic that would persuade the savages to lay down their arms. On the other hand, the bringing down of Zionism and the entire imperial attitude it serves has tremendous potential for reversing the Islamic-fundamentalist tide, which principally defines itself in reaction to Western interventionism.

Those people of good will who recognize the hopelessness of a Palestinian state on present ground and who call instead for the establishment of a decent home for the Palestinian people, rarely take into account the fact that one might as well expect to get milk from a snake as to cajole or pressure the Israeli state as we know it to make such changes. There is simply not one iota of evidence that the existential drive behind Zionism can be put aside for this purpose. Whatever concessions have been made here and there toward such a goal can only convince the utterly naïve or those blinded by ideology. Not once has the state of Israel risen above the flimflam of realpolitik in the provision of a decent home for Palestinians. Look how they treat their own Arab minority, for example, the Bedouins of the Negev, who are already Israeli citizens, albeit ones who stand in the way by trying to retain their nomadic ways. For this affront to Zionism's drive toward total control of the territory, the Bedouins have been dispossessed of their traditional economy and culture and driven, yes, into "'recognized' townships" —or are they "reservations," or "bantustans?"—where their lives can deteriorate according to plan.[17]

So long as Israel remains Zionist, there will never be a viable Two-State resolution. Only a newly minted Israeli state, therefore, would be capable of restoring Palestine—either in a viable two-state configuration, or along some other form. As to what that form may be, we return to the logical antipode to the Two-State solution and revive what has been given various names that can be summed up here in terms of their common meaning, as a *One-State solution*. The One State option is a demand for Israel to cease being a Jewish state that destroys everything worthwhile that went into its making.

The idea of a single state for all the people of Israel/ Palestine was frequently discussed in the early, utopian phase of Zionism.[18] The notion was revived and became formally enunciated shortly before the founding of the present state by an organization, Ihud, under the prestigious direction of Judah Magnes, President of the Hebrew University, and the eminent philosopher Martin Buber. Speaking in 1947 before the Anglo-American Palestine Commission Inquiry, Magnes and Buber stated: "We do not favor Palestine as a Jewish country or Palestine as an Arab country, but a bi-national Palestine as the common country of two peoples."[19] Magnes, who was deeply faithful to this idea and stands as a rare beacon of Zionist humanism, passed on within the year, and it was taken off the table shortly after the founding of the present state.[20] As for Martin Buber, his subsequent behavior does not square with the aura of sainthood that embellishes his memory. By 1958, Buber had washed his hands of the one-state idea and said so at a lecture: "I have accepted as mine the state of Israel, the form of the new Jewish community that has arisen from the war. I have nothing in common with those Jews who imagine that they may contest the factual shape which Jewish independence has taken."[21] This may have been the product of profound philosophical speculation, but it is hard to avoid the conclusion that coarser motives were involved as well. The eminent philosopher had been a tenant in the fine Jerusalem home owned by, of all people, Edward Said's family. In 1947 a dispute arose that ended up in court. Buber lost, and upon handing over the keys to Said's father, ominously said, "Mr. Said, you just wait. I will be back." And after the Nakhba, indeed he was, with a deed from the Jewish Agency, to claim the house as his own for the remainder of his days. It seems that even deep thinkers can engage in ethnic cleansing, and adjust their beliefs accordingly.[22]

The founding of the State of Israel did not put an end to agitation on behalf of radical change. Many non-Zionists of the revolutionary left had also come to Palestine as refugees from Nazism, and their politics came with them. In 1962, a group of dissident Communists founded the Israeli Socialist Organization, better known by the name of its journal, *Matzpen* ("The Compass"), which regarded the war of 1948 in terms of ethnic cleansing, and called, as Michel Warschawski has written, for the "'de-Zionization' of Israel, and its integration into the Arab Middle East." Warschawski became connected with *Matzpen* as a student in 1967, which year also saw its coming to prominence as a radical critic of the Occupation and of Zionist chauvinism, and a forum for dialogue with Palestinian activists.[23] As Israeli society hardened into its imperial form, all sectors united against *Matzpen*'s heresy. Typically, it was the so-called left that led the suppression by declaring their fidelity to the Jewish state. However, the small, persistent voice of universalism never went away, and gathers strength from the ruins of alternatives.[24]

Today, if one goes to anti-government demonstrations in Tel Aviv or Jerusalem, two groups, broadly, will be seen, mingling in comradely fashion then returning to different worlds. One is made up of more or less grizzled veterans of years of standing against Zionist excesses. These are people of good will, tenacious but with a certain resignation. Then there are the young. They call themselves "anarchist," not in the sense of doctrinal ideology, but from a profound rejection of the given system, whether this appears in Israel/Palestine, or globally. Michel Warschawski has written about them:

> For this new, militant generation, whose country is the world, the idea of a Jewish State is obsolete. They abhor racism in all its mani-festations, reject the confines of Jewish identity or Israeli patriotism,

and although the majority still perform military service, they do so without the chauvinism that motivated previous generations. For them, solidarity with the Palestinians is evidence of their engagement with a broader solidarity with all who suffer oppression ...[25]

A similar phenomenon appears beyond the confines of Israel/Palestine. As Esther Kaplan has written, in the United States, "[n]ew emotional and political currents are coursing through the ... struggle for Palestinian rights." Indeed, "[o]nly a quarter of the participants in the International Solidarity Movement [see Chapter 6] are Jewish or Arab."[26]

The watchword is not "post-Zionism," the withering away of classical Zionism as it is subjected to the late-capitalist culture that dissolves all,[27] but "anti-Zionism," that is, an *overcoming* of Zionism through active struggle. This needs to be carried out in the light of a new polity for Israel/Palestine: a single state for all its people.

10

Palesreal: A Secular and Universal Democracy for Israel/Palestine

THE STORY OF AHMAD

I WANT TO TELL you about a Palestinian I met during a visit to Israel/Palestine in May, 2005. He is of course just one man, and I do not mean for him to be representative of Palestinians as a whole—though I have seen enough like him to make his story indicative of something real within this people who have endured more than seems humanly possible and yet retain that spark which allows the flame of hope to be kept alive. Jeff Halper, an estimable American-Israeli activist whose specialty is contending with house destructions, has recently summarized their mood:

> Knowing that the conflict is too destabilizing for the global system to let fester, the Palestinians are saying: We will remain *sumud*, steadfast. Impose on us an apartheid system, blame us for the violence while ignoring Israeli State Terror, pursue your programs of American Empire or your self-righteous notion of a "clash of civilizations"—we Palestinians will not submit. We will not cooperate. We will not play your rigged game. And in the end your power will be for naught. So costly will we make this conflict to Israel, the US and the international community that you will come to us to sue for peace. We will be ready for a just peace that

222

respects the rights of all the peoples of the region, including the Israelis. But you will not beat us.[1]

This resonates with my encounter with Ahmad, which took place on a sunny morning in Jerusalem, where he had been asked by friends to show me the Old City. Tall and impassive, he met me at the Damascus Gate. We passed the IDF guards engaged in their daily harrassment of Arabs, turned left after the first row of stalls, and soon were in the part of Jerusalem considered not worth being seen by the Western tourist, the back alleys of the Muslim quarter. Actually, it comprises more than one-fourth of the designated portions of Jerusalem in terms of population and area, though it is the least in terms of power and wealth and the shakiest in terms of a future. "Smile," says Ahmad (certain features of whose identity have been altered for this account), "you're being watched," and shows me the camera above us, an unblinking reptilian eye, a compound eye as it turns out, for there are some five hundred of the devices gazing on subversive elements. Ahmad went on with some interesting statistics: that of the total population of the Old City, some 34,500 permanent residents, Muslims comprise well more than half, 22,000, while of the other three "quarters," Christians comprise 7000, Jews 3000, and Armenians, 2500. Yet—would you believe it?—of the 40 full-time sanitation workers of Old Jerusalem who haul away the three tons of garbage produced each day, 22 are assigned to the 3000 inhabitants of the Jewish quarter and the other 18 to the 31,500 "others," which means that the average Jewish resident of the Holy City gets 13 times as much garbage removal as the others—and much more than that compared to the Muslims of Old Jerusalem, who live amidst piles of refuse like slum dwellers everywhere.

But wait, there is a neat building just over there. Yes, says Ahmad, that's where Jewish settlers have taken over a Muslim house. "Notice the pillbox on the roof. They keep a round-the-clock armed guard, and report anything suspicious to the police." But how did they come to live here? Ahmad launches into a lamentation on the paths of dispossession. It is the most emotion I have seen from him. There are many such routes, and they are all legal—such is the set-up in Israel, a country built by the expropriation of Arabs. "One man can't pay the tax bill; the next thing you know he is gone; another has to make necessary repairs, but the fee for the permit is $20,000, and he has to sell, because he only earns $400 a month; that house you saw was 200 years old and the owner simply could not do the needed renovations, so the Jews stepped in; once the Arab leaves, he can never come back, because the land is taken forever from him; and if by bad fortune, he should lose his identity card, then he becomes a non-person and loses all rights. There is no end to it. Herzl said it a century ago: 'We will have a state that will destroy everything not Jewish.' They do this every day in the 'only democracy in the Middle East.'"

We left the Muslim quarter after seeing the rare triumph represented by the "Stork" community and health center, which was saved from the bulldozers in 1995 by a 60 day sit-in, and is, with its bright murals, virtually the only cheerful-looking spot I saw in the whole of Old Jerusalem. As we wound through the astonishing variegation of life (for there are considerably more than four ethnicities that live there, including Ahmad's folk, who came from Saharan Africa), we encounter other signs of expropriation, including the imminent dispossession of 20 families whose property is coveted so that another Wailing Wall can be built. The Chief Rabbi has declared it Holy Ground, two million shekels have been raised to do the necessary demolition and reconstruction—and that, in Israel, is that. This one will be for women's wailing only, relieving Zion of the embarrassment of having highly visible segregated facilities for the lesser gender along the inferior portion of the Great Wailing Wall.

I asked to see this famous site. But Ahmad refused to take me: "No, no, I will never go there, I cannot bring myself to do it. But I will show you the Jewish quarter, then point you the route."

The most important fact one needs to know about the Jewish quarter is that whereas in all the other sectors of Jerusalem different kinds of people cohabit with the publically named fraction, this one is for Jews only. As befits its privileged status with respect to the sanitation department, it is also a very sanitary quarter, and a prosperous one, too. One would not immediately think of calling it a ghetto, but a self-imposed ghetto it is. Little sense of history remains, although the old Roman Way, the Cardo Maximus, has been partially restored, any number of memorabilia shops sell historical souvenirs, and a gigantic gold Maccabean candelabrum sits behind heavily fortified glass awaiting transfer to a reincarnated Temple that remains a gleam in the Zionist eye. Mostly the quarter has the glassy homogeneity one comes to expect in neighborhoods reserved for one kind of people. If the dream of Zionism is to destroy everything non-Jewish in the land of Israel/Palestine, the reality of this dream fulfilled is the suffocating aridity of a gated community, each of which, from La Jolla to Johannesburg to Mumbai, eventually becomes like all the others.

Ahmad took me to the terrace overlooking the plaza of the Wailing Wall to bid goodbye. It had been a hot morning and was now high noon. I had largely finished the two-liter bottle of water I purchased upon entry, and Ahmad had declined all refreshment. Surely he would let me buy him a coffee, or even lunch. "No, no," came the reply. "I do not need anything. I am used to going long times without water or food . . ." Really, how so? "I did two hunger strikes, each over thirty days. It was when I was in Israeli prison. I spent seventeen years there."

He was born in 1948 "somewhere on the road to Jordan," a child of the *Nakhba*. His father, recently arrived from Niger, had been a guard at the Al-Aqsa mosque. But then came the great troubles, the ethnic cleansing, and the common fate of displaced people. From Jordan they found their way back to the Palestinian remnant, and there Ahmad grew up, excelled at school, and thought of becoming a doctor.

When war erupted in 1967 Ahmad was working in a cigarette factory. He ran home, then into the streets where he tried to take care of wounded and displaced people. The Zionist victory was swift and followed by a three or four day curfew. He went out, saw bodies still in the street, and tried to help bury them. But the curfew was reinstated. Ahmad's heart hardened: "I saw every kind of humiliation for our people from the Israeli soldiers. They would arrest and beat us for no reason, sexually abuse our women. I became very angry and decided that only by force could we redeem our land."

Ahmad joined a militant faction, the Popular Front for the Liberation of Palestine. He trained in Hebron and participated in guerrilla actions in Jerusalem and Tel Aviv. Ahmad had become an embodiment of the Palestinian terrorist who haunts the Israeli imagination. Betrayed by an informer, he was interrupted while attending a pre-med class at Victoria Hospital two weeks after his last escapade. "They told the schoolmaster that they only wanted to question me for ten minutes; but the ten minutes became seventeen years."

Ahmad was to endure months of torture and privation in a series of 13 prisons. One day his fortunes dramatically improved. He was switched to a better cell, allowed to bathe, and given clean clothes, for a special visitor was coming to see him. Soon afterward, an elegant man wearing a necktie appeared. It was the French Ambassador! Ahmad's father held a French passport and had managed to pull strings on his behalf. The ambassador told Ahmad that the French government had intervened with his captors to secure his release. He could go anywhere he wanted—to Niger, to France, the United States, the USSR, wherever; all he had to do was to name the place and he would be a free man.

Ahmad thought for some minutes, weighing the ambassador's offer against its unspoken implication—that freedom meant leaving his family, Palestine, his comrades and their common struggle. Then he turned to the ambassador and said: "The only place I want to be is in Jerusalem. Can you bring me there?" "You're crazy," said the ambassador, and terminated the interview.

Years later he was released into obscurity in a prisoner exchange, thanks to the intervention of ex-Chancellor Bruno Kreisky of Austria. Even then, he recalls ruefully, "it was hard to go into the outside world and leave my comrades behind." Out of prison, Ahmad joined the human rights community. But his troubles with the state were not over. During the First Intifada he was brought up on charges again and released after another year. Presently he works as a community organizer and lives about thirty kilometers from the sacred city.

I asked Ahmad how he thinks the struggle will go now.

I don't see the struggle here finishing. As long as there are human beings on this earth, they will keep struggling, but in various ways according to circumstances. What I am struggling for now is to see this universe as without borders, so that people can move without anyone stopping you to ask where are you from, where are you going, who are you, Christian, Muslim or Jew? ... This is what I believe—that all these conflicts are monstrous and cannot be justified at all. We are fighting each other as human beings. Yet no human being came into this world willingly; nobody asked us if we wanted to come into this world or not. We are just here; we came naked into the world, we didn't bring with us anything at all. Even our religion we did not bring. How can I believe that this land is mine and that land is his, since we came naked into this world? And since I will leave it naked and will take nothing with me. ...

We are all human beings. If we believe in God, then God created us all. I do not believe God is racist ... Nature is all his creation; we are all a product of nature, and this is not our choice but a fact. Therefore everybody should be seen that way; there should be no discrimination because of sex, color, or whatever.

The only real difference is how you present yourself to your community, and the good you do for your community. That is how we should discriminate between people—in how they serve their community, not just their local community but also the world community. Yes, the whole world. I am not talking about internationalism when I say this, because internationalism is a way to control others. If you say I am Arab then you set yourself off against Europe or America. If I say I am from France, then what about Britain, and if I say I am from Britain, then what about Belgium? That's keeping borders between people. I believe that all the people in the world are one family, that we are all brothers and sisters.

You ask me how to influence the Zionist state? By education and dialogue. Our tradition here, where we have lived side by side for centuries, is to not destroy each other. The people of Jerusalem have committed no massacres. We have not treated the Jews the way Spain or Germany treated the Jews. Why should we suffer now the way they did? If people suffer they should not make other people suffer in the same way.

Through dialogue and mutual respect we can make a better life and put an end to this conflict. It will never be solved with armed conflict, which brings hatred, violence and more violence without end. We should all be allowed to believe what we believe and to be treated with mutual respect. If we want to compete, let it be in sports. Let us play basketball rather than make war. Let us turn our energy to fight illiteracy, famine, disease. Now that we can destroy the whole universe four or five times over, let us turn those resources over to make a better life.

And with that, Ahmad pointed the way to the Wailing Wall and bid me goodbye.

ON OVERCOMING

Our task is to think through what a "just peace" may mean, for which we need to put some flesh on the logical bones of One State for Israel/Palestine, the only meaning under present circumstances of a just peace. In the context of two polities so radically opposed and yet so intertwined, this can be seen either as a *bi-national* state in which the nations of the Jews and the Palestinians coexist, or as something further along a path in which peoples retain a limited recognition of national identity but overcome this through inclusion in a larger whole, beyond chauvinism. In this form of the state, desire no longer attaches to national or tribal identity but becomes non-possessive and is displaced to the universal. The sense of particularity is retained by connection to tradition and memory, and simultaneously transcended through fidelity to a better future. We would call this a *secular-universal* form of the state.

A bi-national state may be thought of as two states folded into one and, because it preserves the essentials of the national aspirations that readily appeal to both sides, may seem rather easier to swallow than its more radical alternative. To swallow, but not to digest, for the notion suffers from all kinds of incompatible lumps. Are we talking about two ethno/theocracies that are supposed to balance each other out? Are there to be distinct legislatures on that basis? How is the executive to be compounded—are Jewish and Arabic prime ministers, etc., to alternate? And the legal system: are there to be two parallel systems of courts, which is to say, will there be no superordinate notion of Law?—a situation that conjures up any number of absurd scenarios, for example, the fate of bi-national divorces. And finally, though the point is implied in all the previous questions, how are we to stop a slide toward disintegration and even civil war once tensions arise, as they must?

And so we would opt for the transcendence of bi-nationality through the secular-universal form of the state. For this there must be a *telos* towards which transcendance aspires: the realization of the inherent dignity shared by each and every person. This is not unworldy utopianism, but a necessity for a practical program. We are talking about what Martin Luther King Jr called the "long arc of justice," and therefore take the long view. Because the notion of a One State is only dimly stirring in present awareness, we need to find a way of illuminating the form of arc that leads to justice in Palestine.

To achieve even a decent outcome in the profoundly traumatized land of Israel/Palestine, one had better offer a vision of something radically better than the present, not to bludgeon people into its mold, but to cause the given to become unstuck and to set change into motion. The process is what matters, because it is what happens in real time. The goal matters chiefly because of the kind of process it directs and sets into motion. Hope tells us that one day the process and the goal may be one. Until then, the truth of democracy in Israel/Palestine has to be a condition of *becoming*; and since what becomes must replace a burden, it is to be seen as a perpetual, and perpetually evolving, moment in the *overcoming* of a tormented history. This demands a visionary movement, in which a sense of what is not yet here can be found prefigured within the given moment.[2] There remains a seed within each person, and within the three Abrahamic religions that grew in this region as well, that can grow so long as a vision of transformation is provided, like a trellis upon which its seedling can take hold. Such is the notion of the secular/universal state. To the degree that its universalizing elements are incorporated into political strategy, so will they enter the oppositional consciousness and serve to overcome Zionism, which is the historically dynamic knot to be untied. This begins the dissolution of the Jewish state in a manner humanly worthwhile. Overcoming is, then, the movement toward the universal. It provides a platform upon which the tactics of anti-Zionism and the goals of a secular/universal state—in other words, the practical side of our work—can be assayed and built.

To concentrate the mind, let us give the new state a name, and call it for now, "Palesreal." If this has a grating sound, so be it, for it reminds that there are difficult changes in the offing. Palesreal comprises a place that is no more now than a word, turned to include four letters of each national home and a shared central "s." But it can also be a spark that is struck every time mutual human recognition takes place within

Israel/Palestine, a spark that can propagate. Needless to say, the reader is free to choose another name should she prefer it.

The status quo in Israel/Palestine is sustained by a toxic brew of retributive fear and fierce joy. National chauvinism is tribal atavism writ large, and both are driven by blood gratification. The history of Zionism is wracked with fear, loathing and ecstatic affirmation, thanks to all that has been packed into the saga of the Jews; this was true even before the Holocaust put the sign of unprecedented horror over it, whence there is no difficulty in recognizing just how powerful the emotional attachments to the Jewish state have been. In the face of these dark desires, the hope for a secular-universal state may appear pallid. However, tribalism does not represent human nature but its stifling. The self which feels joy in chauvinism is not fully realized, but divided and split within itself. In the Zionist regime it is locked by bad conscience into tribalized revenge and paranoia.

Zionism cannot be reasoned away; it has to be confronted, and its lived world has to change through a twofold process: first, creating tension and distress; second, introducing means through which the universal can be appropriated. This is what is meant by truth, in the Gandhian sense: not just the supplying of correct facts, but doing so to enhance the qualities of "soul," and a more universal appropriation of being.[3] It follows that mere denunciation of Zionist crimes is not enough. In itself it just gets the back up and buttresses the bad conscience. It is a question of the "spirit" in which this is done, which is to say, that truth-telling opens to a greater whole, and onto a unity within and between people. Violence in the spirit of vengeance, especially random violence toward innocent civilians, only mirrors Israeli violence, gives Zionism its required daily dose of Jewish suffering, and feeds the Jewish state. A more creative politics dissolves Zionism's shield of legitimacy, destabilizes the regime and builds openings. The same can be said for threatening its lifelines to global capital, also to be combined with truth-telling. Primarily, anti-Zionist politics must foster mutual recognition and restitution of humanity to all, that is, it must undo the racist core of the Zionist state.

THE PRACTICES OF ONE-STATE

Speak the truth about Israel. Gandhi said that truth-telling was the heart of nonviolence. Justice is grounded in truth, and truth inheres in the whole of things, which is not a homogeneous totality but the contradictory, dialectically moving ensemble of the real. There is therefore no single truth, but there are greater and lesser truths. The obligation for people of good will is to find the greater truth and speak it to the power that would suppress it. And one of the greater truths is that there is such a power. For present purposes we may locate its surface in the tentacular Zionist lobby, extending from the upper echelons of the American and Israeli security apparatuses through the chambers of civil society. It follows that every particle of truth about Israeli violations of human rights should also be an exposure of the Zionist lobby. Every truth about Israel needs to be an exposure of the lie that keeps pumping up the leaky gas bag of its legitimacy.

The Lobby intimidates, especially in the United States whose transformation must therefore be a goal of anti-Zionist politics. But once exposed, it can be confronted. Telling the truth about the Lobby is not mere recitation; it should be a guide, rather, to bringing down its corrupt and illegitimate power. We need a campaign to force the Lobby to register as an agent of a foreign power; and another to build data banks to expose those who collaborate with it; and to eliminate the special privileges enjoyed by Israel as tax breaks, technology transfers, indeed, the whole grotesque edifice of handouts, loan guarantees, technologies of death, and the like, which burden US taxpayers while bringing endless misery and destruction to Palestine and Lebanon; and to protest Israel's nuclear arsenal and bring it under international control; and to keep bringing suits for violation of human rights against the likes of Avi Dichter and Moshe Ya'alon; and to insist that the media carry alternative views, and to build alternative media that do; and to expose the Israeli "spies" who clustered around the events of September 11, and even to re-open investigation into the attack on the *USS Liberty* in 1967.[4] There is scarcely any limit to the activism that can be directed against the various arms of the Israel Lobby, just as there is scarcely any limit to the sources that nourish it. And all of these campaigns converge on the necessary step that activists everywhere are tentatively beginning to take: to organize international boycotts against the Zionist state.

Deprive the Zionist state of what it needs. In other words, place Israel where it belongs, in the company of apartheid South Africa, and deprive it, first of its cloak of normalcy, and then, of the capital flows which are its lifeblood. The massive Israeli apparatus is there to protect a very shaky foundation, and the bad conscience is strong but brittle. Hence a central goal of organized Zionism is to block academic, cultural and economic boycotts. To the degree these succeed they have the potential of tipping Israel into the same category as its unlamented apartheid friend. Once this identification happens, matters can go downhill for the Zionist state very rapidly.

This is the context in which we should understand the remarkable cancellation early in 2006 of a major conference in Bellagio, Italy, sponsored by the American Association of University Professors, which had been convened to debate— that is all—the matter of academic boycotts of Israel. Though the AAUP opposes boycotts in principle, it also retains a quaint academic affection for talking things over. But this was jettisoned in the face of a firestorm of protest from the Zionist lobby. Hear Abraham Foxman, veteran watchdog of the Anti-Defamation League:

> We were troubled to learn that eight of the 21 participants in this conference support the use of boycotts against the state of

Israel. We support academic freedom, but one needs to proceed with caution when the views being included are far outside the mainstream, or when the message involves antisemitism, Holocaust denial or questions Israel's right to exist.[5]

Even a rigged conference, then, designed so that the boycott issue would once more be defeated, was too threatening to the thought police. Three major liberal sponsors, the Rockefeller (which owns the Bellagio center), Ford, and Cummings foundations, pulled the plug. It is the kind of story that surfaces almost daily: another battle lost to Zionism. Yet with each instance, a spreading ripple of outrage extends the war.

As this is written, the tactical balance favors the anti-boycott forces, composed as they are of the liberal-left and everything to the right of it, augmented by certain bellwethers of the real left, including Noam Chomsky. No doubt, there are many reasons why these people oppose boycotting Israel: this one because of sentimental affection for a youthful experience as a pioneer at a kibbutz; that one because the image of Holocaust still seizes the mind; another is agitated by the latest news from France about antisemitism; another feels too much fear of the Islamic masses and their potential for vengeance; still another reacts to a suicide bombing, or broods about how everybody picks on the Jews. Then there are those who reason that professors shouldn't take stands, or entertain the quaint belief that the free flow of academics is the best way of convincing Israel to stop being mean to Palestinians—or, though no one mentions it, that it wouldn't be helpful to one's career to support a boycott. And then, of course, there are the considerable number who just think Israel is a good idea for one reason or another. After all, it does have fine symphony orchestras.

Underlying all this is an inability, or disinclination, to recognize that here is a state that produces racism on an expanding scale, and that Israel therefore belongs in the same category as the Republic of South Africa during its apartheid period. Recall the furor that attended the Durban anti-racism conference in 2001, where the United States delegation, led by Secretary of State Colin Powell, and Israel walked out rather than submit to a debate that they knew they would lose badly. The ferocious suppressions of inquiry into Zionism may be regarded as a set of outer defenses to avoid such a confrontation. Remember, too, racist South Africa also had its reasons why it should be left alone. Much of the country was efficiently run and relatively unpolluted, and had trains that ran on time, fine universities and a medical school where the first heart transplant was carried out. The Afrikaners themselves had an indisputable history of being persecuted, indeed, had not Britain built the first identifiable concentration camps during the Boer War, where some 20,000 women and children died?[6] And they, too, could point to a great civilizational threat, of "communism," around which the nations of the West could rally. Nonetheless, a great many people arrived at the conclusion that there was a systematic evil afoot under apartheid, which was irremediable under the terms of its social contract; and that, therefore, more radical measures were necessary. This is the focal struggle for overcoming Zionism, a strategy that necessarily requires cutting the threads of Israel's support systems. Necessary but not sufficient. For that, we require a concrete and nonviolent way Zionism can be overcome.

Bring Palestinians home. Just as Zionism is not identical with apartheid but another instance of state-produced racism, so does the struggle against Zionism require different strategies from those waged in Southern Africa. Some themes are similar in broad perspective, for example, the importance of economic, cultural and academic boycotts in the two instances; or the conjunction of military and non-military strategies in the resistance movments by the oppressed. But just as the "One-or-Two-State" conundrum defines Israel/Palestine and not South Africa, so must there be specific measures to be carried out according to such a context. The point is essential, for the option specifically available to anti-Zionist activism happens to contain within itself both the necessary and sufficient conditions for bringing down Zionism in an entirely peaceful way. The only thing standing in its way is that not enough people in the West have decided that the world would be a far better place without Zionism. When they do, they will find the means of realizing this directly at hand and well worked out.

The Palestinian *Right of Return* (ROR) is an actively pursued and predictably suppressed strategy with the essential quality that it does not seek to "smash" Zionism, but overcomes it by dissolving the logic of Jewish exceptionalism and particularity. It does so by undoing the devices of the bad conscience, then replacing these with the taking of responsibility. A "Jewish Right of Return," according to which, anybody with a Jewish grandmother through the mother's line, is entitled to Israeli citizenship has been a foundation of the Jewish state since its inception, and a mainstay of its demographic strategy. The task is to supplant this narrow right with one grounded in universal justice.

Palestinians today comprise by far the world's largest and oldest refugee population—it is said that one out of every three refugees is Palestinian—and around their predicament has grown an intricate set of rules and conditions, too complex to be recounted here,[7] but of which the essential point is this: that there exists an inalienable human right, inscribed in international law, to return to homes and lands from which one has been forcibly expelled. Thus the ROR is enshrined in both Palestinian desire and international law, in particular, UN Resolution 194. In fact, it is grounded in the most venerable Western tradition of common law itself, the Magna Carta, Chapter 42 of which holds that:

> In the future it shall be lawful (except for a short period in time of war, for the common benefit of the realm) for anyone to leave and return to Our kingdom safely and securerly by land and watere, saving his fealty to Us. Excepted are those who have been

imprisoned or outlawed according to the law of the land, people of the country at war with Us, and merchants, who shall be dealt with as aforesaid.

There was no "law of the land" in 1948 Mandatory Palestine except international law, nor can ethnically cleansed Palestinians be thought of as "people of the country at war with Us," except in the most paranoid of Zionist delusions. And as for "fealty," this would have to be determined on the spot, and in a case-by-case procedure, which is exactly how the planners of the ROR propose to implement it.[8]

The ROR is a more basic strategy than liquidating the Occupation. The latter leaves the Zionist state essentially unchanged except for having less territory. Though we have argued that the implications are actually more radical than this, these are still just implications. On the other hand, the ROR, while requiring the end of the Occupation as a precondition, can directly undo the Jewishness of the state. This fact alone brings one existentially up against the overcoming of Zionism.[9] One cannot ask Palestinians to return without granting them full and equal rights; as these include the franchise, this means that the demographic defenses of the Jewish state are immediately breached. This would remain the case even if some parity with the existing Jewish right of return was stipulated in the interest of fairness. Even within the current borders of Israel and the lands it occupies, and despite everything done to get rid of them, Palestinians have in the last year or so achieved a rough parity of population with the Jewish inhabitants. This fact accounts in part for Ehud Olmert's plan to "draw the final boundaries" of Israel by 2010, and it also means that any reasonable opening for Palestinians to enter the polity now known as Israel will negate its inherent Jewishness.

A One State achieved through the ROR will intrinsically be oriented toward its secular/universal form. From the Palestinian side, the invasion and occupations of 1967 were a reverberation of the Nakhba of 1948, the overcoming of which remains the lodestar of their freedom struggle. To support the ROR, then, means backing the essential human right of self-determination. This changes everything in the agony that is now Palestine, and more broadly, the civilizational struggle wracking the Middle East. A good deal of current opinion holds that fundamentalism, theocracy and the whole paraphernalia of Islamic terror are inherent in the "oriental" Muslim tradition. Bernard Lewis, perhaps the most influential spokesperson for this tendency, writes that "Anglo-French and American influence, like the Mongol invasions, were a consequence, not a cause, of the inner weakness of Middle-Eastern states and societies."[10] No doubt, the Middle East had undergone a long downward turn after centuries of Ottoman rule. But to say that American influence was a consequence of this weakness puts the cart before the horse. The weakness of Middle Eastern society undoubtedly provided an opportunity for Western imperialism. But an opportunity is no consequence; and to deny that imperialism, with its ruthless destruction of traditional community, installation of quisling-like states, and plundering of the resources ("our oil under their soil") has wreaked havoc with Muslim societies and led to the reaction known as political Islam is at best silly, at worst, racist. And of all the intrusions, none has been more drawn-out and consequential than Zionism, the *prima facie* instance of Western aggrandizement at the expense of the Arab/Muslim world.

Fundamentalism and theocracy, of whatever origins, are at heart desperate efforts to reclaim the meaning of existence from the disintegrating effects of modernity, which itself is an instrument of capital's penetration of communities. These are accelerated and can take on the character of terrorism when modernity is the instrument of empire. Then disintegration rules, shattering the life-worlds of indigenous people, and germinating violence as the only way of dignity. A rational hope of self-determination can change everything, however. I do not believe that people given a real choice for freedom with justice (as against, for example, what George W. Bush holds forth under that name) will continue on the path of delusion signified by theocracy and fundamentalism. Indeed, the power of the universal is so great as to catalyze a diminution and even cessation of hostility. We should turn on its head the insulting offer that coercively tells oppressed people to abjure violence in advance before negotiating what is rightfully theirs: Open for them the hope of self-determination, and violence will wither away of itself.

This applied to the South African march to freedom, which was originally guided by Gandhian nonviolence, but added a component of armed struggle after the Sharpeville massacre of 1960. During his imprisonment on Robben Island, Nelson Mandela was tempted with numerous offers of release from captivity and a high position in the Transkei Bantustan if he would authorize a return to pacifism and recognize the Bantustan system (that is, the "multi-state" solution *du jour*). He refused, holding out for the "One-State" solution to South Africa's racism and to the retention of a combined nonviolent/armed struggle as its means, confident, justly so, that violence would wither to the extent that the freedom struggle grew.[11]

For Jews, the Palestinian Right of Return poses an existential choice of whether to abandon the tribalism of Zionism and to become open to the other. This is as it should be, and a tremendous challenge given what has been implanted in the collective psyche. But it is by no means an insurmountable one. At its center, bad conscience is a turning away from responsibility through non-recognition of the basic humanity of the other; therefore the passage defined by the ROR offers a way out of Zionist delusion. Its essence is mutual recognition and the assumption of responsibility, and its means of realization can be incremental and graded through face-to-face interaction. As the illegitimacy of Zionism is brought forth by truth telling and sanctions, the justice entailed in the ROR can be introduced in the spaces left behind by a retreating worldview.

There are countless such "praxes of recognition" extant even now, both within Israel and without, spontaneously arising among people of good will, and representing an emergence of what may be called a politics of good conscience. For example, there is a small but growing organization in Israel, *Zochrot*, which it has been my good fortune to encounter. It is the brainchild of Eitan Bronstein, originally from Argentina, a man upon whom the IDF gave up when he refused duty in Lebanon three times in the 1980s. Eitan is one of the persons of conscience who comprise the saving remnant of Israeli society. "Zochrot" is the feminine form of a Hebrew word that means, roughly, "acknowledgment," that is, a kind of remembering that is also a reconstructing and a taking of responsibility. Its small band of volunteers goes about the country, putting place names fabricated as street signs down where once an Arab village stood (the signs are invariably removed after a few days); or they collect stories and testimonies of displaced persons and bring them into schools; or they train children to make tiles that inscribe lost Arab place names; or they make posters of school photos of the surviving children of Deir Yassin; or they insist upon introducing the taboo word, "Nakhba," into Israel discourse.

Conscience accompanies a person through all the days of life. If bad, it haunts with persecution; if good, it blesses with integrity. For each person, there is a pathway to a transforming of conscience, and the question is how to find this. If the reality of a dispossession can be brought forward as a story attached to a place, which was once someone else's, but has been claimed for Zionism, then, to the degree that such a story registers in the Zionist mind, it must be connected to an associated train of ideas, which may schematically be imagined as: "how did this happen ... who made this happen ... did we make this happen? ... do we not bear some *responsibility* for this?" The notion of responsibility attaches itself directly to each mental quantum whose inner object is now perceived as a fellow being, with a story, universal suffering, and basic right. Once the notion of responsibility enters through mutual recognition, it undoes, by that degree, the denial of guilt and its projection as blame that forms the phenomenological core of Zionism's bad conscience. In the same moment it undermines the fear that pervades Zionism's universe, since fear of this degree is less the product of objective danger than a derivative of inner demonology. This latter implies a threat to the integrity of the ego—the same walled-off ego that must be undone. Mutual recognition is what undoes. It is a dissolving and a transforming, on subjective terrain, that moves away from Zionism. It is a recovery of memory that is also a recognition of history—the recognition Benny Morris couldn't stand when he turned away from the truth he had uncovered about the Nakhba, and toward his nihilist and paranoid defense of Zionism. Recognition, of self and other, often comes, as the common phrase has it, in the form of a "shock" and requires what the psychoanalysts call "working through." But if this can be kept in place—something requiring patient organizing—it can take hold and develop in the direction of nonviolence and reconciliation. It is simply the cowardice of inertia that refuses to take this possibility seriously.

A debate nevertheless remains as to whether the ROR can be implemented. Is the idea practicable, given how upsetting such a change is bound to be, how crowded Israel already is, and the technical issues of tracking down and adjudicating the consequences of dispossession? The best answer I can give is to relay the words of Scott Leckie, Director of an NGO that specializes in this question, the Committee on Housing Rights and Evictions (COHRE). Leckie writes:

Although the prevailing status quo may appear to indicate that the implementation of the rights of displaced Palestinian refugees to return to the homes, lands and properties from which they have been arbitrarily and illegally displaced is nothing more than a pipedream, nothing could be further from the truth. Restitution of refugee property has now become the norm. Millions of refugees and displaced persons have returned to their original homes in recent decades, from Bosnia, South Africa, and Tajikistan to Germany.

Of the dozens of large displaced populations throughout the world who have yet to exercise these rights—Serbs, Ossetians, Congolese, Burundians, Liberians, Afghans and others—no group has anything near the facts, documentation, evidence and legal basis supporting the right to housing and property restitution as those held by the several million-strong Palestinian refugee community. The world has at its fingertips virtually all of the land records, title deeds, historical documents, photographs—even house keys—required to make fair and just restitution a reality for all displaced Palestinians.[12]

No doubt the process of adjudication would require a considerable staff and be expensive, both in the implementation and because monetary claims need to be offered as alternatives to housing on both sides. But consider what it costs to administer the imperial and military side of Israel now, and recall that the future of Palesreal depends on turning the transition into a face-to-face process in which restitution and reconciliation are each the condition for the other. As Leckie has pointed out elsewhere, the success of the South African transition away from apartheid included:

recognition that [white farmers who had to give up land] also had rights. And whatever scenario you have here, this is also going to be a key feature of any restitution program involving the return of Palestinian property. And this is something very important to emphasize in Israel: to take away the fear of any Israelis living inside Palestinian homes now, in terms of the recognition of their rights. International standards say you do not just protect the rights of the returning refugees; you have to also protect the rights of what is called the "secondary occupants"—the ones living inside the homes now. You cannot just kick them out and treat them as if they have no rights. If they have been there one day or thirty years, they also have rights. They cannot be made homeless and they cannot be discriminated against. Their rights need to be protected. This is very important to recognize.[13]

Along these lines, the South African Communist leader Joe Slovo insisted on a "sunset clause" for the new state in which no civil servant (needless to say, white) was to be fired when the ANC took over. This principle, of mitigating the understandable fear in a population undergoing transition by creating an atmosphere of fairness and lawfulness, still holds.[14] Further, there is no expectation that the authorities of the new state will be exclusively or even predominantly Palestinian. Palesreal needs to be seen as a polity whose ethnically driven past is to become subsumed into a universalizing democratic present whose constitution (yes, it will have a constitution, having nothing to fear from one) will include ironclad protection of the right to any belief and practice that does not harm another. The actual moment of transition to the new state can take any number of shapes, including the use of an internationally supervised protectorate as a transitional measure. One should think that the prospect of resolution of what has been the world's most tormenting and divisive conflict for more than a half-century would not lack for widespread and substantial support. As the prospect of a One State grows near, the details of its inauguration can be left to the participants in that happy day.

All well and good. But the momentous implications of granting equal rights to all the people can obscure another matter: Just what kind of a society will Palesreal be? Fidelity to integral human right is an empty abstraction unless its institutional base is specified. For example, we have documented that despite propaganda, Israel is an environmental basket case, and observed that one component of this is the demographic mania to pack the country with as many Jewish citizens as possible. How can matters not be worsened by a strategy one possible outcome of which is to add more people to an already crowded place?[15] Should the return of Palestinians be limited in order to reduce this stress on the Israeli environment?

This line of argument presumes that environmental—or as we should prefer to call them, ecological—problems are essentially quantitative. But this is a wrong-headed way of looking at things. What is "too much" where people are concerned depends essentially on what kind of life these people are living. A lot of people organized around the protection and enhancement of the natural foundation of society (as by a shift to labor-intensive, small-unit organic agriculture) is in fact a very good thing; while smaller numbers of people who live wantonly with respect to nature can be deadly. Just so, does the industrial capitalist North ravage nature far more than the populous South despite lower population density. Our concern with Israel's ecological mismanagement is a quarrel with the Zionist ways of living. Given the attitude of noncompliance and special pleading resulting from its obsession with "security," Israel is environmentally devastating in direct proportion to its population. Palesreal can be a fresh start, which, if it shapes itself according to the principle of recognition and responsibility, cannot but be a great improvement from an ecological as well as a political standpoint. For it is nature, too, that needs recognition, and people who live in mutual self-respect are already well along the road to the rational regulation of their relation to nature.

But the "principle of recognition and responsibility," and the provision of "mutual self-respect"—does this not also point to a society organized along essentially non-capitalist lines? What else is a true democracy except a form of society in which people collectively self-determine their lives, and therefore their means of producing that life? We cannot spell an answer out here, amidst the uncleared debris of twentieth-century socialisms and the tremendously damaged polity of Israel/Palestine. But the question must be posed, and thought through by those who would reclaim a just and decent future for that land.

To struggle for freedom is to undo the forces that bind and deform human being. Capital is that binding in the present epoch—and Zionism has been capital's handservant in the modern world, just as medieval Jews were sucked into this role as usurers and the prototypes of commercialism.[16] Israel is a society whose whole lineage and that of capital have moved in tandem, from the funds advanced to purchase "idle" Ottoman lands in the nineteenth century, to the compact with British imperialism embedded in the Balfour Declaration, to the betrayal of socialist universalising engrained in its nationalist-Zionist form, and on down to the latest shenanigans of the conjoined Zionist and United States state apparatuses as the former seeks a vicarious Greater Israel and the latter plays for oil hegemony. The real history of Zionism has been a working out of the "invisible hand" that has shaped history toward the end of accumulation and has placed the Anglo-Americans at its helm, their Israeli junior partner by their side, attacking here, spying there, doing the dirty work as needed. This is the secret of the so-called Israel, or Zionist, lobby. Not a Jewish lobby, as antisemites would have it, but a dynamic and very unholy gathering of those power-Jews who would hitch their wagon to the star of empire: Democrats, Republicans, phoney intellectuals, all stripes of opportunists exulting in their admission to the inner chambers of power. Thus Martin Peretz, in one of the endless thrashings dealt out to the honest exposers of the Lobby:

> support for Israel is, deep down, an expression of America's best view of itself. Mearsheimer and Walt—who accuse the [sic] Jewish lobby of subverting US foreign policy in Israel's interest—clearly have no clue that American support for the Jewish restoration, rather than a result of Zionist machinations, dates back to the Puritans. And it carries through Woodrow Wilson and Harry Truman to, if you'll forgive me, George W. Bush.[17]

Though not, of course, FDR. In any case the reasoning is atrocious. Does dating back to the Puritans and their life-denying ethos make something good? Would one say that American support of the German restoration known as the Third Reich, as by John Foster Dulles in the 1930s, had nothing important to do with Nazi "machinations" because it dated back to the Puritans (which in fact it did)?[18] Is the continuity of support for Zionism among American presidents to be uncritically celebrated?

But the notion of a "Jewish restoration" is also atrocious. Restored for what? To rape Palestine, to pervert the Holocaust, to become courtiers of an empire that is destroying the planet itself? As they have built their world, the power-Jews have restored nothing so much as Moloch, the child-devouring shadow-form of Yahweh—a verdict all too literal. I'm afraid, though, that forgiveness of Peretz and Benny Morris and Avi Dichter and Moshe Ya'alon will have to wait for the Truth and Reconciliation Commission of the One State to come. Perhaps this will not come for a long time, perhaps it will never come, given the awesome wealth and power at the command of the empire, and its craven press, cowed public, and corrupted political consciousness.

Or perhaps it will ... Given the larger meaning of Israel, its fate will depend on the convulsions awaiting the world-system, upheavals whose content cannot be precisely foreseen but whose coming has been hastened by the phenomenal stupidity and recklessness of the Bush–Cheney regime and its junior partner. Of course, one does not passively wait as they stagger toward their abyss: one patiently organizes, thinks things through, expands the range of associations, and steadily intervenes.

Such is the reality facing dreamers for a better world: a slim chance, and a long haul. As ever, it is the journey that counts, the seeking of good conscience, good will, and good comrades. That, and living out the recognition, which we have scarcely begun to appreciate, much less live, that all humans are brothers and sisters. And particularly the humans of Israel/Palestine, many of whom are literally related across the historical divide—for how many Palestinians are descended from Hebrews who stayed behind after the expulsions of the second century, and later converted to Islam? I recall what my guide Ahmad said as we parted ways:

> I don't see the struggle here finishing ... What I am struggling for now is to see this universe as without borders, so that people can move without anyone stopping you to ask where are you from, where are you going, who are you, Christian, Muslim or Jew? ... This is what I believe—that all these conflicts are monstrous and cannot be justified at all. We are fighting each other as human beings. Yet no human being came into this world willingly; nobody asked us if we wanted to come into this world or not. We are just here; we came naked into the world, we didn't bring with us anything at all. Even our religion we did not bring. How can I believe that this land is mine and that land is his, since we came naked into this world? And since I will leave it naked and will take nothing with me ... We are all human beings. If we believe in God, then God created us all. I do not believe God is racist ... Nature is all his creation; we are all a product of nature, and this is not our choice but a fact.

I think of the schoolchildren I saw in Johannesburg. Bus loads of solemn and wide-eyed black children in blue and grey uniforms, visiting the Constitutional Court newly built on ground that was first a Boer and then a British prison, and then reverted to Afrikaner control, the only prison to have held three Nobel Laureates behind its walls.[19] And I think of the thousands of young Palestinians now held in Israeli prisons, as Ahmad once was, and wonder who will live to see the dawning of their day.

Notes

PROLOGUE

1. From Kevin Anderson and Peter Hudis, eds. *The Rosa Luxemburg Reader* (New York: Monthly Review Press, 2004), p. 390.

2. Seymour Hersh, *The Samson Option* (New York: Random House, 1991), p. 58. Dimona was the underground site in the Negev desert where the bomb was fashioned. The operation was so secret that its funding could not appear on the government's budget. It is remarkable how few people have read this extremely important book, which seems to have not even made it into a paperback edition.

3. Hersh, *Samson*, p. 42. It should be added that we had all cheered on America's acquisition and use of nuclear weapons and would have had little understanding of what was at stake, and therefore little rational ground to oppose Israeli nuclear proliferation. Another major factor was the Rosenberg Atomic Spy case, a virtual show trial of Jewish loyalty to America in the Cold War (defendants, key witnesses, prosecutors, lawyers and judge were all Jewish). See Chapter 6.

4. "Midway through life's path … " The opening line of Dante's *Inferno*.

5. By 1967, I had already moved sharply to the left under the influence of the Vietnam war and my government service within it. The Six Day War was less a manifestation of Zionism than a purging of something that had been deeply bottled inside. It was the last time I felt anything affirmative about Israel. By the 1980s I began writing on the subject. My first essay was "Marx on the Jewish Question," *Dialectical Anthropology*, vol. 8, pp. 31–46 (1983). In 1991, *History and Spirit*, 2nd edn. (Thetford, VT: Glad Day Press, 1998), contained extensive passages on Israel and the First Intifada. The articles which led up to the writing of this book were: "Zionism's Bad Conscience," *Tikkun*, September–October, 2002, 21–4; and "Left-Anti-Semitism and the Special Status of Israel," *Tikkun*, May–June 2003, 45–51, the latter of which was the first time I proposed a One-State solution. The Second Intifada determined me on a path of full-scale confrontation.

6. Isaac Deutscher, *The Non-Jewish Jew, and Other Essays* (London: Oxford University Press, 1968).

1   A PEOPLE APART

1. Ben Caspit, "We will not capitulate," *Maariv*, July 31, 2006.
2. The idea has been widely advanced in Zionist and mainstream American circles that Hizbullah started the bombing, that it used Qana as a launch site, and that it was a "terrorist" organization pure and simple. In fact, Hizbullah "started" things by killing and capturing some Israeli soldiers who had made a border incursion on July 12, 2006. See <http://www.whatreallyhappened.com/israeli_solders.html>. It did so partly in solidarity with the people of Gaza, which Israel was attacking at the time, and partly in the process of bargaining for prisoner exchange, something that had been done with some regularity when Ariel Sharon was PM. Israel responded with a plan that had obviously been gestating for months in collaboration with the United States (who saw this also in terms of its strategic plans against Iran), and which included heavy bombing runs, after which Hizbullah retaliated—but not, however, from Qana. As for the overall character of Hizbullah—which was founded in 1982 to protect Lebanon against Israeli aggression and is a political party and a kind of state within the state—see the particularly good article by Charles Glass, "Learning from its mistakes," *London Review of Books*, August 17, 2006. The real threat to Israel from Hizbullah is precisely that it is not defined by terrorism, nor is Hizbullah's menace the immediate harm it is capable of inflicting. The real threat is that it is a formidable long-term antagonist, the strongest Israel has yet encountered. Many observers from all camps have opined that the July–August 2006 war may prove a kind of watershed in the history of the region.
3. Ran HaCohen, "Israeli Intellectuals Love the War," see <http://antiwar.com/hacohen/?articleid=9486>. Thus famous writer A. B. Yehoshua: "At last we've got a just war, so we shouldn't gnaw at it too much till it becomes unjust" (*Ha'aretz*, July 21, 2006) while Israeli's leading novelist Amos Oz writes, under the Orwellian title "Why Israeli missiles strike for peace": "Many times in the past the Israeli peace movement criticized Israeli military operations. Not this time. [...] This time, Israel is not invading Lebanon. It is defending itself [...]. The Israeli peace movement should support Israel's attempt at self-defense, pure and simple, as long as this operation targets mostly Hezbollah and spares, as much as possible, the lives of Lebanese civilians." (*Los Angeles Times*, July 19, 2006). For the meaning of "self-defense," see the previous note.
4. HaCohen, <http://antiwar.com/hacohen/?articleid=9486>.
5. Robert Alter, *The Five Books of Moses* (New York: W.W. Norton, 2004), p. 1046.
6. Numbers 23: 9. Balaam had been brought in by King Balak of Moab to curse the Israelites camped near his citadel. What the king did not

know was that Yahweh had already appeared to Balaam and convinced him that Israel really was unique, because blessed by so powerful a God as himself, one that could not be compared or interchanged with the Gods of other peoples. The seer told Balak so, confounding him, and Israel escaped harm. Balaam was not thanked for this. We find him slain by the Israelites in the war against Midian (and mocked in later scriptures) evidently related to being blamed for encouraging the men to have sex with women of other nations (Numbers 31: 8, 16). In a characteristic refrain of the harshness that is to increasingly haunt Zionism, we find in the same chronicles Moses issuing the order that because of Yahweh's anger at Israel for extra-tribal sex, he had been commanded to "take all the chiefs of the people, and impale them in the sun before the LORD, in order that the fierce anger of the LORD may turn away from Israel." [Numbers 25: 4] All the males were killed, all the settlements were burned, and all the women, children, animals and other usable possessions were brought to the Israeli camp. Still Moses was angry: "Have you allowed all the women to live? These women here, on Balaam's advice, made the Israelites act treacherously against the LORD ...? Now therefore, kill every male among the little ones, and kill every woman who has known a man by sleeping with him. But all the young girls who have not known a man by sleeping with him, keep alive for yourselves." [Numbers 31: 15–18] This is of piece with the genocidal deeds recounted in Deuteronomy above, except for the gathering of the virgins into sex slavery, a fact which does not greatly improve the moral level, in my view.

7.   Ronald S. Hendel, "Israel among the nations," in David Biale, ed., *Cultures of the Jews* (New York: Schocken Books, 2002), p. 44. This extensive work well documents the great variability of Jewish lives and culture. See also, Peter Machinist, "Outsiders or Insiders: The Biblical view of emergent Israel and its contexts," in Laurence J. Silberstein and Robert L. Cohn, eds, *The Other in Jewish Thought and History* (New York: New York University Press, 1994), pp. 35–60. He writes of the "sharp differentiation between Israel and other inhabitants of the land ... precisely ... to affirm an 'us' whose members ... felt was threatened, and that they may have been hard put to distinguish from a host of 'others.'" [49, 51]

8.   Norman Gottwald, *The Tribes of Yahweh* (New York: Maryknoll, 1979).

9.   *Genesis* 12: 1–3. Later, in 15: 18–21, we learn that "the LORD made a covenant with Abraham, saying, 'To your descendants I give this land, from the river of Egypt to the great river, the river of Euphrates, the land of the Kennites, the Kennizites, the Kadmonites, the Hittites, the Perizzites, the Rephaim, the Amorites, the Canaanites, the Girgashites, and the Jebusites.'"—thereby providing plenty of interpretative fodder

for the advocates of Greater Israel, which is supposed to be Biblically licensed to claim all the territory from Cairo to Baghdad, and, it could be argued, north to Turkey, that is, Lebanon and Syria. All quotes from the Bible in this work, unless otherwise specified, are from the New Revised Standard Version (NRSV) of *The New Oxford Annotated Bible*, eds Bruce Metzger and Roland Murphy (New York: Oxford University Press, 1991, 1994).

10. Or in the case of Buddhism as no-voice-at-all, a distinction we need not pursue here.

11. By the Second Commandment. The theme is elaborated in Deuteronomy, and is extended in Islam, the third of the "Abrahamic religions."

12. 1800 years later, Marx would undertake to challenge this, needless to say, with results that have not yet borne fruit, but may be counted among the aims of this work.

13. I use both terms, depending on context. "Judaeophobia" is important, in part because it reminds us that the hatred in question is really directed against Jews as they have been historically shaped, and not because of their alleged "semitism"—that is, it really cannot be extended racially to Arabs of semitic origins. This is not to say that these are not also afflicted as the objects of racism. They are indeed, but differently from antisemitism/judaeophobia.

14. Quoted in Albert Lindemann, *Esau's Tears* (Cambridge: Cambridge University Press, 1997), p. 7.

15. Marvin Perry and Frederick Schweitzer, *Antisemitism: Myth and Hate from Antiquity to the Present* (New York: Palgrave Macmillan, 2002), p. 3.

16. Lindemann, *Esau's Tears*, has the best discussion of the reciprocity necessary to understand a phenomenon so complex as antisemitism.

17. Israel Shahak, *Jewish History, Jewish Religion, the Weight of Three Thousand Years* (London: Pluto Press, 1994). Page numbers in brackets refer to this edition.

18. Israel Shahak and Norton Mezvinsky, *Jewish Fundamentalism in Israel* (London: Pluto Press, 1999), p. 58.

19. Shahak and Mezvinsky, *Fundamentalism*, ix.

20. Shahak and Mezvinsky, *Fundamentalism*, 59.

21. Shahak and Mezvinsky, *Fundamentalism*, 43.

22. The canonization of Baruch Goldstein is extensively covered by Shahak and Mezvinsky, *Fundamentalism*, pp. 96–112. After he was killed by surviving members of the Mosque, the following was placed on his gravestone: "Here lies the saint, Doctor Baruch Kapal Goldstein, blessed be the memory of the righteous and holy man, may the Lord revenge his blood, who devoted his soul for the Jews, Jewish religion and Jewish land. His hands are clean and his heart is clear. He was killed as a martyr of God on the 14th of Adar, Purim, in the year 5754."

The headstone was finally removed in December 1999, more than five years later.

2   THE UNNATURAL HISTORY OF A BAD IDEA

1.   Clandestinely half-Jewish, Proust writes of France in the time of the Dreyfus trials, a traumatic moment that helped crystallize the elements of Jewish nationalism into Zionism. Proust was largely apolitical, but the Dreyfus case agitated him greatly and he was a prominent defender of the falsely accused Captain. Proust's mother had him baptised and showed no interest in her Jewish past, and the Jewish community in France was Europe's smallest at the time (though the largest today). The most authoritative biographer, Jean-Yves Tadié, *Marcel Proust: A Life* (New York: Viking-Penguin, 2000), denies that Proust's Jewishness meant anything in his sympathies for Dreyfus or in anything else in his life. However, one may argue that Bloch can stand for the split-off Jewishness in Proust himself. Bloch is characterized by a kind of bumptious vulgarity such as antisemites would have ascribed to Jews, in contrast to the Narrator, who effaces himself and is never named. All Bloch's efforts to obliterate the marks of his Jewishness fail; Charlus, the personification of Old Europe, sees right through him.

2.   David Biale, *Power and Powerlessness in Jewish History* (New York: Schocken Books, 1986), p. 120.

3.   Esther Benbassa and Jean-Christophe Attias, *The Jews and Their Future*, trans. Patrick Camiller (London: Zed, 2004), p. 27. Attias is Professor of Jewish History and Culture at the École Practique des Hautes Études, the Sorbonne. See also the massive study edited by David Biale, *Cultures of the Jews*, whose strongly argued thesis is that Jewishness is something that has had to be worked out over innumerable differentiating localities.

4.   One line of interpretation holds that the Ashkenazi Jews are descended from the Khazars, of Turkish and Central Asian origin, who were active in Eastern Europe roughly through the second half of the first millennium, that is, up to the origins of classical rabbinical Judaism. I cannot speak to the veracity of this hypothesis. However, it should be perfectly obvious that as Jews do not have a homogeneous ancestry, neither can they have an actual national home.

5.   Ze'ev Sternhell, *The Founding Myths of Israel*, trans. David Maisel (Princeton: Princeton University Press, 1998), p. 49.

6.   Nur Masalha, *Expulsion of the Palestinians*, (Washington, DC: Institute of Palestine Studies, 1992), gives a detailed and matter-of-fact account of the unrelenting desire within Zionism through the whole course of its history up to 1948 to get rid of the natives of Palestine by all means possible, while yet denying to the world, and to a degree, themselves,

that this was what they were trying to do. From asking the British to do it for them, to opining that the Palestinians would help the Iraqi economy, and that anyhow, being tent-dwellers, it didn't matter where Arabs lived, to speaking frankly that these lower people simply had to be sacrificed so that Great Israel might rise, the notion of "transfer" emerges as the core of Zionism's worldview.

7.   *Sunday Times*, June 15, 1969.

8.   Sternhell, *Founding Myths*, p. 51.

9.   The category of "race," as a biologically grounded sub-speciation, is bogus in itself, and utterly so when applied to the tropes of antisemitism, where it becomes construed as a certain "semitic type" that is supposed to apply to Jewish people. In the real world the fact of diaspora has meant the entrance of innumerable genotypes into the mix of Jewishness over the years—this itself greatly weakening the Zionist claim on the Biblical homeland. See Joel Kovel, *White Racism: A Psychohistory*, 2nd edn. (New York: Columbia University Press, 1984).

10. Arno Mayer gives a particularly fine treatment of the Judaeo-Bolshevik delusion in his *And Why Did the Heavens Not Darken?* (New York: Pantheon, 1988).

11. Amos Elon, *The Pity of it All* (New York: Henry Holt, 2002).

12. Freud and Einstein, as is well known, had Zionist sympathies. The former, deeply apolitical, never committed himself to the project as such; while the latter, who was quite active in Zionist circles in the 1920s and 1930s, had severe misgivings later on, for example, being a signatory of a December 1948 letter to *The New York Times* (along with Hannah Arendt, Sidney Hook and others), which protested a visit to the United States by Menachem Begin and condemned the "shocking example" of the Deir Yassin massacre led by Begin while expressing alarm over the "unmistakable stamp of a Fascist party for whom terrorism (against Jews, Arabs, and British alike), and misrepresentation are means, and a 'Leader State' is the goal." Thanks to Laura Nader of UC Berkeley for this. See also Einstein's epigraph to Chapter 9. In his later years he declined an offer to become the President of Israel.

13. One blushes at the comparison between the cultural advances made under the aegis of Israel and those achieved by Jews who kept faith with their marginality. To be sure, the Zionist state offers a full palette of cultural institutions and opportunities; indeed, along with the claim of being "the only democratic state in the Middle East," Israel proudly trumpets its cultural superiority over everything in the region. But where, in the arts and sciences, has Zionist culture risen above the level of competence, where has it produced the genius evinced by Jews of the Diaspora, who held on to their marginality and used it creatively?

14. For which the political Zionists were taken to task by Rabbi Ahad Ha-Am (Asher Ginsberg), who insistently asked where was the specifically Jewish character of this new state. For Ha-Am, "the salvation of Israel will come through prophets, not diplomats." Herzl, however, saw himself in a messianic way. As he wrote in his diary after the first Zionist Congress, "At Basle I founded the Jewish state." Walter Lacqueur, *A History of Zionism* (New York: Schocken Books, 1972 [2003]), p. 108. For Ha-am, see Arthur Hertzberg, *The Zionist Idea* (Philadelphia: The Jewish Publication Society, 1997) pp. 247–88.

15. Benny Morris, *Righteous Victims* (New York: Vintage Books: 2001), pp. 48–9.

16. Lacqueur, *History*, p. 49.

17. Theodor Herzl, "The Jewish State," reprinted in Herzberg, *Zionist Idea*, trans. Sylvie D'Avigdor, pp. 204–26. Quote cited on p. 213.

18. Hertzberg, *Zionist Idea*, p. 225.

19. A chart indicating American Jewry's contributions to the *Yishuv* up until 1948 can be found in Appendix V, Walid Khalidi, ed., *From Haven to Conquest* (Washington: The Institute for Palestine Studies, 1987), p. 850.

20. Alan Dershowitz, *The Case for Israel* (New York: John Wiley and Sons, 2003), pp. 22–8. A comprehensive critique of Dershowitz's ardent defense of Israel may be found in Norman Finkelstein, *Beyond Chutzpah* (Berkeley: University of California Press, 2005).

21. Their vulnerability was a result of reforms developed by the Ottomans in the mid nineteenth century, which essentially involved a "closure of the commons," and made it easy for new owners to clear the peasantry. Baruch Kimmerling and Joel S. Migdal, *The Palestinian People*, 2nd edn. (Cambridge, MA: Harvard University Press, 2003), pp. 15–21.A

22. Theodor Herzl, *The Complete Diaries*, ed. Rafael Patai (New York: Herzl Press and T. Toseloff, 1960), vol. 1, p. 88. (June 12, 1895).

23. Relations between Bundists and Zionists were to boil for decades. They briefly united during the struggle for the Warsaw Ghetto, then fell apart. Bundists were slaughtered by both Nazis and Soviets, and were eventually overwhelmed by Zionists in the post-war politics of the refugee camps when the latter forced their identity upon Jewish survivors. See next chapter for further discussion. Yosef Grodzinsky, *In the Shadow of the Holocaust* (Monroe, ME: Common Courage Press, 2004).

24. For Borochev, see Hertzberg, *Zionist Idea*, pp. 352–67.

25. The Jewish National Fund, created by Herzl in 1901, and predicted in the diary entry from 1895 quoted above, decreed that all land that it acquired was to remain inalienable Jewish property, to be neither sold nor leased to gentiles.

26. See, for example, Sir John Hope Simpson, "On the Employment of Arab Labour," in Khalidi, *From Haven to Conquest*, pp. 303–7. This official 1930 report to the Mandate concludes that the "present position, precluding any employment of Arabs in the Zionist colonies, is undesirable, from the point of view both of justice and of the good government of the country ... It is impossible to view with equanimity the extension of an enclave in Palestine from which all Arabs are excluded. The Arab population already regards the transfer of lands to Zionist hands with dismay and alarm. These cannot be dismissed as baseless in light of the Zionist policy which is described above."

27. Morris, *Righteous Victims*, p. 52, writes that from the beginning there were "clear echoes of Arab reaction more generally to Zionist exclusiveness, of which Hebrew labor was but one manifestation. Syrian notable Hakki Bey al-Azm ... said: 'We see Jews excluding themselves completely from Arabs in language, school, commerce, customs, their entire economic life. ... [Hence] the [Arab] population considers them a foreign race.'"

28. Sternhell, *Founding Myths*, pp. 7, 111.

29. The painstaking negotiations leading up to the doctrine brought forward major Jewish-American figures like Louis Brandeis, Felix Frankfurter and Stephen Wise, in alliance with the European Zionists led by Chaim Weizmann. Zionists were able to influence Woodrow Wilson through Brandeis, who had appointed him to the Supreme Court in 1916. In addition, the president was predisposed to see things the Judaeo-Christian way thanks to extensive biblical study. All this went a considerable way toward helping American Jews break away from antisemitic discrimination, and allowed the burgeoning of Zionism in the United States. At the same time, it further relegated the Arabs to orientalist oblivion. As for Balfour himself, the former PM and now Foreign Secretary called himself an "ardent Zionist" in a 1919 conversation with Brandeis. Felix Frankfurter, "An Interview in Mr. Balfour's Apartment, 23 Rue Nitot," in Khalidi, *From Haven to Conquest*, pp. 195–9. To prove this, he wrote in 1919 that the interests of the Jewish settlers were "of far profounder import than the desires and prejudices of the 700,000 Arabs who now inhabit that ancient land ..." See also, Frank Manuel, "Judge Brandeis and the Framing of the Balfour Declaration," in Khalid, *From Haven to Conquest*, pp. 165–72; J. M. N. Jeffries, "Analysis of the Balfour Declaration," pp. 173–88. See also Kathleen Christison, *Perceptions of Palestine*, (Berkeley: University of California Press, 1999).

30. This was the second of the major Arab outbursts, following one in Jaffa, in 1921, and preceding a wider revolt from 1936–39, which was put down by the British. Zionists make much of these riots as proof positive of the savagery of the Palestinians, and/or of their manipulation

by vicious leaders, in particular, the Grand Mufti, the "uncompromising Jew-hater Haj Amin al-Husseini" (Dershowitz, *The Case*, p.
42). The reality is depressingly different, and typical: a protracted and
escalating series of tit for tat incidents by one side followed by the
other, focussing in this instance on access to and control of the Arab's
Temple Mount, and the Jew's Wailing Wall, which happened to be
built over the same ground, but which the Arabs were to administer
under the British Mandate, and over which right-wing Zionists were
demanding control, even proposing to rebuild their long-lost Temple
on the site. On August 14, 6000 Jews marched in Tel Aviv, chanting
"The Wall is Ours"; 3000 gathering for prayer that evening. Two
days later, the Arabs began open hostilities, which lasted for a week,
during which period 133 Jews and 116 Arabs violently perished. See
Morris, *Righteous Victims*, pp. 111–20. Morris comments further that
by "1929 the Arabs understood that the disproportionate growth of
the Yishuv, nurtured and sustained by [British] Mandatory government
measures, promised to turn them into a minority in their own land";
and quotes Barbara Smith: "the institutional and ideological basis for
separatism had crystallized ... The economic partition of Palestine
predated geopolitical partition and was well under way."[111]

31.   Arlosoroff's letter is reproduced in full in Khalidi, *From Haven to
      Conquest*, pp. 245–54.

32.   Though not to Jabotinsky himself, who was out of the country and
      in any case had constantly to contend with more extreme elements
      within his group. In fact, he had just clamped down on some of his
      people for their admiration of Hitler, telling them that they had better
      attack Nazism or be expelled. The violent attack on Arlosoroff seems
      to have been a displacement of this. For a comprehensive discussion,
      see Lenni Brenner, *Zionism in the Age of the Dictators* (Westport,
      CT: Lawrence Hill, 1983). The quote from the press appears on
      pp. 128–9. See also Brenner's study of revisionism, *The Iron Wall*
      (London: Zed, 1984). Space does not permit detailing the facts of the
      case. However, Arlosoroff's wife identified one of the assailants as a
      revisionist official, who was convicted and later released upon the
      unsubstantiated confession of an Arab prisoner. In 1944, the murder
      weapon turned up again in the Cairo assassination of Lord Moyne,
      British High Commissioner for the Middle East, by two members of
      the Stern Gang, a revisionist offshoot (and was discovered to have
      also been involved in the killings of two Arabs and four British police
      officers). It is remarkable though unsurprising how little attention is
      given in the standard histories, for example, Sachar, Lacqueur, Morris,
      to Brenner's account despite the fact that he relies heavily on valuable
      primary sources. Without naming him, Lacqueur indirectly dismisses

Brenner's thickly argued thesis that extensive connections existed between Zionism and fascism as "pernicious nonsense."

33.   Howard Sachar, *A History of Israel*, 2nd edn. (New York: Alfred Knopf, 2003), p. 214.

34.   Morris, *Righteous Victims*, p. 120. Lacqueur adds that "after the murder of Arlosoroff, the polarisation in the Palestinian Jewish community brought many new recruits to Irgun." *History*, p. 374.

35.   The phrase is drawn from the diaries of Moshe Sharett, Israel's first foreign minister and prime minister from 1954–55. Livia Rokach, *Israel's Sacred Terrorism* (Belmont, MA: AAUG, 1980). See Chapter 7.

3   THE SPECTRE OF SHOAH

1.   Lacqueur, *History*, p. 384.

2.   Mahatma Gandhi, "The Jews in Palestine 1938." In Khalidi, *From Haven to Conquest*, pp. 367–70.

3.   Lecturing against the Iraq war in Vienna, June 2005, my wife and I were told not to expect any turnout. Why? Because the Austrian "left" supports Bush in Iraq, not for his or America's sake but because this is what Israel wants, and they are still much too guilt-ridden about Austrian complicity in the Holocaust to go against Israel's wishes.

4.   Norman Finkelstein, *The Holocaust Industry* (London: Verso, 2000).

5.   This was a prominent theme of the guilt-ridden European literature of the time, epitomized in Jean-Paul Sartre's *Anti-Semite and Jew*, trans. George Becker (New York: Schocken, 1948 [1965]). This fascinating text deserves much more attention than we can give it here. Sartre's agony over Shoah leads him into undialectical half-truths ("the rationalism of Jews is a passion—the passion for the universal" [111]) and nonsensical falsehoods ("The Jews are the mildest of men, passionately hostile to violence" [117]). According to Betsy Bowman and Bob Stone (personal communication), the question haunted Sartre to the end of his days. He was very sympathetic to the Palestinian cause, and supported their Right of Return, yet could not bring himself to directly criticize Israel. See also Joseph Massad, "The Legacy of Jean-Paul Sartre," *Al Ahram* (Cairo, no. 623, January 30–February 5, 2003).

6.   Tom Segev, *The Seventh Million*, trans. Haim Watzman (New York: Hill and Wang, 1994), provides a vivid portrait of the great range of effects.

7.   Thus Nahum Goldmann, President of the World Zionist Council, in October 1981: "We will have to understand that Jewish suffering during the Holocaust no longer will serve as a protection, and we certainly must refrain from using the argument of the Holocaust to

justify whatever we may do. To use the Holocaust as an excuse for the bombing of Lebanon, for instance, as Menachem Begin does, is a kind of 'Hillul Hashem' [sacrilege], a banalization of the Shoah, which must not be used to justify politically doubtful and morally indefensible policies." Quoted in Noam Chomsky, *The Fateful Triangle* (Boston: South End Press, 1999), p. 98.

8. This consummate charlatan has refused to utter any critical judgment against Israel over the years, claiming he doesn't have complete enough knowledge. If generalized, this tactic would suffice to suppress all criticism of state violence—including that of Nazi Germany, given how unfathomable the Holocaust is said to be. As a correspondant in the hire of Irgun from 1947–49, one might think Wiesel to be in a position to say something interesting about the Deir Yasin massacre carried out by that body in 1948, but for some obscure reason he holds back. On the other hand, he has no hesitation in praising the United States for its venture into Iraq and in doing so, shows no hesitation in unctuously proclaiming that he fully understands that war. In a recent column (July 4, 2004) in *Parade* Magazine, titled "The America I Love," Wiesel deals with mounting atrocity stories such as the "abuses" in Abu Ghraib prison with the following: "Well, one could say that no nation is composed of saints alone. None is sheltered from mistakes or misdeeds. All have their Cain and Abel. It takes vision and courage to undergo serious soul-searching and to favor moral conscience over political expediency. And America, in extreme situations, is endowed with both. America is always ready to learn from its mishaps. Self-criticism remains its second nature. Not surprising, some Europeans do not share such views. In extreme left-wing political and intellectual circles, suspicion and distrust toward America is the order of the day. They deride America's motives for its military interventions, particularly in Iraq. They say: It's just money. As if America went to war only to please the oil-rich capitalists. They are wrong. America went to war to liberate a population too long subjected to terror and death." Here Wiesel, a man dedicated to the recovery of memory, seems to have forgotten the war was said to be about stanching the flow of weapons of mass destruction. This is a man who was granted the Nobel Peace Prize in 1986, not so subtly acting as an Israeli agent in goading the United States on to the destruction of Iraq.

9. Of course, family and other directly personal bonds are extensively distorted; but these are either the product of individual mental pathologies, or remain particularized and can only be drawn together in some intermediate rubric like tribe or nation. As for the universal, this, too, is obviously imperfectly realized both in practice and theory. However, its intrinsic nature is such that the more we realize it as a

goal, the further removed we become from these kinds of pathologies of splitting.

10.   Hitler and Stalin are included among this type.

11.   The Italian dictator, who was not known for antisemitism, was very fond of the revisionists. In 1935 Mussolini told David Prato, who later became the chief rabbi of Rome: "For Zionism to succeed you need to have a Jewish state, with a Jewish flag and a Jewish language. The person who really understands that is your fascist Jabotinsky." Brenner, *Dictators*, p. 117.

12.   Mayer, *Heavens*.

13.   The definitive study of Nazi mentality in this regard is Klaus Theweleit, *Male Fantasies*, 2 vols (Minneapolis: University of Minnesota Press, 1987, 1989); and for the Jewish side, Daniel Boyarin, *Unheroic Conduct* (Berkeley: University of California Press, 1997). In Proust's extraordinary (even for Proust) 20 page meditation upon homosexuality in which the Narrator engages at the beginning of *Cities of the Plain* after discovering that this is the secret of M. de Charlus, no fewer than eight references are made to Jews as exemplars of those whose exclusion and corresponding banding together are of the same type as that forced upon "inverts." Two of these pertain to Zionism, and in the final one of the series he refers to Zionism as a "lamentable error": "We shall study them [ie, the homosexuals] with greater thoroughness in the course of the following pages; but I have thought it as well to utter here a provisional warning against the lamentable error of proposing (just as people have encouraged a Zionist movement) to create a Sodomist movement and to rebuild Sodom. For, no sooner had they arrived there than [sic] the Sodomites would leave the town so as not to have the appearance, would take wives, keep mistresses in other cities where they would find, incidentally, every diversion that appealed to them." Marcel Proust, *Remembrance of Things Past*, trans. C. K. Scott Moncrieff and Terence Kilmartin, vol. 2 (New York: Random House: 1981), pp. 655–6.

14.   Segev, *Seventh Million*, p. 96.

15.   Segev, *Seventh Million*, p. 28.

16.   Grodzinsky, *Shadow*, pp. 9, 11. The phrase reveals that reduction of humanity to a thing-like status that regularly accompanies grandiose plans of social engineering.

17.   Including the shameful record of the United States vis-à-vis the human costs of fascism—whether by not getting aid to the Spanish Republic, not bombing the rail lines to Auschwitz, not freely admitting earlier waves of Second World War refugees, etc. There was, besides nativism, a twofold root to these lapses, both sides underappreciated: first, the widespread alliances between the Western democratic ruling classes and their fascist counterparts; and second, the influence of pro-Nazi

Pope Pius XII and his American henchman, Francis Cardinal Spellman, who controlled the loyalties of FDR's Catholic working-class base. See John Cooney, *The American Pope* (New York: Crown, 1984).

18. This section is drawn from Morris L. Ernst, "F.D.R.'s International Plan for Jewish Refugees," in Khalidi, *From Haven to Conquest*, pp. 489–94. Reprinted from his 1948 memoir, *So Far So Good*.

19. This section is drawn from Grodzinsky's valuable study, *Shadow*.

20. Grodzinsky, *Shadow* p. 85.

21. Grodzinsky, *Shadow* p. 207.

22. Though as Grodzinsky, *Shadow*, pp. 222–6, emphasizes, fully 60 percent ended up elsewhere despite all the efforts to prevent this.

23. Michael Melchior, MK, "An immoral state," *Ha'aretz*, August 19, 2004. I do not know if Melchior factors in the religio-ethnic distinctions that pervade Israel and bring down the burden to a vastly disproportionate degree upon the 18 percent of the country comprised by Arab Muslims and Christians, but assume this to be the case. Again, "Thirty-eight percent of families did not have enough money to heat their homes, and 16 percent of prescriptions were not used because people could not pay for the drugs. Some 45 percent of those in need of dental treatment didn't seek it, and 50 percent of those who didn't have comprehensive health insurance gave up on it because of financial constraints." Stuart Winer, *The Jerusalem Post*, August 9, 2004.

24. Dan ben-David, "The State of Israel's Education," *Ha'aretz*, June 20, 2006. The author is Professor of Economics at Tel Aviv University.

25. Tony Karon, "Where do France's Jews Belong?" *TIME* Online edition, July 21, 2004. See <http://www.time.com/time/columnist/karon/article/0,9565,671180,00.html>.

4 THE ONLY DEMOCRACY IN THE MIDDLE EAST

1. From a letter to his son, Amos, October 5, 1937. Quoted in Joel Beinin, *Was the Red Flag Flying There?* (Berkeley: University of California Press, 1990), p. 14.

2. Yehoshafat Palmon, advisor to the Mayor of Jerusalem on Arab affairs, on how to proceed after the 1967 war placed most of the city in Israeli hands. Quoted in David Hirst, *The Gun and the Olive Branch* (New York: Thunder's Mouth Press/Nation Books, 2003), p. 358.

3. Biale, *Power*, has a comprehensive discussion of these developments.

4. The literature on Gramsci is huge. For a compilation of his essential writings, see Antonio Gramsci, *Selections from the Prison Noteboooks*, eds, and trans. Quintin Hoare and Geoffrey Nowell Smith (New York: International Publishers, 1971). For a biography and general study, see Alastair Davidson, *Antonio Gramsci: Towards an Intellectual Biography* (London: Merlin Press, 1977).

5. The distinction between accumulation and legitimation in the functioning of modern states is well drawn by James O'Connor, *The Fiscal Crisis of the State*, 2nd edn. (Somerset, NJ: Transaction Publishers, 2001).

6. Finkelstein, *Chutzpah*, pp. 207–20.

7. Bernard Avishai, *The Tragedy of Zionism* (New York: Helios Press, 2002), pp. 189–90.

8. The story is told in Avishai, *Tragedy*, pp. 184–90. The publisher lists 29 favorable comments, from left, right, Jewish and non-Jewish sources.

9. Avishai, *Tragedy*, p. 185.

10. Avishai, *Tragedy*, p. 188.

11. See Hirst, *The Gun*, pp. 283–90, with references to other studies. Jews in Iraq enjoyed a prosperous, well-integrated position consistent with their ancient lineage as citizens of Mesopotamia. The only significant violence against them in modern times occurred in 1941, in association with a spell of social chaos brought about by Nazi machinations, following which the sense of tension abated. Insofar as there was hostility from the Arabs, it was, entirely understandably, against Zionism—which fit nicely into the young Israeli government's need to entice Arab Jews after the Holocaust deprived it of the desired Ashkenazi. In Ilan Pappe's judgment, a combination of Iraqi government hostility to potential Zionism amongs its Jewish citizens and bombs set off by the Jewish Agency did the trick. Ilan Pappe, *A History of Modern Palestine* (Cambridge: Cambridge University Press, 2004), pp. 175–82.

12. As recently as 2004, Sharon was beating the drums to encourage immigration by calling attention to—and grossly exaggerating—French antisemitism. The word, terrorism, does not appear in the index to Avishai's book; while Deir Yassin is dismissed (p. 177) as a "horrible act [which] is still shrouded in mystery," a preposterous claim in view of extensive investigation by the British, as well as many first-hand accounts, etc. (See Chapter 7).

13. Pappe, *History*, p. 175.

5 FACTS ON THE GROUND

1. Jonathan Nitzan and Shimson Bichler, *The Global Political Economy of Israel* (London: Pluto Press, 2002), p. 91.

2. To reiterate, the land, though legally purchased from mainly absentee owners, was, insofar as it was desirable, thickly populated with Palestinians who had to be forced off if the new owners were going to use it to become settlers of their own. This was the launching point of the actual Zionist-Palestinian conflict.

3. Net profit for the Leumi Group in 2004 was $433 million, not huge as banks go, but a 62.8 percent increase from 2003. The Bank has branches in 18 countries, on all continents. See <http://english.leumi. co.il/Home/0,2777,1415,00.html>.

4. Nitzan and Bichler, *Political Economy*, p. 299. By 1995, "the bank had a vast array of precious holdings, operating across the economy. All and all, it had stakes in more than 770 companies …."

5. Pappe observes further that the kibbutzim, the mainstay of Zionist utopian vision, was forced to used Mizrahi labor. However, the Kibbutzniks couldn't tolerate adult African Jews, and so used young children, who were separated from their parents and made to work the least desirable lands. *History*, p. 180.

6. Tom Segev, *The First Israelis*, trans. Haim Watzman (New York: Hill and Wang, 1984), p. 157.

7. Nitzan and Bichler, *Political Economy*, p. 276.

8. Estimates run as high as 300,000 non-Jews, whose immigration is facilitated by fake documents and the never-ending hunger for non-Arab bodies. A number of antisemitic incidents are blamed on the gentile newcomers.

9. The reader will perhaps recall the mild flap over the ascent in 2005 of Amir Peretz, a leftist-Sephardic Jew, to the leadership of Labor. Did this mean a turn in the direction of Israel's progressive party? Well it did, but not the direction imagined. As this is written, Peretz sits as Minister of Defense, in charge of destroying Gaza and Lebanon, though apparently under the thumb of his generals.

10. Nitzan and Bichler, *Political Economy*, p. 351. During the 1950s, the top 20 percent of the Israeli population earned only 3.3 times as much as the bottom 20 percent; while the United States, by the same standard, went as high as 9.5. By 1995, however, the situation was reversed. Israel had reached a ratio of 21.3 between the top and bottom, while the United States had only gone to a factor of 10.6. According to *World Wealth Report 2005*, there are now 7400 millionaires in Israel, twice the world per capita average. Where the net assets of the world's millionaires rose by 8.5 percent between 2004 and 2005, the rise in Israel was 20 percent.

11. Joel Kovel, *The Enemy of Nature* (London: Zed, 2002).

12. Allon Tal, *Pollution in a Promised Land* (Berkeley: University of California Press, 2002), p. 77. This work, by an insider in Israel's environmental movement, is distinctly magisterial, though less successful in its discussion of the Occupied Territories than of Israel itself.

13. By the 1990s, in part due to the immigration of many highly trained Russians, Israel had achieved the world's highest proportion per

capita of engineers and PhD's in science. Nitzan and Bichler, *Political Economy*, p. 347.

14.   Tal opens his book with the hair-raising story of the 1997 incident when a bridge over the Yarkon River near Tel Aviv broke during ceremonies for the Maccabiah Games which Israel was proudly hosting for Jewish athletes from across the world, plunging a good portion of the Australian team into waters of unfathomable malignancy. Three athletes died of acute toxicity and many others suffered horrendously (pp. 1–17).

15.   Chris McGreal, "Once mighty Jordan reduced to a trickle," *Guardian*, March 9, 2005. "Fifty years ago," writes McGreal, "1.3bn cubic metres of water flowed through the lower Jordan each year. Today, environmentalists say that if 200m cubic metres travel the lower Jordan then it is a good year, and nearly half of that is raw sewage from Palestinian villages and Jewish settlements, the effluent from commercial fish farms and other untreated waste water." As a result, the Dead Sea is becoming dead-er, losing a meter a year and down to one third its old area. There is talk about sacrificing Israeli agriculture to save the Dead Sea—for tourism.

16.   I have offered an account of this in Joel Kovel, *The Enemy of Nature*. Strictly speaking, every capitalist-industrial nation has its own profile of how the reigning mode of production destabilizes ecosystems. We do no more than draw that profile for Israel here.

17.   With the highly significant exception of Israel's unacknowledged nuclear arsenal, which somehow never gets taken into account in the various tribulations of the Middle East.

18.   Avi Shlaim, *The Iron Wall* (New York: W.W. Norton, 2001), pp. 228–32, summarizes the extensive backdrop to this, mainly with Syria.

19.   Masalha, *Expulsion*, p. 17.

20.   The notion of wilderness exists only within the culture of the West. Other civilizations, and certainly indigenous peoples, do not regard nature as radically Other and an antagonist to civilization—with the exception of the people described in the Pentateuch of the Old Testament, whose estrangement from nature figures in the history they initiated.

21.   David Ben-Gurion, "The Imperatives of the Jewish Revolution," in Hertzberg, *Zionist Idea*, p. 617.

22.   Ethan Ganor, "Pollution, Apartheid and Protest in Occupied Palestine," *Earth First! Journal*, September, 2005. Ganor writes: "Because Israel's own, generally stringent, environmental laws regulating industrial processes and waste discharge are not enforced inside the Occupied Territories, the West Bank has become a sacrifice zone. Many of the factories have no environmental safeguards and unleash solid waste burned in open air, wastewater that flows into watersheds, or hazardous

waste dumped and buried at outdoor sites. Lands near the foothills of industrial zones are especially vulnerable. One of the largest zones, Barqan, near Nablus, encompasses 80 factories and generates 810,000 cubic meters of wastewater per year. The wastewater flows into a wadi (a watercourse that is dry except during the rainy season) and pollutes the agricultural lands of three Palestinian villages." As Tal documents, the stringency of environmental laws within Israel, proper, is relative to what is in effect a free-fire zone in the Territories.

23. For a summary prepared for the UN, see, Center for Economic and Social Rights, *Thirsting for Justice: Israeli violations of the human right to water in the Occupied Palestinian Territories*, May, 2003. See <www.cesr.org>.

24. The Israeli human rights group, B'tselem, has the most useful compilation of this. See <www.btselem.org>.

25. Zafrir Rinat, "Survey shows environmental hazards spreading throughout the Dan region." See <www.Haaretz.com 09/03/2005>.

6 PARTNERS IN ZION

1. From an email to her mother, February 27, 2003. The complete correspondence can be read in *Monthly Review*, May, 2003, pp. 50–60.

2. According to Amira Hass, in *Ha'aretz*, May 19, 2004, there is such a network, which chiefly serves to smuggle in food, medicines and other necessities of life forbidden because of Israeli blockade. Hass further emphasizes that the Palestinians are capable of regenerating the tunnels faster than the IDF can rub them out.

3. Tanya Reinhart recounts a blood-curdling interview with a D9 bulldozer driver from *Yediot Aharonot*. The unit in question received medals for its work in the Jenin refugee camp in 2002. The driver, who was on duty for 75 continuous hours and more or less continuously drunk, reports: "For three days I just destroyed and destroyed ... They were warned by loudspeaker to get out of the house before I come, but I gave no one a chance. I didn't wait. I didn't give one blow, and wait for them to come out. I would just ram the house with full power, to bring it down as fast as possible. I wanted ... to get as many as possible ... Others may have restrained themselves, or so they say. Who are they kidding? ... I didn't give a damn about the Palestinians, but I didn't just ruin with no reason. It was all under orders ... If I am sorry for anything, it is for not tearing the whole camp down." *Israel/Palestine: How to end the war of 1948* (New York: Seven Stories Press, 2002), pp. 161–5.

4. Naomi Klein, "Rescuing Jessica Lynch, Forgetting Rachel Corrie," in Tony Kushner and Alisa Solomon, eds, *Wrestling with Zion* (New York: Grove Press, 2003), pp. 69–72.

5. Most recently, we have the near 100 percent Congressional support of Israel's devastation of Lebanon in July 2006, only eight Representatives dissenting. This blank check for mayhem was accompanied by the predictable increase in Israeli aggression.

6. Martin Peretz, "Traveling With Bad Companions," *Los Angeles Times*, June 23, 2003.

7. Using the official Israeli press report as evidence, the ISM states that although some of their people had a "brief social encounter" with the bombers at Rafah, they knew nothing of the bombers' intentions, had no other links and provided no other support—indeed, "Israeli military and security had much more contact with the two than we did." They deny any link with any armed Palestinian group and affirm that "all ISM statements and actions clearly demonstrate our commitment to non-violence." As for the allegation that ISM has supported the Palestinian right of "legitimate armed struggle," their website says: "As enshrined in international law and UN resolutions, we recognize the Palestinian right to resist Israeli violence and occupation via legitimate armed struggle. However we believe that nonviolence can be a powerful weapon in fighting oppression and we are committed to the principles of nonviolent resistance." Peretz substitutes "support" for "recognize," then fragments the statement so that what the ISM emphatically does support as an alternative to armed struggle—nonviolence—is left out. See website links for Rachel Corrie, <http://www.palsolidarity.org/main/category/rachel-corrie/>. For information about the Israeli house demolitions that Rachel Corrie and the ISM sought to counter, see <http://web.amnesty.org/library/Index/ENGMDE150332004>; <http://electronicintifada.net/v2/article2700.shtml>; <http://www.freepalestinecampaign.org/attacks_on_ISM.htm>.

8. See <www.RachelsWords.org> for details. Strenuous agitation succeeded in restoring the play's appearance in the autumn of 2006. Indeed, Rachel's cause has been taken up by a dedicated group of activists, including her family.

9. Matt Wolf, "Requiem for an Idealist (and a Cause Celebre)," *The New York Times*, March 31, 2006 (E3).

10. For a well-researched and thorough compilation of British-Zionist ties in the Blair government, see <www.spinwatch.org/index.php>; and particularly, Muhammad Idrees Ahmad, "Labour Friends of Israel in the House," <http://www.spinwatch.org/modules.php?name=Content&pa=showpage&pid=345>. I am grateful to David Miller for this information.

11. David R. Francis, "Economist tallies swelling cost of Israel to US," *Christian Science Monitor*, December 9, 2002.

12. Richard Curtiss, *The Cost of Israel to U.S. Taxpayers* (Los Angeles: If America Knew, n.d.); see <http://www.ifamericansknew.org/stats/cost_

of_israel.html>. Curtiss concludes that when hidden costs are factored, "the nearly $14,630 every one of 5.8 million Israelis received from the U.S. government by Oct. 31, 1997 has cost American taxpayers $23,240 per Israeli."

13. Joel Kovel, *Red-Hunting in the Promised Land*, 2nd edn. (London: Continuum, 1997).

14. The second bombing occurred in July 2006, during Israel's assault on Lebanon. As for the indictment: "On December 15, 2005, in New York, the Center for Constitutional Rights (CCR) served process papers on Lt. Gen. (ret.) Moshe Ya'alon, former Head of the Intelligence Branch and former Chief of Staff of the Israel Defense Forces (IDF), for war crimes and other human rights violations. The class action lawsuit is in connection with the hundreds of civilian deaths and injuries in the 1996 shelling of a United Nations compound in Qana, in the south of Lebanon. The complaint was filed in the U.S. District Court for the District of Columbia, and process was served on the defendant this afternoon in Washington, D.C. The charges include war crimes, extrajudicial killing, crimes against humanity, and cruel, inhuman or degrading treatment or punishment." See Belhas vs Ya'alon at <http://www.ccr-ny.org/v2/legal/human_rights/rightsArticle.asp?ObjID=eqV BNxvlcx&Content=682>. On March 7, 2006, Ya'alon gave a talk at the prestigious right-wing Hudson Institute that began, "Since the 1979 Iranian Revolution, the Islamist regime in Tehran has continually declared its aspiration to annihilate the State of Israel," and took off from there. See <http://www.washingtoninstitute.org/templateC07. php?CID=287>.

15. James Bennet, "Israel says war on Iraq would benefit the region," *The New York Times*, February 27, 2003. The article refers to a speech made by Defense Minister Shaul Mofaz to the Conference of Presidents of Major Jewish Organizations, beating the war drums on the eve of the invasion.

16. The report, called "A Clean Break: A New Strategy for Defending the Realm," was issued in 1996. Written in a messianic tone and with a steady eye on further forging the relationship with the United States, it is obsessed with "containing" Syria and also Iran, militarily if warranted. The report also calls for the "*right of hot pursuit* for self defense into all Palestinian areas"... " [this included as well a call to remilitarize the Lebanon border, as did indeed happen in 2006] "a justifiable practice with which Americans can sympathize"; a "focus on removing Saddam Hussein from power in Iraq — an important Israeli strategic objective in its own right"; and a radical shift in relations with the United States: weaning itself from foreign aid by moving full tilt into neoliberal globalization. "Israel can become self-reliant only by, in a bold stroke rather than in increments, *liberalizing its economy*,

cutting taxes, relegislating a free-processing zone, and selling-off public lands and enterprises — moves which will electrify and find support from a broad bipartisan spectrum of key pro-Israeli Congressional leaders, including Speaker of the House, Newt Gingrich." The report is widely available on the internet. For the original, see <http://www.israeleconomy.org/strat1.htm>.

17.   Alan Wald, *The New York Intellectuals* (Chapel Hill: University of North Carolina Press, 1987). See also, Kovel, *Red-Hunting*.

18.   As successor to an immensely powerful FDR, Truman floundered about for some time looking for support. Well-organized Zionist contributors lept into the breach and established effective control. This provided the context for his manipulation of the UN in 1947 to promote partition on terms favorable to Israel, because, as he admitted, there were hundreds of thousands of Jewish votes clamoring for this and scarcely any Arab ones opposing it. Harry Clark, "How it all began: Truman and Israel," *Counterpunch*, June 3, 2006. As for Eisenhower, though he enraged the Israelis in 1956 by squashing the Suez invasion, he was unable to stop the making of the nuclear bomb, as observed above. See Hersh, *The Samson Option*. Kathleen Christison describes Eisenhower's "aloofness" with respect to Israel and his utter lack of feeling for its drama. He felt that "no group should have a 'caretaker' at the White House." However, he felt even less for Palestinians, who got nowhere at all with his administration. *Perceptions of Palestine* (Berkeley: University of California Press, 1999), p. 97.

19.   Akiva Eldar, "People and Politics," *Ha'aretz*, June 27, 2002.

20.   Christison, *Perceptions*, has an excellent discussion. She is sympathetic to Carter but critical of his abstract and moralistic approach.

21.   Jeff Blankfort, personal communication.

22.   Tom Tugend. See <http://www.jewishjournal.com/home/preview.php?id=15285>. As Jeff Blankfort has pointed out (personal communication), such contributions are tax deductible under US law. Calling Lebanon a "terrorist state" is akin to calling Rachel Corrie a supporter of terrorism.

23.   See <http://www.ccr-ny.org/v2/legal/human_rights/rightsArticle.asp?ObjID=ccDzL2NjXs&Content=678>.

24.   Yossi Verter, "Rabin rally may be delayed to allow Bill Clinton to take part," *Ha'aretz*, October 6, 2005. See <http://www.sourcewatch.org/index.php?title=Haim_Saban>. Andrew Ross Sorkin, "Shlepping to Moguldom," *The New York Times*, September 5, 2004. Writes Sorkin, "This year, [Saban] invited Germany's most prominent advertising executives to his home in Los Angeles for dinner with Mr. Clinton. The executives, he said, were stunned."

25. Recent studies of this phenomenon include Esther Kaplan, *With God on their Side* (New York: New Press, 2004); and Kevin Phillips, *American Theocracy* (New York: Viking, 2006).

26. Ernest Tuveson, *Redeemer Nation* (Chicago: University of Chicago Press, 1968). See also, Kovel, *History and Spirit, Red-Hunting*.

27. See <http://people-press.org/reports/display.php3?PageID=725>. The site as a whole, <http://pewresearch.org/>, contains a wealth of poll data on this crisis (at least 250 studies), including the finding from July 2006, that the US citizenry remain supportive of Israel in its bombing and invasion of Lebanon despite losing support for virtually all other aspects of American foreign policy.

28. Sorkin, "Shlepping".

29. By 1971, the United States had supplanted world Jewry as Israel's largest donor and unilateral source of capital transfers. Joel Beinin, "The United States-Israeli Alliance," in Tony Kushner and Alisa Solomon, eds, *Wrestling With Zion* (New York: Grove, 2003), pp. 41–50.

30. The United States closely monitored the 1982 invasion of Lebanon, which Reagan supported using the Cold War logic that the PLO was a Soviet tool. It paid profoundly in 2001, Osama bin Laden having said that he conceived the idea of flying planes into American buildings at the time as an act of revenge. It is characteristic that the 2006 invasion of Lebanon has been carried out insouciantly in spite of this.

31. Beinin, "The United States-Israeli Alliance."

32. Israel played the Samson card in the 1973 war when their army was facing a devastating defeat at the hands of Egypt and Syria. The threat to use nuclear force was taken very seriously by Henry Kissinger, who saw to it that reinforcements were rushed into the fray. This constituted a major escalation of United States military aid. Hersch, *The Samson Option*.

33. Nachman Ben-Yehuda, *The Masada Myth: Collective Memory and Mythmaking in Israel* (Madison: University of Wisconsin Press, 1995). According to Ben-Yehuda, a professor at the Hebrew University in Jerusalem, the "heroes" of Masada were a group of robbers and assassins, the Sicarii, who terrorized and massacred Jewish villages and escaped to Masada after being forced by other Jews to leave Jerusalem. Thus they did nothing to protect the capital from Roman aggression. Although there were instances of heroic resistance against the Roman legions, none of these took place at Masada, which essentially was a gangster camp, the occupants of which took their lives once the Romans laid siege. In other words, the event more resembles the 1978 mass suicide at Jonestown, in Guyana, than the myth dear to Israeli identity. Whether this expresses a deeper truth about Israel is a matter I leave to the reader.

34. The most useful guide to the literature and essential features of the incident is Wikipedia: <http://en.wikipedia.org/wiki/USS_Liberty_incident#_ref-5>.

35. Seymour Hersh, "The Traitor," *The New Yorker Magazine*, January 18, 1999, pp. 26–33. See <http://www.freerepublic.com/focus/fr/576453/posts>. See also Hersh, *The Samson Option*.

36. Justin Raimondo, *The Terror Enigma* (New York: iUniverse, 2003).

37. Jerry Markon, "DoD Spy for Israel given 12 years," *Washington Post*, January 21, 2006.

38. John Mearsheimer and Stephen Walt, "The Israel Lobby," *London Review of Books*, March 23, 2006. The essay had been previously rejected by the *Atlantic Monthly*, once owned by Mortimer Zuckerman. A whole monograph could be written about its reception, the storm attending which was not due to the originality of its findings (which are available from many sources all over the internet) but to the fact that it represented at least a temporary breach of the gentlemen's agreement to never discuss Israel seriously in mainstream circles. Walt was the academic dean of Harvard's Kennedy School. His impending resignation was mysteriously announced shortly after the essay appeared, even as Harvard was withdrawing its logo from the article's website. An excerpt from Martin Peretz's contribution to the attack appears at the close of Chapter 10. As for AIPAC, its former executive director Morris Amitay pooh-poohed the essay in the *New York Sun*: "I would be worried if Henry Kissinger was saying this. But who are these guys? As far as I'm concerned this is a tribute to the Jewish community. We couldn't do anything about Auschwitz, but look, we now control foreign policy for a region of the world so vital to American interests"—thus barefacedly admitting what he is supposed to deny. Eli Lake, "David Duke Claims to Be Vindicated By a Harvard Dean," *New York Sun*, March 20, 2006.

7 BAD CONSCIENCE AND STATE RACISM

1. Morris, *Righteous Victims*, p. 209. According to Israeli human rights sources, the number of 93 is the best current estimate, though some believe that the true number was 130–40. An original number of 254 was proclaimed by the Jews as well as Arabs and became a factor in the Exodus. See Hirst, *The Gun*, pp. 248–56, which contains eyewitness reports and official British records.

2. From Yossi Meman and Dan Raviv, *Friends in Deed: Inside the U.S. Israeli Alliance* (New York: Hyperion, 1995), p. 354. Quoted in Phyllis Bennis, "Of Dogs and Tails: The Changing Nature of the Pro-Israeli Lobby, The Unchanging Nature of the U.S.-Israeli Alliance," in Tony Kushner and Alisa Solomon, eds, *Wrestling With Zion* (New York:

Grove, 2003), p. 127. The Reagan administration was supporting Saddam Hussein at the time as an instrument against the Iranian revolution and had been forced to denounce the attack.

3. Cf. Shlaim, *Iron Wall*, p. 419. Begin blamed himself for pre-empting medical care that should have gone to her.

4. Brenner, *The Iron Wall*, p. 195. The Germans rejected the proposal, which Brenner aptly calls one of "the most grotesque productions ever concocted by the human mind" [198], arguing that they had to respect Arab sensibilities. When he became prime minister, Shamir claimed that he had nothing to do with this tendency within the Stern Gang. The flimsiness of the argument is readily disposed of by Brenner.

5. Shlaim, *Iron Wall*, p. 91; Beinin, *Red Flag*, p. 11.

6. According to Shlaim, *Iron Wall*, p. 92, the dashing Dayan was "the main architect of the policy of reprisals."

7. According to our etymological dictionaries, the English word has no cognates in other languages; and the origins in Old English may stem from *bæddel* and *bædling* meaning "effeminate man, hermaphrodite, pederast."

8. Kovel, *White Racism*. Edward Goldsmith recalls that "in Alsace I went to villages where there was a drinking fountain for Christians and a drinking fountain for the Jews, because we mustn't pollute ... we were ritually unclean, we might have killed God, you see. So we were untouchables; my family were untouchables for 500 years in the city of Frankfurt. So we were confined to this little area ..." From an interview with the author, Mumbai, India, January, 2004.

9. Shlaim, *Iron Wall*, pp. 96–7.

10. Rokach, *Sacred Terrorism*, p. 36. Italics in original.

11. I recall hearing Naomi Chazan, who as a member of the Knesset earned a reputation for progressiveness, saying in answer to a question from the floor at the Socialist Scholar's conference in New York City, March 2003, that while she was opposed to the idea of a "Jewish State," she still wanted "a state with a permanent Jewish majority"—a marvellous feat of intellectual legerdemain.

12. Finkelstein, *Image and Reality of the Israel–Palestine Conflict* (London: verso, 1995), pp. 88–120, provides a good comparative summary of these mythologies for Israel, the United States, Germany and South Africa.

13. Raphael Eitan, in 1983, when he was Chief of Staff of the IDF; crude racist statements by the ultra-Orthodox are as plentiful as olive trees in old Palestine. One example will do here: the comment by Rabbi Ovadiyah Joseph, leader of the fundamentalist SHAS Party in March 1993, that "There is no animal worse than the Arabs." Quoted in Davis, *Apartheid Israel*, (London: Zed, 2003), p. 166; *Ha'aretz* editorial, April 7, 2005; Chris McGreal, "41% of Israeli Jews Favor Segregation,"

Guardian, March 24, 2006. The *Ha'aretz* editorial deserves quoting, as it reveals both racism and the forthrightness to honestly denounce it. It states: "Betar Jerusalem's fans showed this week that Israeli society—or at least part of it—is severely ill, infected with blatant, contemptible racism. At a soccer game between Betar and Bnei Sakhnin, some Betar fans did not hold back racist curses against Abbas Suan, Bnei Sakhnin's midfielder. They didn't like the fact that an Israeli Arab scored the equalizing goal against Ireland, thus leaving Israel still in the race for the World Cup. They did not like the fact that the Arab team has twice defeated Betar Jerusalem. 'You can go crazy over the fact that Arabs beat us,' said one of the fans, repeating the same kind of contemptible racist remarks made for generations about Jews in the countries where they were in the minority. ... in Israel, the most terrible things get said in public about Arabs and the prime minister is silent. The president is silent. The speaker of the Knesset is silent. And the police do nothing, even though there are suitable laws for dealing with the matter."

14. A resolution that Zionism was a form of racism had been passed by the UN in 1975. It never succeeded in penetrating the consciousness of the West and, after a furious counter-attack spearheaded by John Bolton, later UN Ambassador of the United States, was rescinded in 1991. In Durban, where racism was seen in global context, the matter returned front and center to the agenda. This included major attention to matters such as the Dalit question in India and reparations for chattel slavery, in addition to reopening the issue of Zionism as racism. The most striking feature was the identification of the United States as the cockpit of world racism. This was met with a great deal of arm twisting and manipulation by the United States—including the withdrawal of Secretary of State Powell from the conference—all of which largely succeeded in neutralizing the issues. See Eric Mann, *Dispatches from Durban* (Los Angeles: Frontline Press, 2002).

15. The most striking example was the need to quantify the black slaves as three-fifths of a person for the purposes of regulating the vote in the new American republic. This act more or less set the standard for modern racism.

16. In *White Racism*, I develop the theme as it has been worked out in the United States as a transition from *dominative* to *aversive* racism, and then beyond, to a withering of racial awareness, combined with the sustenance of racist institutions, called *metaracism*.

17. Norman Finkelstein has done a definitive debunking of this notion, first in his critique of Joan Peters' *From Time Immemorial*, a 1984 work that caused a sensation by "proving" that Palestinians weren't really an indigenous people but essentially came to get ahead by working for Jews. Finkelstein, among others, succeeded in dispatching Peters to the dustbin of histories. See Finkelstein, *Image and Reality*, (London: Verso,

1995), pp. 21–50. In *Beyond Chutzpah* he takes on Alan Dershowitz in a reprise of the theme, demonstrating that Dershowitz plagiarized Peters, a book already revealed to have been a hoax.

18. Davis, *Apartheid Israel*, p. 174. Until 1948, Sakhnin owned or had access to 70,000 dunums (17,500 acres). By 2000 this had shrunk to 10,000 dunums.

19. Davis, *Apartheid Israel*, p. 106.

20. Davis, *Apartheid Israel*, p. 48. See discussion in Chapter 4.

21. Barry Chamish, "The Ringworm Children: How the Israeli Government Irradiated 100,000 Israeli Kids," *Israel Insider*, October 28, 2005. This essentially recounts the findings of an Israeli documentary film, "The Ringworm Children" (translated in Hebrew as "100,000 Rays"), directed by David Belhassen and Asher Hemias, which won the prize for "best documentary" at the Haifa International film festival and is gradually making its way into the national consciousness.

22. A notion coined by Chaim Weizmann at the Versailles Peace Conference when he called for a Palestine "as Jewish as England is English." Masalha, *Expulsion*, p. 12.

23. Personal communication.

8 SLOUCHING TOWARD JERUSALEM

1. Name withheld. Date of email transmission,18 June, 2003.

2. This characterization is drawn from Shahak and Mezvinsky, *Fundamentalism*, to whom much of the present section is indebted—although I take exception to their somewhat linear treatment of the subject, in which the behavior and writings of Orthodox Jews tend to be directly extrapolated from medieval to modern conditions. For a good critique, see Joseph Massad, <http://web.mit.edu/cis/www/mitejmes/issues/200105/br_massad.htm#fn1>. About three-quarters of Israeli Jews are Orthodox, of which the politically dominant faction, and the one sent to the Occupied Territories, are the Religious-National Jews. Gush Emunim, founded in 1974, is the best-known organization of this tendency. The other, more strictly observant, are the *Haredim*. Both factions are extensively and intricately represented in Israeli political life, and field a number of parties who hold seats in the Knesset and often provide crucial swing votes.

3. See <http://www.ict.org.il/inter_ter/orgdet.cfm?orgid=19>.

4. Quoted in Shahak and Mezvinsky, *Fundamentalism*, p. 106.

5. Shahak and Mezvinsky, *Fundamentalism*, p. 100.

6. They can be seen in Ashwin Desai, *We are the Poors* (New York: Monthly Review Press, 2002), marching alongside Palestinians in the 2001 World Conference Against Racism, carrying, among other

banners, a sign reading "Authentic Rabbis have always opposed Zionism and the State of Israel." Following p. 81.

7. Kovel, "Zionism's Bad Conscience."

8. C's "objective" proof of God's word is, in my view, purely subjective and arbitrary. God's word is what the Jew hears, and his sect reinforces. The doctrine of exceptionalism and the Covenant keep this from being universal, hence it can never rise above the level of opinion. These larger questions cannot be addressed here, except to say that the "humanism" that animates the present account is grounded not in the separateness of humanity from being, but in our participation in the formativity of nature. It thus moves toward universality, for which reason, a nonviolent solution to the dilemma of Israel/Palestine is eminently conceivable, C's fears notwithstanding, and however slender the hope. Further thoughts about these matters are offered in the remainder of this work, though not systematically.

9. Jeffrey Goldberg, "Among the Settlers," *The New Yorker*, May 31, 2004, pp. 46–69. Lenny Goldberg's remarks are virtually identical to the notorious statement made by a senior member of the Bush administration in 2004, who disdained the "reality-based community," because "we make our own reality," that is, have already taken events to the next place, thus making the critics irrelevant. Given the theocratic tendencies of G. W. Bush (see Chapter 6), this is much more than a casual resemblence.

10. Ari Shavit, "Survival of the fittest," *Ha'aretz*, January 9, 2004. The ostensible purpose of the interview was to discuss the release, first of the Hebrew translation of Morris' work, *Righteous Victims*, extensively used herein; and also the second edition of his famous "revisionist" history, *The Birth of the Palestinian Refugee Problem Revisited* (Cambridge University Press). All quotes in this section are from this interview.

11. Morris also discovers that there were more instances in which Arab leadership urged evacuation than he had previously thought, a finding that does not change the dynamics of what is going on in the interview.

12. Note how uncritically Morris skips back and forth between "Arabs" and "Islam" in his Crusade, forgetting that many Palestinians are Christian, and the majority of Muslims—Iranians, Afghanis, Central Asians, Pakistanis, Indians, Indonesions—are not Arab. As they say, any stick to beat a dog.

13. The Holocaust itself has to be reckoned as a consequence of the Nazi invasion of Russia—see Chapter 3. The race hatred directed against Slavs was comparable to that against the Jews, and a definite genocidal impulse was at work. Russia lost about 28 million people during the war, and tens of thousands of hospitals, libraries, etc., were flattened,

as the Nazis sought to convert the Soviet Union into a *tabula rasa* for the resettlement of Teutons. Stalingrad was the momentous battle when the Nazi advance was definitively stopped, and probably the bloodiest ever fought, Russian casualties exceeding the German.

14. The comparison is powerfully developed by Ward Churchill, "An American Holocaust? The Structure of Denial," *Socialism and Democracy*, vol. 17, no. 1, Winter–Spring, 2003, pp. 25–75.

15. For studies of the Iroquois heritage, see Oren Lyons and John Mohawk, eds, *Exiled in the Land of the Free* (Santa Fe: Clear Light Publishers, 1992); for a study of movements from below, see Peter Linebaugh and Marcus Rediker, *The Many-Headed Hydra* (Boston: Beacon Press, 2001); see also, Barry Unsworth, *Sacred Hunger* (New York: W. W. Norton, 1993), a remarkable Booker Prize-winning historical novel; also Kovel, *Red-Hunting*.

16. See, for example, William Blum, *Rogue State* (Monroe, ME: Common Courage Press, 2005).

17. As this is written, we read of plans underway in Israel to build a fancy museum promoting "religious tolerance." Alas, the ground chosen for this project is one of the leading cemeteries for Palestinians. But then, one cannot make an omelette without breaking eggs.

18. Jonathan Kaplan, *The Dressing Station* (London: Picador, 2001). In this documentation of Kaplan's work as a surgeon in the world's trouble spots, he gives a vivid description of the brutal wounds inflicted by Israeli-made weapons upon black Africans who threatened the hegemony of the racist state. See p. 103.

19. Edward Herman, "Ethnic Cleansing and the 'Moral Instinct,'" Z Magazine, March, 2006, p. 36.

9 BEYOND THE TWO-STATE SOLUTION

1. From an interview with Steve Zeltzer, October 2005, San Francisco; see <http://www.radio4all.net/proginfo.php?id=16276>.

2. King Ibn Saud of Saudi Arabia urged President Roosevelt when the latter was on his way home from the Yalta Conference to give the Jews their state by taking a piece of land out of Germany for the purpose ("F.D.R. meets Ibn Saud," in Khalidi, *Haven*, pp. 509–13). FDR showed interest, gave assurances of fairness, then died a few weeks later. In the fall, Truman scotched the idea with the coarse excuse of having hundreds of thousands of Zionist constituents and few Arabs. In other words, there is a place for colonial expansion, and it is not in the metropolis.

3. William Robinson has developed this useful term to describe formally manipulated oligarchies (most often by the United States), in which *comprador* elites are recycled through a facade of simulated democratic institutions. The notion has wide provenance. William Robinson,

Promoting Polyarchy (Cambridge: Cambridge University Press, 1996).

4. Many questions arise here, including the status of Cuba. My view is that there are many formal blockages in Cuba against what is ordinarily construed as democracy, for example, one-party rule, lack of freedom of the press, and so forth. But the context, which is decisive in forming judgments of this sort, makes it abundantly clear that these defects arose in order to preserve a real degree of socialism against the assault of US imperialism; hence the class structure enforced by Cuban the state is fundamentally different from the others under consideration. Any country that sends doctors around the world to afflicted areas (a thousand, for example, to far-away Pakistan after the 2005 earthquake), or whose infant mortality is at least as good as the United States, despite its US-imposed poverty, must rank high on the scale of relative legitimacy.

5. The American South after the civil war, and Germany and Japan after the Second World War, lay in ruins and passed through a period of statelessness and stewardship, to be reconstructed on a fundamentally different basis, in each case retooled to foster a more functional capitalism. By contrast, Communist Czechoslovakia, Poland, Hungary, etc., had "velvet" revolutions and moved into a different kind of social contract (also centered on the restoration of capitalism) in which hardly anyone lost their lives. In the transformation of apartheid South Africa deplorable black on black violence fomented by a dying racist regime marred the process (which again centered about bringing the logic of the new state and that of capital into a harmonic relation), but does not change the point developed here. Although few lost their lives in the immediate wake of the Bolshevik triumph in Russia, tens of millions perished in the nightmare of counter-revolution, civil war, and foreign intervention that ensued.

6. By far the most comprehensive and astute analysis of the One-State/Two-State conundrum is given in Virginia Tilley, *The One-State Solution* (Ann Arbor: University of Michigan Press, 2005).

7. It goes without saying that this is not a complete inventory. The Islamist state of Saudi Arabia is obviously structurally illegitimate, and is so, moreover, through connivance with the US. Zimbabwe countenances violent expropriations against white farmers, that is, lacks the path of reconciliation taken by South Africa after overthrowing white rule. China's occupation of Tibet may be less odious than Israel's of the West Bank and Gaza because the Chinese have been back and forth over that territory for centuries, but it is still odious. The four countries discussed at greater length herein are chosen because they form a family of special relevance to the phenomenon of Zionism and its racism. See Theses 7 and 8, above.

8. Now come back to haunt everybody as gambling casinos.
9. Works in which this argument has been analyzed include Davis, *Apartheid Israel*; Mona N. Younis, *Liberation and Democratization: The South African and Palestinian National Movements* (Minneapolis: University of Minnesota Press, 2000); and Tilley, *One-State Solution*. Recently an extensive journalistic study has appeared by Chris McGreal, "Jo'burg and Jerusalem … Worlds Apart?" *Mail&Guardian* [South Africa], March 3–9, 2006, 18–21.
10. Davis, *Apartheid Israel*, p. 86.
11. Davis, *Apartheid Israel*, p. 87.
12. McGreal, "Jo'burg and Jerusalem."
13. The two nations jointly exploded an atomic device in the South Atlantic on September 22, 1979. Israel gave technical assistance and received enriched uranium for its program in return (having had to resort to theft in the past). As a leader of the anti-apartheid movement put it in 1982: "Israel is now the biggest hole in the growing fence of sanctions surrounding apartheid South Africa. Israel is forcing the anti-apartheid movement—even in UN corridors—to ask: will we have to boycott Israel in the future to support the liberation of South Africa?" Penny Johnson, "Israel and South Africa: The Nuclear Axis," in Shahak, *Israel's Global Role*, pp. 49–51. See also, Hersh, *The Samson Option*.
14. McGreal, "Jo'burg and Jerusalem."
15. It is also the case that the black underclasses were somewhat better treated under apartheid than since the formation of the new state in 1994, guided by neoliberal globalization. This has made millions into "useless" subproletarians.
16. It is worth emphasizing that every American president from Nixon on has made some effort to reverse the tide of Israeli expropriation of the Occupied Territories. This was not the result of any passion for justice, but reflected geostrategic apprehension about the effects on the Arabs. In each instance an extraordinary blitz by the Zionist lobby, often employing its control over Congress, nullified the effort. See Mearsheimer and Walt, *Israel Lobby*.
17. "In the ten year period between 1949 and 1959, hundreds of thousands of Bedouins were expelled from the Negev and other parts of the country, adding to the displaced refugee population." Today, more than forty years later, "tens of thousand of Bedouins, living in what Israel has called 'unrecognized villages,' have come under renewed siege. Israel has announced plans to remove all Bedouin from these communities, resettle them in 'recognized' townships, and build new Jewish settlements on the sites." And so it goes. *Ruling Palestine: A history of the legally sanctioned Jewish-Israeli seizure of land in Palestine*," Centre on Housing Rights and Evictions (COHRE); BADIL

Resource Center for Palestine Residency and Refugee Rights, 244 pages, May 2005, pp. 36, 148. Copies from COHRE International Secretariat, 83 Rue de Montbrillant, CH-1202 Geneva, Switzerland.

18.   For example, Arthur Ruppin, a socialist, founded the Brith Shalom movement in the 1920s, which called for a bi-national state and included Martin Buber and Gerschon Scholem among its members. Unfortunately, Ruppin was also active in calling for the transfer of Arabs out of Palestine. Masalha, *Expulsion*, p. 11. Also in the 1920s, the radical and utopian HaShomer HaZair called on Histadrut to explore the possibility of a bi-national state. "Little came of the scheme," writes Howard Sachar, *History*, p. 181.

19.   Judah Magnes and Martin Buber, "Testimony Before the Anglo-American Inquiry Commission," in Arab-Jewish Unity (Westport, CT: Hyperion Press, 1976), p. 12.

20.   For Magnes, see Hertzberg, *Zionist Idea*, pp. 440–9.

21.   Martin Buber, "Israel and the Command of the Spirit", *Israel and the World* (Syracuse: Syracuse University Press, 1997), p. 257. He goes on to hope for "cooperation" between the peoples, an empty claim given his endorsement of the Jewish state.

22.   Uri Davis, "Martin Buber's Paths in Utopia—The Kibbutz: an experiment that didn't fail?" *Peace News*, no. 2446, March–June, 2002. Davis' larger point is to make a very sharp critique of Buber's famous paean, in *Paths in Utopia* trans. R. F. C. Hull (Boston: Beacon Press, 1958 [1946]), to the kibbutz, Zionism's most famous contribution to social organization. "The uniqueness of this Zionist co-operative venture is not, as Buber alleged, in that 'it alone has proved its vitality in all three spheres' of 'internal relationships, federation and influence on society at large,' or that in establishing the Jewish village commune 'the primary thing was not ideology but work.' Nor is the uniqueness of the venture represented in its ability to constantly 'branch off' into new forms and new intermediate forms.' Rather, the unique feature of the Zionist co-operative enterprise was and remains: a) its utility as a strategic colonial instrument directed to alienate the indigenous Palestinian Arab population from their lands, and b), its racism—membership in these co-operative village communities was (and remains) only open to Jews. ... It is clear to me that the Zionist co-operative movement in Palestine has been a primary driving force in the development and consolidation of Israeli apartheid; playing a role similar to that played by the Dutch Reform Church in the development and consolidation of South African apartheid. In recent decades the falsehood of Buber's assessment of the Zionist co-operative venture in Palestine has became progressively transparent. The Kibbutz collective dining room has now become a paying cafeteria and, under privatisation, sections of the Kibbutz membership (e.g., the elderly) have been pauperised to the

extent that some are not able to afford to pay for a full meal. There have been reports in the Israeli Hebrew press of elderly Kibbutz members covering their meat portion with a heap of rice in order to save money at the till. A 'signal non-failure,' as Buber would have it."

23. Michel Warschawski, *On the Border* (Cambridge, MA: South End Press, 2005), p. 25. Warschawski has stayed with this fight right through the present. Currently, his Alternative Information Center in Jerusalem continues to promote universalism and cooperation between Palestinians and Israelis.

24. Tilley, *One-State Solution*, pp. 183–94, reviews the recent stirrings of the One-State idea among a wide range of Israeli intellectuals (including those alarmed enough by it to mount harsh attacks); as well as in Palestinian opinion. In the United States, Tony Judt, "Israel: the Alternative," *New York Review of Books*, 50, no. 16, October 23, 2003, calls attention to the growing logic of the One-State.

25. *On the Border* Warschawski, pp. 193.

26. Esther Kaplan, *"Globalize the Intifada,"* in Tony Kushner and Alison Solomon, eds, *Wrestling with Zion* (New York: Grove, 2003), pp. 81–8.

27. Ephraim Nimni, ed., *The Challenge of Post-Zionism* (London: Zed, 2003), provides a range of views on this phenomenon.

10 PALESRAEL: A SECULAR AND UNIVERSAL DEMOCRACY FOR ISRAEL/PALESTINE

1. Jeff Halper, "Elections in Palestine and Israel: *Sumus* vs Apartheid," *The New Internationalist*, April, 2006.

2. Ernst Bloch, *The Principle of Hope*, trans. Neville Plaice, Stephen Plaice and Paul Knight, 3 vols, (Cambridge: MIT Press, 1986), was the philosopher of this dialectic.

3. For an introduction to Gandhi in these matters, see M. K. Gandhi, *Non-Violent Resistance* (New York: Schocken, 1961). To Gandhi, Truth and God were different aspects of the same spirit-force. This is clearly not the place to take up these questions in depth, especially for a figure who remains as controversial as he is great. Further reflections may be found in Kovel, *History and Spirit*. When we speak of the "universal" here, we mean something of the same, albeit not the God Yahweh of the Old Testament.

4. I am grateful to James Petras for conceptualizing many of these strategies in internet postings. See also <http://www.cnionline.org>.

5. David Macfarlane, "Sponsors quash boycott debate," *Mail&Guardian* [South Africa], February 17–23, 2006, p. 7.

6. It is worth recalling that the Great Trek of 1834, which led to the settlement of the country's interior and became an event equivalent in

Afrikaner mythology to the Mosaic wanderings of the ancient Hebrews, was a reaction to Britain's insistence that the Boers give up their black slaves. Thus it was a "freedom" march.

7. Much information can be found at the following websites: COHRE <www.cohre.org>, Badil <www.badil.org>, Al-Awda <www.al-awda. org>. A thorough and practically oriented study appears on the latter's site. See also <http://www.plands.org/books/citizen/introduction. htm>.

8. I am indebted to Peter Linebaugh for sharing information about the Magna Carta, drawn from his forthcoming book, *The Magna Carta and the Commons* (in press, University of California Press).

9. For a variant that attempts to evade this, see Yoav Peled and Nadim Rouhana, "Transitional Justice and the Right of Return of Palestinian Refugees," *Theoretical Inquiries in Law*, 5: 2, 2004, pp. 317–32. The authors postulate an initial phase in which Palestinian in-migration would stop short of the attainment of the majority that would dissolve the Jewish state. They introduce the notion of "transitional justice," in which the *Right* of return is acknowledged but the *means* of return are negotiated to some mid-point at which both sides are given reassurances and grounds for hope, this allowing for the undoing of anxiety and the unfolding of recognition, and thereby preparing the ground for the next, deeper phase. So long as this is carried out in good-faith recognition that the Jewishness of the state comprises the heart and soul of the problem, that is, eventually has to go, it would be acceptable. The question, however, is the degree to which this principle will avoid the existential core posed by the maintenance of the Jewish state, turn into prevarication, and lead to another swindle of the Palestinian people.

10. Bernard Lewis, *What Went Wrong?* (New York: Oxford Univesity Press, 2002), p. 153.

11. Nelson Mandela, *Long Walk to Freedom* (Johannesburg: Macdonald Purnell, 1994), pp. 469, 509.

12. Personal communication.

13. From a lecture at Zochrot, May 6, 2005. See <http://www.zochrot. org/index.php?id=335>.

14. It will be pointed out that a degree of retributive violence against whites, with the threat of more to come, has occurred in South Africa. But no claim is being made that the new South Africa did the best possible job of transition, only that it remains a huge improvement over apartheid. As to what went wrong, that is lucidly given in a lesson that remains to be learned: do not think you are successfully transforming a society unless you also transform its class structure.

15. But by no means necessary. A good portion of the ROR will be excercised by Palestinians who live either in Israel proper (the "present absentees") or the Occupied Territories. It is quite uncertain how many Palestinians

from the diaspora will want to return—or whether other arrangements for them may be included in the countries where they now reside. The NGOs, all needless to add, scarcely non-partisan, who are most involved in the ROR—Al-Awda, COHRE, Badil—are all firmly of the opinion that there is no demographic barrier to implementation.

16. Benjamin Nelson, *The Idea of Usury: From Tribal Brotherhood to Universal Otherhood* (Chicago: University of Chicago Press, 1969). This nexus comprises one of the deepest roots of judaeophobia. It is very much entangled with Nazi antisemitism in relation to the inflationary shocks of the 1920s. It also pertains to a surge of antisemitism during the capitalist crises of the 1930s in the United States and England as well as Germany.

17. Martin Peretz, "Realist school's conspiratorial minds deviate wildly from reality," *The Australian*, April 22, 2006. Mearsheimer and Walt do not refer to the lobby as Jewish, but properly, as representing Israel. Is Peretz trying to smear them with the label of antisemitism? Does he himself think of the lobby as inherently Jewish, as antisemites would hold? Or is he just being sloppy?

18. See Kovel, *Red-Hunting*.

19. Gandhi, Chief Albert Lutheli, founder of the ANC, and Nelson Mandela.

Bibliography

BOOKS AND ARTICLES

Alter, Robert, *The Five Books of Moses* (New York: W.W. Norton, 2004)

Anderson, Kevin, and Peter Hudis, eds. *The Rosa Luxemburg Reader* (New York: Monthly Review Press, 2004)

Arlosoroff, Chaim, "The Stages of Zionism and Minority National Rule," in Khalidi, ed., *From Haven to Conquest* (Washington, DC: The Institute for Palestine Studies, 1987), pp. 245–54

Avishai, Bernard, *The Tragedy of Zionism* (New York: Helios Press, 2002)

Beinin, Joel, *Was the Red Flag Flying There?* (Berkeley: University of California Press, 1990)

Beinin, Joel, "The United States-Israeli Alliance," in Tony Kushner and Alisa Solomon, eds, *Wrestling With Zion* (New York: Grove, 2003), pp. 41–50

Benbassa, Esther, and Jean-Christophe Attias, *The Jews and Their Future*, trans. Patrick Camiller (London: Zed, 2004)

Ben-Gurion, David, "The Imperatives of the Jewish Revolution," in Arthur Hertzberg, *The Zionist Idea* (Philadephia: The Jewish Publication Society, 1997), pp. 606–19.

Bennis, Phyllis, "Of Dogs and Tails: The Changing Nature of the Pro-Israeli Lobby,The Unchanging Nature of the U.S.-Israeli Alliance," in Tony Kushner and Alisa Solomon, eds, *Wrestling With Zion* (New York: Grove, 2003)

Ben-Yehuda, Nachman, *The Masada Myth: Collective Memory and Mythmaking in Israel* (Madison: University of Wisconsin Press, 1995)

Biale, David, *Power and Powerlessness in Jewish History* (New York: Schocken Books, 1986)

Biale, David, ed., *Cultures of the Jews* (New York: Schocken Books, 2002)

Bloch, Ernst, *The Principle of Hope*, trans. Neville Plaice, Stephen Plaice and Paul Knight, 3 vols, (Cambridge: MIT Press, 1986)

Blum, William, *Rogue State* (Monroe, ME: Common Courage Press, 2005)

Boyarin, Daniel, *Unheroic Conduct* (Berkeley, University of California Press, 1997)

Brenner, Lenni, *Zionism in the Age of the Dictators* (Westport, CT: Lawrence Hill, 1983)

Brenner, Lenni, *The Iron Wall* (London: Zed, 1984)

Buber, Martin, *Paths in Utopia* trans. R. F. C. Hull (Boston: Beacon Press, 1958 [1946])

Buber, Martin, "Israel and the Command of the Spirit", in *Israel and the World* (Syracuse: Syracuse University Press, 1997), pp. 253–7

Chamish, Barry, "The Ringworm Children: How the Israeli Government Irradiated 100,000 Israeli Kids," *Israel Insider*, October 28, 2005

Chomsky, Noam, *The Fateful Triangle* (Boston: South End Press, 1999)

Christison, Kathleen, *Perceptions of Palestine*, (Berkeley: University of California Press, 1999)

Churchill, Ward, "An American Holocaust? The Structure of Denial," *Socialism and Democracy*, vol. 17, no. 1, Winter–Spring, 2003, pp. 25–75

Clark, Harry, "How it all began: Truman and Israel," *Counterpunch*, June 3, 2006

Centre on Housing Rights and Evictions (COHRE); BADIL Resource Center for Palestine Residency and Refugee Rights, *Ruling Palestine: A history of the legally sanctioned Jewish-Israeli seizure of land in Palestine,"* 244 pages, May 2005.

Cooney, John, *The American Pope* (New York: Crown, 1984)

Corrie, Rachel, "I am in the Midst of a Genocide": E-Mails from Gaza, *Monthly Review*, May, 2003, pp. 50–60

Davidson, Alastair, *Antonio Gramsci: Towards an Intellectual Biography* (London: Merlin Press, 1977)

Davis, Uri, "Martin Buber's Paths in Utopia—The Kibbutz: an experiment that didn't fail?" *Peace News*, no. 2446, March–June 2002

Davis, Uri, *Apartheid Israel* (London: Zed, 2003)

Dershowitz, Alan, *The Case for Israel* (New York: John Wiley and Sons, 2003)

Desai, Ashwin, *We are the Poors* (New York: Monthly Review Press, 2002)

Deutscher, Isaac, *The Non-Jewish Jew, and other essays* (London: Oxford University Press, 1968)

Einstein, Albert, *Ideas and Opinions*, (New York: Modern Library, 1954)

Elon, Amos, *The Pity of it All* (New York: Henry Holt, 2002)

Ernst, Morris L., "F.D.R.'s International Plan for Jewish Refugees," in Khalidi, ed., *From Haven to Conquest* (Washington, DC: The Institute for Palestine Studies, 1987), pp. 489–94

Finkelstein, Norman, *Image and Reality of the Israel-Palestine Conflict* (London: Verso, 1995), pp. 21–50

Finkelstein, Norman, *The Holocaust Industry* (London: Verso, 2000)

Finkelstein, Norman, *Beyond Chutzpah* (Berkeley: University of California Press, 2005)

Frankfurter, Felix, "An Interview in Mr. Balfour's Apartment, 23 Rue Nitot," in Khalidi, ed., *From Haven to Conquest*, (Washington, DC: The Institute for Palestine Studies, 1987), pp. 195–9

Gandhi, M. K., *Non-Violent Resistance* (New York: Schocken, 1961)

Gandhi, M. K., "The Jews in Palestine 1938," in Khalidi, ed., *From Haven to Conquest* (Washington, DC: The Institute for Palestine Studies, 1987), pp. 367–70

Ganor, Ethan, "Pollution, Apartheid and Protest in Occupied Palestine," *Earth First! Journal*, September 2005

Glass, Charles, "Learning from its mistakes," *London Review of Books*, August 17, 2006

Goldberg, Jeffrey, "Among the Settlers," *The New Yorker*, May 31, 2004, pp. 46–69

Gottwald, Norman, *The Tribes of Yahweh* (New York: Maryknoll, 1979)

Gramsci, Antonio, *Selections from the Prison Noteboooks*, eds, and trans. Quintin Hoare and Geoffrey Nowell Smith (New York: International Publishers, 1971)

Grodzinsky, Yosef, *In the Shadow of the Holocaust* (Monroe, ME: Common Courage Press, 2004)

Halper, Jeff, "Elections in Palestine and Israel: *Sumus* vs Apartheid," *The New Internationalist*, April 2006

Hendel, Ronald S., "Israel among the nations," in David Biale, ed., *Cultures of the Jews* (New York: Schocken Books, 2002)

Herman, Edward, "Ethnic Cleansing and the 'Moral Instinct,'" *Z Magazine*, March 2006

Hersh, Seymour, *The Samson Option* (New York: Random House, 1991)

Hersh, Seymour, "The Traitor," *The New Yorker Magazine*, January 18, 1999, pp. 26–33

Hertzberg, Arthur, *The Zionist Idea* (Philadelphia: The Jewish Publication Society, 1997)

Herzl, Theodor, *The Complete Diaries*, ed. Rafael Patai (New York: Herzl Press and T. Toseloff, 1960)

Hirst, David, *The Gun and the Olive Branch* (New York: Thunder's Mouth Press/Nation Books, 2003)

Jeffries, J. M. N. "Analysis of the Balfour Declaration," in Khalidi, ed. *From Haven to Conquest*, (Washington, DC: The Institute for Palestine Studies, 1987), pp. 173–88

Johnson, Penny, "Israel and South Africa: The Nuclear Axis," in Shahak, *Israel's Global Role: Weapons for Repression* (Belmont, MA: Association of Arab-American University Graduates, 1982), pp. 49–51

Judt, Tony, "Israel: the Alternative," *New York Review of Books*, vol. 50, no. 16, October 23, 2003

Kaplan, Esther, *"Globalize the Intifada,"* in Tony Kushner and Alisa Solomon, eds, *Wrestling With Zion* (New York: Grove, 2003), pp. 81–8.

Kaplan, Esther, *With God on their Side* (New York: New Press, 2004)

Kaplan, Jonathan, *The Dressing Station* (London: Picador, 2001)

Khalidi, Walid, ed., *From Haven to Conquest* (Washington, DC: The Institute for Palestine Studies, 1987)

Kimmerling, Baruch, and Joel S. Migdal, *The Palestinian People*, 2nd edn. (Cambridge, MA: Harvard University Press, 2003)

Klein, Naomi, "Rescuing Jessica Lynch, Forgetting Rachel Corrie," in Tony Kushner and Alisa Solomon, eds, *Wrestling with Zion* (New York: Grove Press, 2003), pp. 69–72

Kovel, Joel, "Marx on the Jewish Question," *Dialectical Anthropology*, vol. 8, 1983, pp. 31–46

Kovel, Joel, *White Racism: A Psychohistory*, 2nd edn. (New York: Columbia University Press, 1984)

Kovel, Joel, *History and Spirit* 2nd edn. (Thetford, VT: Glad Day Press, 1988)

Kovel, Joel, *Red-Hunting in the Promised Land* 2nd edn. (London: Continuum, 1997)

Kovel, Joel, *The Enemy of Nature* (London: Zed, 2002)

Kovel, Joel, "Zionism's Bad Conscience," *Tikkun*, September–October, 2002, pp. 21–4

Kovel, Joel, "Left-Anti-Semitism and the Special Status of Israel," *Tikkun*, May-June 2003, pp. 45–51

Lacqueur, Walter, *A History of Zionism* (New York: Schocken Books, 1972 [2003])

Lewis, Bernard, *What Went Wrong?* (New York: Oxford Univesity Press, 2002)

Lindemann, Albert, *Esau's Tears* (Cambridge: Cambridge University Press, 1997)

Linebaugh, Peter and Marcus Rediker, *The Many-Headed Hydra* (Boston: Beacon Press, 2001)

Lyons, Oren, and John Mohawk, eds, *Exiled in the Land of the Free* (Santa Fe: Clear Light Publishers, 1992)

Machinist, Peter, "Outsiders or Insiders: The Biblical view of emergent Israel and its contexts," in Laurence J. Silberstein and Robert L. Cohn, eds, *The Other in Jewish Thought and History* (New York: New York University Press, 1994)

Magnes, Judah, and Martin Buber, "Testimony Before the Anglo-American Inquiry Commission," in *Arab-Jewish Unity* (Westport, CT: Hyperion Press, 1976)

Mandela, Nelson, *Long Walk to Freedom* (Johannesburg: Macdonald Purnell, 1994)

Mann, Eric, *Dispatches from Durban* (Los Angeles: Frontline Press, 2002)

Manuel, Frank, "Judge Brandeis and the Framing of the Balfour Declaration," in Khalidi, ed. *From Haven to Conquest* (Washington, DC: The Institute for Palestine Studies, 1987) pp. 165–72

Masalha, Nur, *Expulsion of the Palestinians* (Washington, DC: The Institute of Palestine Studies, 1992)

Massad, Joseph, "The Legacy of Jean-Paul Sartre," *Al Ahram* (Cairo, no. 623, January 30–February 5, 2003)

Mayer, Arno, *And Why Did the Heavens Not Darken?* (New York: Pantheon, 1988)

Mearsheimer, John, and Stephen Walt, "The Israel Lobby," *London Review of Books*, March 23, 2006

Metzger, Bruce, and Roland Murphy, eds, *The New Oxford Annotated Bible* (New York: Oxford University Press, 1991, 1994. New Revised Standard Edition [NRSV])

Morris, Benny, *Righteous Victims* (New York: Vintage Books: 2001)

Nelson, Benjamin, *The Idea of Usury: From Tribal Brotherhood to Universal Otherhood* (Chicago: University of Chicago Press, 1969)

Nimni, Ephraim, ed., *The Challenge of Post-Zionism* (London: Zed, 2003)

Nitzan, Jonathan, and Shimson Bichler, *The Global Political Economy of Israel* (London: Pluto Press, 2002)

O'Connor, James, *The Fiscal Crisis of the State*, 2nd edn. (Somerset, NJ: Transaction Publishers, 2001)

Pappe, Ilan, *A History of Modern Palestine* (Cambridge: Cambridge University Press, 2004), pp. 175–82

Peled, Yoav and Nadim Rouhana, "Transitional Justice and the Right of Return of Palestinian Refugees," *Theoretical Inquiries in Law*, 5: 2, 2004, pp. 317–32

Perry, Marvin, and Frederick Schweitzer, *Antisemitism: Myth and Hate from Antiquity to the Present* (New York: Palgrave Macmillan, 2002)

Phillips, Kevin, *American Theocracy* (New York: Viking, 2006)

Proust, Marcel, *Remembrance of Things Past*, trans. C. K. Scott Moncrieff and Terence Kilmartin, vol. 2 (New York: Random House: 1981) [*Cities of the Plain*]

Raimondo, Justin, *The Terror Enigma* (New York: iUniverse, 2003)

Reinhart, Tanya, *Israel/Palestine: How to End the War of 1948* (New York: Seven Stories Press, 2002)

Robinson, William, *Promoting Polyarchy* (Cambridge: Cambridge University Press, 1996)

Rokach, Livia, *Israel's Sacred Terrorism* (Belmont, MA: Association of Arab-American University Graduates, 1980)

Sachar, Howard, *A History of Israel*, 2nd edn. (New York: Alfred Knopf, 2003)

Sartre, Jean-Paul, *Anti-Semite and Jew*, trans. George Becker (New York: Schocken, 1948 [1965])

Segev, Tom, *The First Israelis*, trans. Haim Watzman (New York: Hill and Wang, 1984)

Segev, Tom, *The Seventh Million*, trans. Haim Watzman (New York: Hill and Wang, 1994)

Shahak, Israel, *Israel's Global Role: Weapons for Repression* (Belmont, MA: Association of Arab-American University Graduates, 1982)

Shahak, Israel, *Jewish History, Jewish Religion, the Weight of Three Thousand Years* (London: Pluto Press, 1994)

Shahak, Israel, and Norton Mezvinsky, *Jewish Fundamentalism in Israel* (London: Pluto Press, 1999)

Shlaim, Avi, *The Iron Wall* (New York: W. W. Norton, 2001)

Simpson, Sir John Hope, "On the Employment of Arab Labour," in Khalidi, ed., *From Haven to Conquest* (Washington, DC: The Institute for Palestine Studies, 1987), pp. 303–7

Sternhell, Ze'ev, *The Founding Myths of Israel*, trans. David Maisel (Princeton: Princeton University Press, 1998)

Tadié, Jean-Yves, *Marcel Proust: A Life* (New York: Viking-Penguin, 2000)

Tal, Allon, *Pollution in a Promised Land* (Berkeley: University of California Press, 2002)

Theweleit, Klaus, *Male Fantasies*, 2 vols (Minneapolis: University of Minnesota Press, 1987, 1989)

Tilley, Virginia, *The One-State Solution* (Ann Arbor: University of Michigan Press, 2005)

Tuveson, Ernest, *Redeemer Nation* (Chicago: University of Chicago Press, 1968)

Unsworth, Barry, *Sacred Hunger* (New York: W. W. Norton, 1993)

Uris, Leon, *Exodus* (New York: Doubleday, 1958)

Wald, Alan, *The New York Intellectuals* (Chapel Hill: The University of North Carolina Press, 1987)

Warschawski, Michel, *On the Border* (Cambridge, MA: South End Press, 2005)

Younis, Mona N., *Liberation and Democratization: The South African and Palestinian National Movements* (Minneapolis: University of Minnesota Press, 2000)

FROM THE PRESS

ben-David, Dan, "The State of Israel's Education," *Ha'aretz*, June 20, 2006

Bennet, James, "Israel says war on Iraq would benefit the region," *The New York Times*, February 27, 2003

Caspit, Ben, "We will not capitulate," *Maariv*, July 31, 2006

Editorial, *Ha'aretz*, April 7, 2005

Eldar, Akiva, "People and Politics," *Ha'aretz*, June 27, 2002

Francis, David R., "Economist tallies swelling cost of Israel to US," *Christian Science Monitor,* December 9, 2002

Hass, Amira, *Ha'aretz,* May 19, 2004

Lake, Eli, "David Duke Claims to Be Vindicated By a Harvard Dean," *New York Sun,* March 20, 2006

Macfarlane, David, "Sponsors quash boycott debate," *Mail&Guardian* [South Africa] February 17–23, 2006, p. 7

Markon, Jerry, "DoD Spy for Israel given 12 years," *Washington Post,* January 21, 2006

McGreal, Chris, "Once mighty Jordan reduced to a trickle," *Guardian,* March 9, 2005

McGreal, Chris, "Jo'burg and Jerusalem ... Worlds Apart?" *Mail&Guardian* [South Africa], March 3–9, 2006, 18–21

McGreal, Chris, "41% of Israeli Jews Favor Segregation," *Guardian,* March 24, 2006.

Melchior, Michael, "An immoral state," *Ha'aretz,* August 19, 2004

Peretz, Martin, "Traveling With Bad Companions," *Los Angeles Times,* June 23, 2003

Peretz, Martin, "Realist school's conspiratorial minds deviate wildly from reality," *The Australian,* April 22, 2006

Shavit, Ari, "Survival of the fittest," *Ha'aretz,* January 9, 2004

Sorkin, Andrew Ross, "Shlepping to Moguldom," *The New York Times,* September 5, 2004

Wiesel, Elie, "The America I Love," *Parade* Magazine, July 4, 2004

Winer, Stuart, *The Jerusalem Post,* August 9, 2004

Wolf, Matt, "Requiem for an Idealist (and a Cause Celebre)," *The New York Times,* March 31, 2006 (E3)

REFERENCES WITH WEBSITES (LAST ACCESSED OCTOBER 1, 2006)

<www.al-awda.org; http://www.plands.org/books/citizen/introduction.htm>; (Al-Awda)

<http://web.amnesty.org/library/Index/ENGMDE150332004>

<http://antiwar.com/hacohen/?articleid=9486>; Ran HaCohen, "Israeli Intellectuals Love the War"

<http://www.badil.org>; (Badil)

<http://www.btselem.org/English>

<http://www.ccr-ny.org/v2/legal/human_rights/rightsArticle.asp?ObjID=eqV BNxvlcx&Content=682> [Belhas v. Ya'alon]

<http://www.ccr-ny.org/v2/legal/human_rights/rightsArticle.asp?ObjID=ccD zL2NjXs&Content=678> [Matar v. Dichter]

<http://www.cnionline.org>

<http://www.cesr.org>; (Center for Economic and Social Rights), *Thirsting for Justice: Israeli violations of the human right to water in the Occupied Palestinian Territories*, May 2003

<http://www.cohre.org>; (COHRE)

<http://electronicintifada.net/v2/article2700.shtml>

<http://en.wikipedia.org/wiki/USS_Liberty_incident#_ref-5>

<http://www.freepalestinecampaign.org/attacks_on_ISM.htm>

<http://www.Haaretz.com, 09/03/2005>; Zafrir Rinat, "Survey shows environmental hazards spreading throughout the Dan region"

<http://www.ict.org.il/inter_ter/orgdet.cfm?orgid=19>; Israeli (Foreign Ministry Information Service)

<http://ifamericansknew.org/stats/cost_of_israel.html>; Richard Curtiss, *The Cost of Israel to U.S. Taxpayers*

<http://www.israeleconomy.org/strat1.htm>

<http://www.jewishjournal.com/home/preview.php?id=15285>; Tom Tugend, "Gala for IDF," *Jewish Journal of Los Angeles*, January 2006

<http://web.mit.edu/cis/www/mitejmes/issues/200105/br_massad.htm#fn1>; Joseph Massad, A Review of Shahak and Mezvinsky, *Jewish Fundamentalism in Israel*

<http://www.palsolidarity.org/main/category/rachel-corrie/>

<http://people-press.org/reports/display.php3?PageID=725>; (Pew Research Center)

<http://www.RachelsWords.org>; (Rachel's Words)

<http://www.radio4all.net/proginfo.php?id=16276>; Ilan Pappe, interview by Steve Zeltzer, October 2005, San Francisco

<http://www.sourcewatch.org/index.php?title=Haim_Saban>; Yossi Verter, "Rabin rally may be delayed to allow Bill Clinton to take part," *Ha'aretz*, October 6, 2005

<http://www.spinwatch.org/modules.php?name=Content&pa=showpage&pid=345>; Muhammad Idrees Ahmad, "Labour Friends of Israel in the House"

<http://www.time.com/time/columnist/karon/article/0,9565,671180,00.html>; Tony Karon, "Where do France's Jews Belong?", *TIME* Online edition, July 21, 2004

<http://www.washingtoninstitute.org/templateC07.php?CID=287>

<http://www.whatreallyhappened.com/israeli_solders.html>

<http://www.zochrot.org/index.php?id=335>; Scott Leckie, Zochrot, May 6, 2005

Index

Compiled by Sue Carlton